LEGITIMATION
OF REGIMES

LEGITIMATION OF REGIMES

International Frameworks for Analysis

Edited by Bogdan Denitch
City University of New York, USA

 SAGE Studies in International Sociology 17
sponsored by the International Sociological Association/ISA

For information address

SAGE Publications Ltd
28 Banner Street
London EC1 Y 8QE

SAGE Publications Inc
275 South Beverly Drive
Beverly Hills, California 90212

British Library Cataloguing in Publication Data

Conference on Legitimation and Delegitimation of Regimes,
City University of New York, 1977
Legitimation of regimes. — (Sage studies in international sociology; 17).
1.   Legitimacy of governments — Congresses
I.   Title   II.   Denitch, Bogdan
320'.01   JC328.2   78-63117

ISBN 0-8039-9898-8
ISBN 0-8039-9899-6 Pbk

First Printing
Printed in Great Britain by
Biddles Ltd., Guildford, Surrey

CONTENTS

FOREWORD

This volume of essays is the result of a Conference on Legitimation and Delegitimation of Regimes which was held at City University of New York in April 1977. All of the essays have been specifically commissioned for the volume and are the result, in some part, of the collective discussions of the participants. The Conference itself was generously supported by a grant from the Joint Committee on Eastern Europe of the American Council of Learned Societies and the Social Science Research Council, and was co-sponsored by the PhD Program in Sociology of the Graduate Center of City University, and the Research Institute on International Change of Columbia University. As if this were not enough in the way of organizational sponsorship, the Conference also represented an activity of the Committee on Political Sociology of the International Political Science Association and the International Sociological Association. The volume, therefore, is the seventeenth volume of publications of the Committee on Political Sociology.

The multitude of sponsorship reflects the fact that the theme of Legitimation and Deligitimation has assumed a centrality and urgency in the work of political scientists and sociologists in a number of countries and operating with diverse analytic frameworks ranging from traditional systems analysis to Marxism and neo-Marxism.

What turned out to be particularly fruitful during the conference was precisely the diversity of approaches that the varying participants brought in. Not only were Marxists and non-Marxists able to find a common language for addressing the theme but what was even more cheering was the fact that the debate and the concern cut across traditional disciplinary lines, and the contributors came from departments of Sociology, Political Science, History and Economics.

To sound a parochial note, it is my belief that this debate is central to political sociology and that the other disciplines only illustrate how narrowly political sociology is practised by practitioners who do not range across the social science disciplines.

It remains only to reiterate the editor's gratitude to the participants, the sponsors and, not least, to Selma Lenihan, without whose patient labors the volume never would have been produced.

Bogdan Denitch
New York City
March, 1978

I

THE DIMENSIONS OF
THE PROBLEM

1

LEGITIMACY AND THE SOCIAL ORDER

Bogdan Denitch
Graduate School, City University of New York, USA

The contributions to this book on legitimacy and social order range
over much of the terrain covered by the major debates on legitimacy,
social stability and political order today. These are debates which were
always latent in political sociology but which have been sharply
refocused by the events of the past decade in Eastern and Western
Europe. While the West European polities are increasingly facing class
cleavages and challenges to the legitimacy of the social order from an
organized Left, the East European societies — monocratic as they are —
face unorganized challenges from dissident intelligentsia, remnants of
the traditional middle classes and, with increasing urgency, from the
proudest creation of their social system — the massive new industrial
working class.

In the Fifties, the generally accepted thinking about these ideas was
quite different. On the one hand, it was almost self-evident to most
Western political observers of the period that the East European social
and political systems were hardly legitimate at all, imposed as they were
externally over a restive and grumbling population. In the West, on the
other hand, the economic miracle and the political stability appeared to
create societies with little prospect for social transformation, where the
domestication of the mass working class parties and trade unions
seemed to provide a broad consensual basis for the support of the rules
of the game which appeared to be working.

The dominance in Western political science of Parsonian paradigms
which emphasized social cohesion and stability as the societal norms
were linked to what appeared to be the social and economic realities of
the day. If there were challenges to the legitimacy of the social order,
they were to be found in the Third World, the unfolding colonial
revolution, and the movements to create new and, presumably, legiti-

mate nation-states on the ruins of a colonial order.

By the 1960s this social and political tranquillity began to be challenged by the emergence of an adversary culture within the student Left in the industrial societies. This adverse new Left political culture appeared to be almost the only discordant note in societies characterized by the quiescence of the mass class-based parties and institutions within a Europe and a United States which were said to be moving steadily into a society described as post-industrial where the classic cleavages would be absent entirely. The extremism of the student protest movement in part reflected the same consensus. The student radicals saw themselves as isolated from the mass social forces, limited generationally, and doomed to probable failure since linkages with massive social forces outside of the universities were non-existent and, in practice, not desired. This was the era where it was commonly accepted that the working class was conservative, that the communist parties were securely and eternally ensconced in their ghettoes, and where social democracy had given up all but a vestigial claim to represent an alternative social order. The alternative, in short, was between neat, well-managed, welfare states, sometimes run by social democrats, sometimes by Left-Center governments or even conservatives, which had solved the basic problems of an industrial economy. Political and social issues were marginal, focusing on the role of minorities, cultural stagnation, and the need to aid the development of the Third World out of a disinterested civic conscience, if for no other reason.

When social movements of any substance emerged, they certainly did not appear to challenge the basis of social order; rather, they sought their fair share of the benefits. Thus, the mass civil rights movement in the Southern states of the United States based its appeal on the truisms learned in civics classes of their own society. They demanded an extension of the rights granted to the majority to themselves, and although the tactics of such movements were often confrontational, the goals were moderate and subject to easy co-optation.

The student activists, in challenging the existing norms and values, seemed to represent a blend of neo-Luddite resistance to the encroaching homogenization of an industrial society and, therefore, had little relevance to the under-privileged groups of their own societies since they challenged the need for economic reform which would 'merely' extend the living standards, and thus presumably the problems, of the prosperous middle classes to other strata. This puritanical objection to consumerism was the stigmata of a movement whose isolation was underlined by the fact that it did not even see poverty and exploitation in their own societies as substantive problems. Thus, for the more extreme student Left, the hero figures were outsiders — the Third World revolutionaries, the Fanons, the Che Guevaras, the Vietnamese revolutionists; in the United States, not the mass civil rights movement, but rather Malcolm X and the Black Panthers. If there was to be a social transformation at all, it would be based on a loose, undefined alliance of these forces with the ideologically purified children of the middle classes in the universities. The working class, in so far as it was interesting at all, was only interesting where it found itself excluded from the main paths of social development — the Chicano farm workers, the immigrant workers in Western Europe, the lumpen-proletariat of the inner cities, and the like.

It was possible for entire schools of thought to gain visibility and notoriety in the Sixties based on the idea that the only challenge to the social order was a cultural one with culture perceived narrowly. How many scholars took the *Greening of America* seriously in their day? It certainly had its run. Peripheral Marxist theorists unconnected with parties and movements of any social substance kept producing increasingly abstract works on alienation as the main single weakness of the social order created in industrial societies. The tolerance characteristic of bourgeois consensus was, we were told, repressive. The norms of debate in the academy were a sham, and the student adversary culture sought to turn the universities into oases of social criticism reserved for those social scientists and political thinkers who reflected this adversary culture.

The Sixties also produced a plethora of studies on the convergence of all industrial societies. In so far as the university-based Left defined weaknesses within the monocratic regimes of Eastern Europe and the Soviet Union, they lay in the prevalence of alienation and the spread of consumerism. Thus, Western student-radicals warned the reformers in Prague of 1968 that the 'real' danger the Czechs faced was that they would merely duplicate the sterile prosperous societies of the West. The criticism of the mass Left parties which emerged during the hectic and heroic days of barricades on the Left Bank in May 1968 in France centered on the fact that those parties merely wanted to improve the economic lot of the underclasses and the workers in their society.

What was curious even then was the fascination of the media and of the broader elements in the society with these marginal challenges.

Shelves of works were published on the nature of the student rebellions, and endless dull dissertations were produced on student radicalism. And yet, the form of rebelliousness proved to be transitional, left few residues, and is hardly mentioned at all when one thinks of challenges to the industrial social order today. The reason seems to be clear: if the social order is in question, it is because of major structural problems which it cannot solve and because major social forces organized in parties, trade unions, and mass institutions challenge the basis of the social consensus and demand a transformation.

The Seventies are a period when challenges to system legitimacy appear all the more destructive because of the collapse of faith in their own legitimacy by many of the defenders of the social order. The economic miracle has come to an end. Substantial unemployment appears to be the norm. The underclass and the lumpenproletariat are expanding. The problems which appeared subject to technocratic welfarism are increasingly intractable. Neither the conservatives nor the liberal critics of the social order appear to have any confidence that their formulas work any more. The vision of the future is increasingly one of scarcities, grim accumulation of problems, and the inability of the social order to create consensuses which would make the demands upon it settleable through normal channels.

The general optimism of the ruling elites which characterized Western Europe of the past decades is replaced by an increasingly fashionable pessimism. In this there appears to be a real convergence; the situation of their opposite numbers in state socialist societies is not markedly different. The era of high growth rates seems to be behind us, and therefore an increasingly harsh tone emerges in the debates on redistribution and social amelioration.

There are many symptoms of this. In the United States the collapse of the traditional liberal consensus and the emergence of neo-conservatism is but one. The society, we are told, has tried to do too much; the poor will always be with us; welfare measures have unanticipated and unpleasant consequences; even the goals of ethnic and racial integration have taken a back seat when it becomes clear that in multi-racial societies substantial redistribution is required and the haves are increasingly unwilling to make sacrifices, if they ever were, on behalf of the have-nots. Long-submerged ethnic groups have emerged in the Seventies, and demand, urgently and often violently, recognition and a share of power. Traditional societies which prided themselves on their integration suddenly find ethnic cleavages emerging which were all but forgotten. Scots, Welsh, Breton, Basque, Flemish and other nationalisms, which were antiquaries' delight in the past, are transformed into political problems, and serious intellectual journals pose the question: is the motherland of parliamentary democracy – Great Britain – governable at all? The social peace imposed by DeGaulle crumbles for his successors, and the long reign of Christian democracy in Italy and of Franco in Spain is challenged by massive parties of the working class.

The internal challenges and stresses within the industrial polities are paralleled by shifts in the world order which are equally destabilizing. Not only is there a persistent demand for a new economic order posed by the Third World countries to an increasingly defensive and mean advanced world, but the previously stable balance of the Cold War is upset by the emergence of new forces which are unwilling to permit the world to be ordered by any 'Metternichian' arrangement between the two colossi – the Soviet Union and the United States. Trans-national movements that were movements – world communism and world capitalism – are internally rent and, at least in the case of the world communist movement, we are dealing with a phenomenon which is historical rather than actual.

In short, major challenges to national institutions, the international order, and major faiths are characteristic of the present period, and seem to have no readily acceptable solutions. In summarizing the basic challenges, one is of course focusing on the symptoms; the causes are more complex, and seem to be organically linked to the social order itself. If one were to group them, a useful categorization might be the following.

Challenges to the political order and the nation-state. These are more intense in multi-ethnic polities but, then, much of the world is governed by multi-ethnic polities. They range from the Soviet Union, where a non-Russian majority is emerging, to the African states, where the boundaries have little if any relevance to national and ethnic divisions. They include states with submerged ethnic national groups where the entire basis of the political agreement is questioned by the insistence of particular sub-groups on group representation and group cohesion within what were previously seen as universalist societies with a common citizenship. These challenges vary in intensity but in essence put into question the whole nineteenth-century nation-building effort of Jacobin and Mazzinian liberalism. Simply stated, the liberal state was

based on an assumption that common citizenship rights and a common
language would create an integrated nation whose institutions would be
legitimate in so far as they were accepted by the majority. That is an
untenable proposition if the state is seen as a coalition of ethnic groups
which bargain for their rights collectively and where the central loyalty
is based on a consensus among the component national units rather
than on a common electorate cutting across ethnic divisions. Such a
non-unitary model has been seriously attempted only in Switzerland
and Yugoslavia, and appears to work only in cases where the federal
authority is reduced to a stark minimum and the basic unit of governance is a geographically more or less homogeneous national unit. The
game of multi-ethnicity probably works better where there are more
than two partners, and where it is not perceived as a zero-sum game. It
is far more difficult to manage in situations where there are two
unequal partners, i.e. Quebec and the rest of Canada, or where there is a
preponderantly larger and more powerful partner, i.e. Britain in relation
to Scots-Welsh and Northern Irish questions. The reason for this
appears quite simple — in those cases the multi-ethnic solution is
unacceptable to the majority and unenforceable by the minority. This
leads to separatisms which are themselves an extreme challenge to state
legitimacy.

A second problem which is emerging within nation-states as such is
based on the relevance of the geographic representation model itself.
That model emerged in societies which are predominantly rural, where
the units are more or less equivalent. Increasingly in Western Europe,
consociational or neo-corporatist solutions are in the air. Whatever the
virtue of such solutions, they exist uneasily, if at all, side by side with a
parliamentary democracy based on one man-one vote. Interest representation of one kind or another may well be the wave of the future in
advanced industrial societies, but whatever else such representation
poses, a new type of social contract would have to underlay the rules of
the game.

Challenges to the economic and social order. These exist on both
the international and national scale and, while the international
challenges may in the long run be more disturbing, in immediate
political terms it is the internal challenge that is more difficult to
manage, if for no other reason than that it is based on massive political
and social forces within the state. Put a little differently, while there
may be a great deal of moral force behind the demand for a new world
order which would involve a redistribution of wealth between the have

and have-not nations, there is little if any practical force behind such demands and, passionate debates in the UN notwithstanding, the Third World nations are if anything less capable of imposing their wishes on a world economy today than they were in the past. This can be seen in part by the disarray of the non-aligned bloc and is a reflection of a reality that the Third World nations are often in bitter competition among themselves and only a few have the good fortune to sit on vast reserves of fuel which enable them to demand new terms. Internally, these challenges are more difficult to channel off into debating arenas because they are based, where effectively posed, on mass parties of the Left and their institutions and, all futurologists to the contrary notwithstanding, at least in Western Europe the Left appears to have a natural majority and therefore can use the levels of state control to press for redistribution.

The difficulties here fall into two categories: the first covers demands posed in the advanced welfare states, particularly Scandinavia, Great Britain, Holland, etc. where any major move towards redistribution within the economy or of political power would have to substantially affect the standard of living not only of the elites but of the more prosperous sections of the middle class. Redistribution under these circumstances involves raising the tax burdens of the more prosperous strata which see themselves as overtaxed already, pushing a greater share of consumption into the social sector and, most difficult of all, a move into a redistribution of political and economic power within complex industrial economies. The real problem is that after emptying the basket of popular welfare state demands, the next stage requires measures over which there is far less consensus and, therefore, postulates far sharper societal cleavages. In the second category – the less developed European countries – precisely because these are less developed as welfare states, there are large backlogs of basically egalitarian social and economic demands which are popular beyond the traditional base of the Left parties. Thus, in an Italy or a France, because of the greater inequities, measures extending social welfare and a fairer taxation would probably gain middle class adherence to the Left parties rather than set them into opposition and, at least in the initial stages, Left governments in the Mediterranean countries should be able to generate broad enough consensuses to remain reasonably stable.

A further difficulty exists with redistribution in advanced industrial societies in that one is not dealing here with stark cases of poverty and need which can appeal to other strata on a mutually accepted moral basis. Redistribution in welfare states, on the contrary, involves requiring the state to tilt in favor of the industrial working class and its allies in a way which would be perceived by the other strata as being illegitimate. Cynically stated, the problem is that one is not proposing to give largesse to the deserving and deferential poor but that a relatively prosperous and aggressive working class demands that the gap between itself and the middle class professionals and industry owners be drastically lowered. Experiences with professional and middle class reaction, when faced with such demands, are hardly sanguine. There have been strikes and protests by engineers and doctors in West European welfare states, not directed at a lowering of their own standard of living but rather protesting at the decreasing gap between their wages and those of skilled workers. They regard that gap as indispensable to maintaining a social order familiar to them and, therefore, sharp resistance to egalitarian advances is likely. On the other hand, an increasingly combative Left in Western Europe guarantees that the push in that direction is on the agenda, and the entire basis of social peace in the past two decades will be increasingly challenged.

Analogous challenges will exist increasingly in Eastern Europe. The harbinger here can be seen in the massive strikes in Poland and the less dramatic work stoppages in Rumania and the Soviet Union. The problem is somewhat different. A social order which bases its legitimacy on the claim to be ruling in the name of the working class finds it extremely disruptive and difficult to deal with working class unrest and working class claims. The monocratic states of Eastern Europe have found it relatively easy to deal with intellectual discontent; intellectuals are co-optable, relatively easy to intimidate, and do not form a stratum the size and cohesiveness of which can engage in more than guerrilla probes in challenging the legitimacy of the social arrangements. The industrial working class, on the other hand, not only is increasingly massive but in its present manifestation increasingly assumes the appearance of a classic proletariat since the systems are now dealing with sons of industrial workers and not with former peasants barely integrated into an industrial society.

This challenge is all the more difficult to contain because it is couched within the value system and the norms of the society itself. It is not outside agitators but working conditions and the texts of Marx, Engels and Lenin which focus the workers' grievances into collective action. A state claiming to be socialist which engages in massive direct suppression of the very class in the name of which it is supposed to rule faces a challenge to its legitimacy which affects the elite itself. And while East European elites can retain a great degree of homogeneity, vis-à-vis external challenges, and challenges seen as anti-socialist in nature, these challenges tend to fragment the elite.

Challenges within the educational systems and the future elites of the societies. Characteristic of advanced industrial societies has been the massive expansion of education which has created increasingly difficult problems for all of the advanced industrial polities. Quite simply stated, the implicit promise that higher education will provide a readily accessible road to social mobility into professional and satisfying jobs has simply ceased to work the way it used to. Increasingly, the unemployment of educated cadres has turned what would have been future recruits into the elites, into embittered adversaries of the social system. This rebelliousness, unlike the student rebellions of the Sixties, is linked to the structural problems of the society and is extraordinarily difficult to manage because a reduction of the growth of educational opportunity would be seen as a betrayal of democratic values, while an expansion of these opportunities would aggravate the problem of the oversupply of persons who claim that education has prepared them for non-manual work.

This problem is more acute in Western Europe at the moment but has an East European concomitant which is equally painful. One of the bases of the legitimacy of the social order in Eastern Europe has been the relatively rapid social mobility which these systems have provided for the children of the working class and the peasants. This has linked the new elites and the new middle classes to the social and political system, and created a loyal or, at the very least, a passive stratum whose personal advances were the result of the social transformation in Eastern Europe. However, once a second generation has been created by the mass university systems, a dilemma is posed: either to expand the educational system still further and to continue making room for the children of the working class and peasantry who want to use this avenue for social advancement, in which case increasing surpluses of persons overtrained for the administrative and professional jobs which are available will be created. Alternatively, restrictive numerical quotas could be imposed which would, if based on 'objective' examinations, have the unacceptable effect of excluding working class and peasant candidates from this escalator and thus sharpen the class cleavages in those societies. If the quotas were class-biased in favor of the working class and peasantry, a downward mobility would then be imposed on the children of the new middle class and technicians which would turn *those* strata into increasingly embittered opponents of the social order. Thus, the very instrument which was designed to maximize social mobility, and thus the legitimacy of the system, has become a problem.

In the Third World huge universities spawn an ever-increasing number of ill-trained malcontents who are unemployable but believe that their diplomas should spare them from a life of manual labor and propel them into the government bureaucracy. Since such post-university careers are all but closed for most, a generation of perpetual student 'political' activitists has been created. Since new openings in the system can only be created by the removal of the old elites, or by a vast expansion of the white collar strata, that activism is almost always extremist. Since anti-system language today is Leftist, that activism expresses itself in crude Marxist slogans which have no real content other than rationalizing the replacement of an old ruling elite with a newer one. It is symptomatic that the 'leftism' of university students tends to be anti-democratic, anti-working class and opposed to the mass parties of the Left where they do exist. The concessions student activists do get in most societies are usually the expansion of the universities, abolition of the already symbolic examinations, and some degree of student control of the universities. This aggravates the problem, making the universities even less useful to the economies of underdeveloped countries, making the graduates unemployable abroad, and making education consume an ever-increasing share of limited resources. Large universities exist in countries where massive illiteracy prevails, where secondary school systems continue to provide a classical education for a small elite, and where no technical or vocational schools exist. But even where vocational and technical education does exist parallel to the secondary or university education, it is relegated to a lower class status. Successful adolescents attain an MA in literature or a law degree; failures get the vocational degrees which the society needs.

In Western Europe and the United States, the same massive expansion of university education has caused increasingly insoluble social and political problems. The Italian universities have become parking lots for the unemployed. Some have expanded tenfold without expanding capacities for job opportunities. This is one of the several reasons for the growing number of terrorists of the Right as well as of the Left who have turned the universities into strongholds immune from the police and university administration. That hardly any education takes place is the least of the resulting problems. While Italy is admittedly an extreme case, less pathological versions of this alienation can be found in other university systems. Even where students and graduates are for the most part docile, as in the United States, the long-run effect will be the massive underemployment of university graduates. The most benign consequence so far has been the increasing tendency of university-trained US professionals to turn to unionization and collective bargaining to improve or maintain their status. As timid a profession as university professor has begun unionizing. In France, Italy, Spain, Holland and Sweden the consequence has been to increase the proportion of middle class and professional voters who vote for the Left parties. This enhances the prospects of the Left in its revitalized challenge to the legitimacy of the social order. Dissatisfied university graduates also contribute to the revitalized separatist and nationalist parties such as the Scots, Basque, Bretons, Welsh and the Quebec separatists.

Thus, in this respect there does seem to be a convergence between societies as diverse as state socialist and West European industrial democracies, and as different as industrial and non-industrial societies. All find it increasingly difficult to deal with the ever-growing and ever-bitter army of betrayed clerks.

Challenges to the patriarchal dominance of the traditional family in modern societies. The massive influx of women into the economies of advanced industrial societies provides a backdrop for another serious challenge to the societal arrangements which have long been familiar. As masses of women enter into the work process, and as the percentage of women who are educated in universities for technical and elite occupations increases, the traditional patriarchal domination of the family and male monopoly of power in society is increasingly subject to attack. Some of this attack takes the form of a guerrilla war within the institutions and the family itself, with feminists' ideological myths being counterposed to the previously universally accepted view of the inevitability of patriarchy; some of the challenges are limited to affirmative action drives in employment and education. But the most fundamental challenge is in the organization of the family which cannot sustain its traditional arrangement in a world where both parents are increasingly bread-earners and where the traditional division of labor — with the woman taking care of the home and the family and the man coping with the outside world — becomes the exception.

The social indicators of this crisis are all around us to see. The growing divorce rates, the growing control of family size, including abortion and contraception, the increased dispersal of women to professions previously reserved for males, and the symbolic entry of women into limited posts within the elites themselves. But while this particular challenge is probably more co-optable on a superficial basis than the class pressures for economic power and redistribution, nevertheless a serious reordering of social institutions will be required to replace the role of the traditional family in nurturing and socializing of children, and in assuring the social reproduction of future workers. While there is no logical reason why an industrial society cannot make such reforms, and some have gone a long way in that direction, pressures in this direction tend to strengthen those forces challenging the justness of the present social arrangement and are more in tune with the traditional parties of the Left than with the defenders of the existing social order.

One can conceive of this challenge as coming in two stages. In the first broad stage of demands for economic and social equity the demands of the feminists coincide roughly with those of the traditional parties of the Left. They thus help weaken the hold of the traditionalist parties and the churches on that part of the population where they were historically strongest, i.e. the women. At the second, and more complicated, stage of attempting to alter the power relations within the family, the feminist movements will find quite often that they have to attack their erstwhile allies and have a much harder row to hoe. This is because at that point they are not merely in the game of asking for a fairer social and economic arrangement but posit far more radical demands about the readjustment of deeply-held traditional values and norms. In any case, the reservoir of traditional supporters of authority and stability which the women have represented in industrial societies now becomes yet one more source of anti-systemic demands which question the validity of the system itself.

Most of these and other challenges are transsystemic and are equally directed at the capitalist welfare states and the state socialist societies. This gives ground for arguments for convergence theories, although the responses to these challenges will differ and the outcomes will probably produce different social arrangements. The convergence theories have had, at their base, the notion that advanced industrial societies, no matter what the formal political organization, basically have problems which are similar and which are increasingly subject to apolitical, technical expertise for management. The vision of a convergent world is the vision of a technocracy triumphant both in the economy and in the civil and political society.

There have been trends in that direction, trends which in the West are underlined by the increasing irrelevance of parliamentary government as ever-greater shares of power and problem-solving go to bodies of presumably apolitical experts. It is this technocratic trend, however, which has exacerbated the challenges to the legitimacy of social order. The 'apolitical' experts are, of course, never apolitical. Their very definitions of what are problems and legitimate options for solutions are linked to consciously and unconsciously held political and social values. An *unacceptable* cost is, after all, only unacceptable if one presumes the present social and economic arrangement to be in essence *acceptable*. An expert, gradual approach in dealing with social priorities will always be more reasonable, moderate and gradual if one does not perceive oneself to be in a burning house. This may explain why well-housed and well-paid urban housing experts in the United States have been able to dither for decades while areas like the South Bronx in New York City turned into desert.

The disenchantment with technocracies and the real or pretended expertise which they bring to bear to the management of human affairs has deep-seated structural roots which are a part of the entire package of problem overload which the industrial societies face today. As the workforce gets increasingly well educated, and as university education itself becomes more broadly diffused, much of the previous claim of the elites to rule through a monopoly of expertise and information is challenged. In large industrial enterprises and agencies, even more in the vast bureaucracies of modern welfare states, substantial sections of the workforce have an education which is superior to that of those who have authority over them.

Authority ultimately, if it is not to rest on traditional legitimacy but on rational-bureaucratic legitimacy, must assume that there is some rationality behind the hierarchical structures. This is increasingly and more obviously not the case. It hardly matters which example we pick, but to take a parochially American one: whatever the qualities of the bright young staff surrounding President Carter, one can hardly seriously argue that it is their greater capacity, intellectual training or managerial expertise which has placed them where they are.

Nothing is more disillusioning for sociologists than elite studies. In Britain, the incapacity of the managerial and political elites has been a national scandal for decades, but societies which were able to bumble through when the governments governed less can hardly expect to do that when assaulted with contradictory and continual demands for more effective outputs.

The communications explosion in the past decade has added to the unrest and the critical stance taken towards one's own society by large sections of its population. It hardly does any good now for a ruling elite in a moderately successful East European country to point to the indisputable real growth of living standards and improvement of services in its society. That is not the criterion by which they are judged. The Polish, Hungarian and Yugoslav workers, not to speak of the East Germans covered by the West German television networks, compare their standard of living with that of the most advanced industrial societies of Western Europe. So, for that matter, do middle classes, technicians and experts. And since the whole world cannot live in Sweden, it means that increasingly the demands placed on the systems are beyond any reasonable capacity of those systems to satisfy. This international comparison of performance does not aid the more advanced industrial democracies because they in turn are seen as grossly inegalitarian and socially mean, given their wealth and ability to produce an even better and more satisfactory standard of living.

That particular point was unwittingly recently underlined in a special issue of *Time* (7 March, 1978) which compared socialist and non-socialist societies. The issue was supposed to illustrate the crisis of socialism, and used three numerical indicators to make its point. The first was gross national product per capita; the second, a collapsed scale based on life expectancy, child mortality and literacy, called quality of life. This scale, of course, obviously reflected other services as well, such as medicine, education, housing and the degree with which those were distributed through the population as a whole. And, finally, there was a political freedom index. While the last was parochial and clearly flawed, stressing as it did the Freedom House criteria which are limited to political freedom of expression, the first two told what was a disastrous tale as far as the West European and North American industrial societies were concerned. By this 'quality of life' criteria the state socialist societies, including the Soviet Union, had a standard of life equal and sometimes superior to those of societies which had GNPs six and ten times larger. Whatever else this showed, the performance of the capitalist industrialized West was niggardly and poor, given its capacities. It also showed that whatever else was wrong with the state socialist societies, the problem of relatively rapid massive and dramatic increases in living standards is not unsolvable.

This argument, of course, puts many of the challenges directed at the inegalitarian social orders of the West in a different light. Surely dramatic increases in living standards of the lower half of the population are possible, and when it is argued that the present socio-economic system makes them impossible, the result is a questioning of whether such a socio-economic system is worth preserving at all. Surely, for the masses on welfare, for the unemployed or underemployed, for the lower-paid workers, for those who are housed in a grossly inadequate way, for those deprived of minimal decent health care and education, to be told that the satisfaction of *their* demands would overload the capacity of the political system and economy is not an argument calculated to strengthen their acceptance of the system's legitimacy in today's world. The ordering of social priorities in non-traditional societies is, after all, the work of men and institutions created by them, and must therefore ultimately rest on a general assumption that minimal social justice and fairness pervade the rules of the game.

The social and economic justice of the social order can be questioned in an amorphous, unorganized way but, in much of Western Europe today, it is challenged by organized parties of the Left, giving this challenge therefore a great impact and organizational potential for the transformation of present-day West European society.

The delegitimation of an old social order may lead to deep-seated political and economic malaise without, at the same time, producing the will to transform that order. The particular aspect of today's crisis is that the alternatives to the present social order have lost much of their chiliastic appeal both among the masses and the alternative political elites. If there is a crisis of welfare state capitalism and its liberal ideology underlined by the growth of neo-conservatism and the idea that societies are increasingly ungovernable, there has also been an erosion of faith within the political elites in the state socialist societies and mass working class parties of the West as well. The challenges do not have the same certainty that their alternatives are viable either. We live in an era of the decline of mass secular faiths, where communism itself is in an internal crisis of legitimacy which previously attached to the concept of a world movement with a world center, and social democracy having exhausted its welfare state short-range program, seemingly incapable of addressing itself to what lies or should lie beyond the welfare state.

The social democratic dilemma is particularly relevant for Western Europe at this time since the most sustained, organized challenge to the existing capitalist order is based, in all countries other than Italy, primarily on the massive working class-based socialist and social democratic parties. It is, after all, they and not the ultra-Left grouplets which offer a viable, visible, political alternative. Their problem, however, is that the moderate and reasonably effective welfare states which they have governed have merely governed and adapted societies which have in their essence remained capitalist. There were many good political reasons for this, including the Cold War and exigencies of a world market. But whatever those reasons were, the social democratic parties, and even the moderate West European communist parties, have not been able to arouse and sustain an enthusiastic support for their alternatives. They are seen as the better option, as the superior way of dealing with the social problems, but they have not offered effectively a vision of a new social order which is convincing. The democratic pluralist polities probably do function better if there is not too much 'enthusiasm', and if the alternatives debated are not too drastic. However, when a societal crisis is on hand, moderate and lukewarm alternatives hardly provide organizing values for the transformation to a different social order.

The point here is a familiar one. The working class parties have not conquered the moral and political hegemony within the civil society but merely occasionally been given the opportunity to run the state and some economic institutions. Therefore, there is a standoff in much of the industrial West. While the old order is losing its legitimacy, a new one has not yet won it. And this explains, in good part, the glacial slowness with which social transformations are taking place, and the cautious programs of the parties of the Left. What is absent here is a radical imagination which can visualize a society which is fundamentally different in its hierarchies both on the micro and the macro level. This is a price which decades of moderate 'socialism from above' has extracted. It is this bureaucratized, hierarchical socialism which has been the real life alternative in the post-World War II world. Whether it took the authoritarian form of state socialism in Eastern Europe or the moderate democratic form of social democratic and labor governments in Western Europe, socialism in the post-World War II world has maintained the value systems and priorities of the old social order, and distributed social welfare and varying doses of equality from the top down, resisting any spontaneous impulses from below and any attempts at a creative reconstruction of the rules of the game.

The effect is obvious. In Eastern Europe the elites have copied the life styles and manners of the pre-revolutionary elites or of their capitalistic equivalents in the West today. The bureaucracies of the social democratic and communist parties in the West are manned by enlightened, decent administrators every bit as addicted to hierarchy and engaged in manipulation of the masses as the civil servants of the society itself.

I am arguing that Gramsci, in one essential argument, was right — that for a new class to replace the existing ruling class, it must make itself fit to rule. It must attain a dominance in culture, in the civil society, in the basic institutions before it can effectively wield political power to make social transformations. The bourgeoisie replaced the feudal order *after* they had clearly become dominant economically, intellectually and morally. A part of the crisis of legitimacy lies in the fact that the exhaustion of the moral, political and intellectual capital of the old ruling elites has not been replaced by the conquest of those arenas by those who pose themselves as the carriers of the new social organization of advanced industrial societies. And the crisis of legitimacy of the capitalist West is therefore simultaneously a crisis of modern socialism.

One can argue that the crisis of socialism, in turn, is an historical penalty being paid for the fact that the first conquest of power by a socialist party in Russia took place in a backward, unprepared society where the civil society was not conquered by the Bolsheviks before their seizure of state power. As a consequence, a socialism — if it can be called that — was created which, whatever its successes, was monstrously unattractive to the more advanced working classes of the West and North America. It is also an historical penalty paid for the straitjacket imposed on social democracy after World War II; for the pruning and limitation of Western social democracy to pare it down to those measures acceptable within the framework of a US-led capitalist world economy, counterposed in a Cold War to the Soviet-led bloc.

The crisis of legitimacy in the West requires, for its solution, a dramatic breakthrough and reordering of the social order on a scale analogous to that which followed the breakdown of feudalism and the development of capitalist democracies. That breakthrough, if it occurs, will probably occur in the advanced West European industrial polities and, if successful in developing a new social order and civilization, cannot but have an effect beyond its geographic confines. If a new post-capitalist socialist system is built in Western Europe, it will represent the beginning of a dramatic stage of the crisis of legitimacy in the state socialist societies to the East and posit a new historical alternative on a world scale. Just as the Bolshevik revolution, with all its problems, posed an alternative which was visible and available to modernizing elites throughout the Third World, this breakthrough in Western Europe would be posed on a world arena. For it to occur, it is obviously not enough simply to have parties of the Left govern advanced West European societies within more or less the present political, economic and social framework. If they are to cope with the crisis of legitimacy, they must offer an alternative social organization, an alternative system of values and, ultimately, a new civilization.

2

THE NORM OF ILLEGITIMACY - TEN YEARS LATER

Irving Louis Horowitz
Rutgers University, USA

In the study of legitimacy we are the children of Max Weber; just as in the study of revolution we are the offspring of Karl Marx. This is as might be expected: since if there is any truth to the phrase that Weber is the 'bourgeois Marx', it shows up in the analysis of how social systems come to sustain themselves over time through a combination or permutation of traditional, bureaucratic, or charismatic modalities. That Weber himself appreciated the complexities of the problem of legitimacy is indicated by his allusion to the special circumstances surrounding the Papacy. He saw such church forms of legitimacy as a function of the 'charisma of the office'; the so-called magical leadership potency is less derived from the personal qualities of any given Pope, as it is from the institutional properties of a world historic church.

My initial foray into the problem of legitimacy was thus suggested by Weber. Since if charisma of office is a fourth distinct type, then a little discussed present-day secular variant of that type is the charisma of party. In the preparation of *Three Worlds of Development* I emphasized how throughout the Third World and non-aligned nations, such a phenomenon seemed to have arisen (Horowitz, 1966: 225-53). Even in such clear instances as Egypt under Nasser, India under Nehru, and Tito in Yugoslavia, it is clear that the major binding single party units survive intact after the demise of an originating leadership. Indeed, it is a tribute to the innovating potentials of Third World political systems that they have managed to address problems of succession and leadership in such an innovative manner.

Yet, it soon became apparent that the notion of party charisma was a special condition, rather than a general law of political development. Where institutions were durable and powerful in their own right, such a

concept has great operational worth: whether in describing the leadership of the Roman Catholic Church or a representative socialist or
Third World country. However, in other nations, ranging from Ghana to
Brazil, the party apparatus itself was subject to extreme pressures, and
with the fall of charasmatic figures like Nkrumah or Goulart, party
dissolution also occurred. This happened to a lesser degree to be sure —
sometimes as absorption in new political formations; yet it was no
longer possible to subsume all or most Third World or non-aligned
powers under the rubric of party charisma.

   This need to reach out for a more embracing concept, one that took
into account the phenomena of party, class, and state under
praetorian conditions, led to my discussion of the norm of illegitimacy
the following year. For it became evident by the late 1960s that
military might in the Third World had become pre-eminent. Furthermore, its management of the political system was not based on anything remotely resembling a Rousseauian social contract, but was
simply a rearrangement of elites lacking in either electoral or popular
support. These new structural configurations in the Third World were,
and remain, of such a profound nature that it was no longer feasible to
speak of a crisis in legitimacy. Rather, it became necessary to explore
what the new configurations of power were, and how they contributed
to the formation of the new normative framework, quite unlike what
characterized Western and socialist societies alike. To these new states I
affixed the term: norm of illegitimacy.

   The original utilization of the norm of illegitimacy concept was to
explain what appeared to be the aberrant and yet permanent political
climate of crisis throughout Latin America (Horowitz, 1968; Horowitz,
1969).[1] It was clear then, and I am convinced even more so now, that
the model employed has a range of applicability to many parts of the
Third World, and certainly beyond the Latin American orbit originally
covered. For the so-called crisis of legitimacy that has become common
parlance with respect to the Third World, has now clearly invaded
intellectual discourse in the First and Second Worlds as well. We have
an expanding literature of growing significance on the breakdown of
legitimacy in the West (Wolfe, 1977), and a similar sort of doomsday
literature covering contemporary communism (Jacobson, 1972).

I

My concern is not so much with the breakdown of legitimacy as the normative standing of militarized politics equal to, if not greater than, the older capitalist and socialist orders alike. What we are witness to is less a crisis of legitimacy than new forms of institutionalizing power. Seen in this way, problems of legitimation do not necessarily evaporate, but they do take on a more specialized meaning; since we can now examine the problem of legitimacy as long standing rather than the conventional mode of crisis-thinking on ways of maintaining legitimate authority.

The crisis factor in the legitimation process has common roots, yet different forms of expression, given the structural differentiation of political systems in the 'three worlds'. In Western capitalism and democracy, those societies most characterized by parliamentary representation, the problem has been that within a mass society there has been a stretching out effect of representational government. When a constituency is small, the relationships between the representative and those who are represented are direct and organic. But as the size of parliamentary governments is held constant, and citizen size continues to grow, the ratios of representation change. As a result, those who represent constitutencies are themselves nearly as anonymous, remote, and removed from popular consensus as executive officers or even appointed officials. This stretching out effect generates a problem of non-choice, a feeling of helplessness before world historic events presumably beyond ordinary control. This, in turn, leads to at least a short term fall-off of interest more conventionally labelled by political scientists as a problem of political alienation in a democracy (cf. Schwartz, 1976: 18-53). But whatever labels are attached, widespread agreement exists that the sense of distance between those who rule and those who are ruled is in large part the source of the legitimacy crisis in the West.

When we turn to the Second World, basically the universe of socialist economies and political authoritarianisms, the problem of legitimacy shifts. At least in nations where an independent communist movement seized power the basis of legitimacy is not electoral so much as based on the doctrine of direct popular participation, alternatively called the dictatorship of the proletariat, socialism of the whole people, the rights of the masses, and so on (Denitch, 1976: 41-48). Characteristic of the socialist situation, with nearly 100 percent electoral turnout

on behalf of a single party, and parliamentary government reduced to
rubber-stamping executive authority, different political structures yield
the same sort of outcomes. Socialism also reveals the problem of
non-choice, and a problem of a fall-off of popular interest. We need
only witness the constant efforts of the Soviet government to stimulate
participation to realize how serious this problem of apathy, alienation
and, ultimately, a crisis in legitimate authority has become.

One should not confuse political legitimacy with national hegemony. Neither the classic models of the American nor Soviet revolutions could boast hegemonic rule by the *de jure* procedures of claiming
legitimacy for a revolutionary elite or party. In the case of the
American revolution claims of legitimacy for the 'first new nation'
divided the colonists and resulted in the emergence of united empire
loyalists who, for the most part, settled in Canada. One authority,
Leslie F. S. Upton (1967: 1-7) put the matter thus:

> The American Revolution was a civil war between British subjects and
> particularly between British Americans. The Loyalists were the losers. They
> were the first 'unAmerican' Americans, interrogated by committees, con-
> demned without judge or jury, smeared in the press, expelled from their jobs,
> and deprived of their possessions. The American mind can tolerate any crime
> but that of failure: the grand sweep of American history covered the loyalists
> in oblivion.

And the Soviet Revolution revealed even deeper cleavages between
bolshevik legitimists and social democratic hegemonists. As David Lane
notes (1971: 59-61) the immediate consequence of the Soviet State was
civil war.

> From 1918 to 1921, the country was enveloped in the chaos of civil war and
> foreign intervention: it was a period known as 'War Communism'. For much
> of the time the Bolsheviks ruled only one-seventh of Russian territory, mainly
> the Great Russian areas of the country, the remainder being occupied by other
> governments.

Thus, even at points of maximum revolutionay fervor, legitimacy is
never quite holistic.

The success of a revolution is itself a phase of legitimizing a regime.
This may be followed by institutionalization, which operationally refers
to the emergence of hegemonic rule, or at least a broad-based consensus
between the holders of power. Creating an institutional framework is
often as difficult and exacting a task as leading a successful revolution.

Indeed, it has become an iron law of socialist revolutionary politics that the cadre formed in making a revolution is inevitably displaced by one formed to carry through its stated tasks. In that post-revoluntionary process very few of the original 'old revolutionists' survive the bureaucratic processing. But quite beyond legitimating and institutionizing phases is what might be termed the 'highest stage' of revolution-making: solving the riddle of succession.

The crucial point in the revolution comes when there is a need to transfer power from one person or group to another person or group; and to do so without the destruction of the governing and bureaucratic networks as a whole. The serious problems that arose in the transference of power after the death of Lenin in the Soviet Union and of Mao in the Peoples Republic of China is a clear indicator of just how serious a matter succession can be in non-democratic regimes. Far even beyond Dahl's question: 'after the death of original leader, then what?' This is clearly not the place for a full-blown discussion of problems of leadership and succession. It is sufficient to note the three phases of post-revolutionary morphology: legitimation, institutionalization, and succession.

When viewed against such an historical background, urging older forms of legitimation upon the Third World is a far less attractive moral imperative than would at first seem apparent. It might well be argued that the function and structure of military politics in Latin America has increasingly come to provide a solution to the crisis of legitimacy by turning the political structure upside down: by institutionalizing forms of illegitimate authority that are admittedly derived neither from the electoral process, nor the direct will of the people, but simply by a presumed national need best understood by those who lead, and best implemented by those who are led. Thus, the Third World, faced with monumental problems of modernization at the economic level, mobilization at the political level, and militarization at the organizational level, has moved toward a style of governance that deserves to be understood on its own terms. The arrogant presumption that such Third World forms only provide a benchmark on an evolutionary scale which is still considerably behind either Western or socialist forms of government, does not appreciate the ironic situation that has ensued: legitimacy, like illegitimacy, is a problematic and not a given.

II

I have attempted to extrapolate, by way of assumptions and hypotheses from my earlier papers, just what the norm of illegitimacy entails. In order to avoid excessive repetition I have reduced those earlier efforts to ten propositions that seem central to present-day concerns, and that should provide an adequate measure of the worth of this concept in currect discussions of this topic.

(1) The norm of illegitimacy arises in a context where structural requisites for legitimate authority are absent. When authority can neither be institutionalized through the mechanism of class/mass, nor through law/authority, then illegitimacy exists in fact.

(2) The norm of illegitimacy is serviceable both to the internal needs of the political/military order which gives direction to national policy, and to an international/multinational order which delimits the directions of any one nation in the world economy.

(3) The norm of illegitimacy, like that of legitimacy, is intended to produce mass political mobilization and, at the same time, reduce unsponsored violence or acts of terror. Illegitimacy becomes an instrument to prevent rather than to stimulate untrammeled social change.

(4) The norm of illegitimacy is guaranteed and underwritten by a combination of internal and international elites which view a circulation of government power as beneficial to larger global interests.

(5) The norm of illegitimacy is usually carried forth by military or quasi-military forces, sometimes overturning civilian regimes, and other times overturning military regimes; but always circulating elites while minimizing the risk of civilian authority in the Third World.

(6) The norm of illegitimacy serves as a political distributive mechanism without being an economically distributive mechanism. Since no government undergoing a constant set of political rotations at the top can legitimate itself, either electorally or through direct participation, political illegitimacy becomes institutionalized.

(7) The norm of illegitimacy serves to prevent any undue entrenchment of special, sectarian interests. Hence, it serves to overcome structural deformities in the political system, and does so without risking social revolution or systemic overhaul.

(8) The norm of illegitimacy is a mechanism for problem management rather than problem solving. Its purpose is to institutionalize elite authority without the conventional calcifying effects of either older civilian or military formations that are attached to race, class, or

religious interests instead of the profession of State power directly.

(9) The norm of illegitimacy presupposes a conflict model, just as theories of legitimation for the most part presuppose consensus models. In propositional forms: when a consensus apparatus becomes inoperative, political-military regimes turn to a norm of illegitimacy rather than risk normlessness and widespread upheaval as a whole.

(10) The norm of illegitimacy permits the institutionalization of crisis as a normative political pattern, rather than presume a norm of legitimacy which is not only inoperative in most parts of the Third World, but increasingly subject to wide-scale pressures in the First and Second Worlds.

A considerable amount of work on illegitimacy took place outside the framework of political sociology, particularly by political anthropologists. I confess that in doing my own work I did not take proper account of the efforts of these scholars, specifically Clifford Geertz (1963) and George Balandier (1970). They have served to provide a deeper understanding of the subjective side of the processes which accompanies the breakdown of legitimacy and, parenthetically, makes possible the emergence of a norm of illegitimacy.

Geertz pointed out that for virtually every person in every society some attachments flow more from a sense of natural, even spiritual, affinity than from social or political interaction. He went on to note that in modern societies the shifting of such ties to the level of political supremacy has increasingly come to be considered as pathological. An increasing percentage of national unity is maintained not by calls to blood and land, but by a vague, intermittent and routine allegiance to a civil or military state supplemented to a greater or lesser extent by the government use of police powers and ideological exhortation. In modernizing societies where the tradition of civil authority is weak, and where technical requirements for effective welfare are poorly understood, primordial attachments serve to demarcate autonomous political units. What finally emerges, according to Geertz, is a theory that authority comes only from the inherent coerciveness of such primordial attachments, or what in fact in my own terms I have come to call the norm of illegitimacy.

George Balandier enriches this notion of the primordial or spiritual source of permanent strife by speaking of the desacralization of power. This process of desacralization of traditional leadership of Kings and Chiefs was inevitable since the power of those sovereigns and chiefs was legitimated by reference to colonial governments rather than native groupings. Such authority rarely rested on any intrinsic merits of such systems of rule. Hence, the transition from the patrimonial to the bureaucratic type of authority does not take place in the Third World the way it did in either the First or Second Worlds. Because these colonial political systems were so varied, different reactions to the experiences of post-colonial transformation were inevitable. Bureaucratic desacralization did not bring about the terrible effects feared by former rulers; but it did result in types of rule that attempted to combine hierarchical and egalitarian forms rather than displace the latter by the former.

Balandier notes that the process of modernization was set in motion by the colonial adventure. But that very adventure created political distortions that led political parties, social ideologies, and military regimes to seek out forms of institutionalization quite different from the older European and American societies. All human societies produce politics, and none are resistant to historical processes. On the other hand, this universal proposition comes upon the particular: namely, that Third World politics produces national, ethnic, racial, and religious demands that lead to a very different set of norms in the Third World than in either the First or Second Worlds.

III

Even if we confine these remarks to Latin America, it will be apparent that the norm of illegitimacy is deeper and more pervasive than a decade ago. The sterling examples of Argentina, Brazil, and Peru, the hardy perennials of the 1960s, have now been joined by presumably bedrock democratic regimes, such as Uruguay and Chile, in the 1970s. In part, the failure to recognize the growing militarism of Latin America, even in former democracies such as Chile and Uruguay, rests on an inability to appreciate the extent to which these countries shared with the rest of Latin America demands for wider popular participation and greater economic growth without the wherewithal to deliver the goods and services. But it also reflects an inbred tendency on the part of scholars to live in a world of labels: not to take seriously the potency and power of militarism in the history of countries such as Chile and Uruguay (cf. Lowenthal, 1976; Nunn, 1976, and Kaufman, 1977).

An area in need of far greater emphasis than it received in the past is the relationship between electoral politics and the norm of illegitimacy. Specifically, why should it be that elections, that monument to constitutional legitimacy, should fail to prevent military dominion, authoritarian takeovers, and the constant rotation of self-appointed leaders? Alfred Stepan (1971: 79-84) found that in Brazil a regime is more likely to be overthrown the smaller its margin of victory. Later Martin Needler (1977: 115-16) broadened this observation into a generalization by noting that 'the narrowness of an electoral victory seems to impair a government's legitimacy, thus making a military coup against it more likely'. Yet, in North America and Western European political democracies, where the system itself and not the party process provides legitimation, similarly close elections, while engendering bitterness and charges of vote tampering, ironically serve to unite the nation and prevent militarist outcomes. While a tradition of competitive elections may itself reduce differentials of winning from losing, it also stimulates a norm of illegitimacy based on charges, often launched by military technocrats, that the electoral process is wasteful, divisive, and fruitless. And if one examines the sad roster of Latin American nations which once had vigorous presidential elections, and far from routine campaigns, few of them have endured. It is the quasi-democracies, the basically single party states (Mexico, Cuba, and to a lesser extent Venezuela and Costa Rica) that have shown greater resistance to illegitimate authority than the former democracies of the area. But then, one might well argue that single party states are themselves a special case of illegitimate authority.

This is not to equate military technocracy with the norm of illegitimacy. Although the norm of illegitimacy invariably requires high military participation, many military systems were and remain transitional — such as in Greece, Spain, and Portugal. It is conceivable that military rule can become institutionalized and hence develop a sense of quasi-legitimacy without the constant rotation of power. This is certainly what has taken place in Brazil. The military regimes essentially institutionalize their power, regularize the political processes in order to solve the problem of succession, and in this way create political forms that stabilize rather than rotate elites in power. The recent directives of President Ernesto Geisel are intended to prevent civilian opposition from reaching power in the foreseeable future; but also serve to move away from the highly personal military dictatorships of previous years, and incorporate themselves as the only institution capable of leading the economic and social transformation of Brazil. Since time is a crucial element in legitimation, the ability of the Brazilian military to maintain itself in power far longer than either they or their opponents originally thought possible, represents a move away from the norm of illegitimacy to a type of authoritarian legitimacy far less prevalent a decade ago.

The situation in Argentina which provided the classic model for the norm of illegitimacy a decade earlier remains just that under the present rule of its military President, Rafael Videla. What makes Argentina's military government different from those in Chile and Brazil, and other countries with similar military rule, is its refusal to be branded as a permanent military regime. It constantly defines itself as a transformational movement. It is this insistence on transition which gives continuing substance to the norm of illegitimacy in theory as well as fact in a nation such as Argentina. For as soon as civilian rule is threatened, the coup-within-a-coup phenomenon occurs; and the norm of illegitimacy is preserved.

The crucial test for the norm of illegitimacy is the same as for all societies: can such a framework achieve high levels of productivity without inflation or labor unrest? Can it achieve political stability without mass apathy and alienation? Can it create a stable pattern of succession without recourse either to the democratic distemper of the West, or without resorting to the authoritarian repression of the East? Here the evidence for the success of the norm of illegitimacy is impressive, at least in the economic arena.

Nations such as Argentina, subject to intense political pressures and a nearly endless round of mass terrorism, have yet managed during the past year to achieve significant goals. Argentine monetary reserves in 1977 are more than two billion dollars, one of the highest in its history. Fair trade, which has been subject to a constant deficit for years, has been improved to the point where a 1.2 billion dollar surplus was achieved in the Argentine balance of payments at the close of 1976. The present rate of unemployed in Argentina is 4 percent, thus resolving a nearly chaotic issue of underemployment as well as unemployment of the Argentine past. And the forecast is for an economic growth rate of 4.5 percent in 1977, 5.7 percent in 1978, levelling off to around 5 percent for the years 1979 and 1980.

The situation in Chile is more complex since the inherited economic problems are more chronic. The inflationary rates have been reduced from 400 percent per annum to less than 50 percent per annum. Unemployment has been reduced to roughly 6 percent of the work force. Industrial absenteeism has been reduced from 40 percent to roughly 5 percent. While the Chilean situation hardly presents the same sense of economic miracle as Brazil, or even stability such as in Argentina, it remains a fact that despite all sorts of international pressures, the Chilean military junta has achieved a consequential economic stability.

Calls for human rights have not only largely fallen on deaf ears, but have resulted in summary rejection of American foreign policy pleas, and a direct assertiveness characteristic of successful rather than unsuccessful regimes. This is especially true in the case of Brazil which, by virtue of its economic strength, a gross national product averaging more than 10 percent, is able to go directly into the financial market and bypass foreign aid from the United States government. The Brazilian economy is no longer dependent on foreign-aid handouts, and the best proof of this is that the United States, which in the 1960s provided 35-40 percent of all armaments sold to Brazil, and financed yet additional purchases of dollar grants, today provides only 14 percent of such arms purchases, even though the amounts involved are running at two billion dollars. In short, the very success of military rule and illegitimate political norms has made possible a level of Third World assertion inconceivable a decade ago. Hence, the norm of illegitimacy, far from signifying the existence of widespread dependency of Latin America on the United States, on the contrary has come to illustrate a style of rule intended to create autonomy and independence from the United States.

The same problems exist now as a decade ago — only with a greater sense of urgency. Whether or not short-run tendencies can produce long-range economic benefits to large numbers; whether the costs of maintaining a norm of illegitimacy (high military and police power) dry up economic distributions rather than expand services; and finally whether the very success at the economic level may engender new classes and social formations and hence new demands for legitimacy and the institutionalization of authority based on democratic or populist premises — these remain as elusive now as before. But for the present, the norm of illegitimacy has served to institutionalize military authority and stabilize the mixed economy.

One can only conclude in a spirit of caution: certainly in a world in which the United States is viewed as both the bête noire of autonomous Latin American development and, at the same time, the leading proponent of human rights in these areas, to be met in turn by intransigent Latin American elites demanding more in the way of economic development and political nationalism, and less in the way of human rights. This bizarre paradigm has come to characterize the present moment, and would indicate that we are confronting not only the crisis of legitimation, but a crisis in the labelling processes used to describe the world.

Elite structures, which are responsible for both the so-called crisis in legitimacy and the consequent norm of illegitimacy, serve to promote ideology at the expense of polity. The central lesson, the basic outcome, of viewing the norm of illegitimacy ten years later, is to face the end of politics — its relatively complete displacement by policy-making elites. Whether this end to politics in the Third World is limited to that large chunk of the universe, or endemic to the current stage of universal political history, thus becomes a new element to observe and examine — more in fear than in delight, more in trembling than in tranquility.

NOTES

First presented before the Conference on the Legitimation and Delegitimation of Regimes at the City University of New York, Graduate Center. Sponsored by the American Council of Learned Societies, 22-24, April 1975.

1. Initially, I presented 'The Norm of Illegitimacy' at the American Sociological Association meetings on 31 August, 1967 at San Francisco, California. The paper entitled 'Political Legitimacy and the Institutionalization of Crisis in Latin America' in fact preceded the other in idea formation by a good six months. It was first presented at the American Political Science Association meetings on 8 September, 1977 at Chicago, Illinois. Earlier drafts of each study were given at various invited conferences and lectures; but it is fair to say that the relatively final versions of each were delivered at these back-to-back meetings.

REFERENCES

BALANDIER, G. (1970) *Political Anthropology.* New York: Pantheon Books (A Division of Random House).

DENITCH, B. D. (1976) *The Legitimation of a Revolution: The Yugoslav Case.* New Haven and London: Yale University Press.

GEERTZ, C. (ed.) (1963) *Old Societies and New States: The Quest for Modernity in Asia and Africa.* New York: The Free Press/Macmillan, pp. 105-57.

HOROWITZ, I. L. (1966) 'Party Charisma: Practices and Principles, Ideological and Institutional Bases of Party Charisma', and 'Intra-Country Variations in Party Charisma', in *Three Worlds of Development: The Theory and Practice of International Stratification.* New York and London: Oxford University Press.

— —, (1968) 'Political Legitimacy and the Institutionalization of Crisis', *Comparative Political Studies,* 1 (1): 45-69.

— —, (1969) 'The Norm of Illegitimacy: The Political Sociology of Latin America', in I. L. HOROWITZ, J. de CASTRO and J. GERASSI (eds.), *Latin American Radicalism: A Documentary Report on Left and Nationalist Movements.* New York: Random House; London: Jonathan Cape, pp. 3:29.

JACOBSON, J. (1972) *Soviet Communism and the Soviet Vision.* New Brunswick: Transaction Books/E. P. Dutton.

KAUFMAN, E. (1977) *Uruguay in Transition: From Civil to Military Rule.* New Brunswick: Transaction Books.

LANE, D. (1971) *Politics and Society in the USSR.* New York: Random House.

LOWENTHAL, A. F. (ed.) (1976) *Armies and Politics in Latin America.* New York and London: Holmes and Meier Publishers, Inc.

NEEDLER, M. C. (1977) 'The Closeness of Elections in Latin America', *Latin American Research Review,* XII (1): 115-21.

NUNN, F. N. (1976) *The Military and Chilean History: Essays on Civil/Military Relations, 1810-1973.* Albuquerque: University of New Mexico Press.

SCHWARTZ, D. C., J. ABERBACH, A. W. FINIFTER et al. (1976) 'Political Alienation in America'. A special supplement to *Transaction/Society,* 13 (5) (July/August).

STEPAN, A. (1971) *The Military in Politics: Changing Patterns in Brazil.* Princeton, New Jersey: Princeton University Press.

UPTON, L. F. S. (ed.) (1967) *The United Empire Loyalists: Men and Myths.* Toronto: Copp Clark Publishing Company.

WOLFE, A. (1977) *The Limits of Legitimacy: Political Contradictions of Contemporary Capitalism.* New York: The Free Press/Macmillan Publishing Company.

3

POLITICAL LEGITIMACY IN CONTEMPORARY EUROPE

Joseph Rothschild
Columbia University, USA

Before, during, and immediately after World War II, the viability of states was much discussed in political literature. Recently, however, that issue has waned as the international community has lowered its threshold requirements and definitions of what constitutes viability. States that would formerly have been deemed non-viable by virtue of their small size, awkward and indefensible frontiers, or meager human and material resources, are now normally and as a matter of course subsidized and sustained by the international community. Corresponding to this process in political life, there has occurred a simultaneous shift in the focus of political theory and political analysis away from the question of viability, and toward the issue of legitimacy as particularly important and problematical.

The attention currently devoted to this problem of political legitimacy stems in part from a widespread sense that the contemporary state, while viable enough in terms of that older concern and its newer standards, is nevertheless somehow out of phase with the world's travails — seemingly too small and weak to solve such global issues as inflation, yet apparently too big and remote to evoke that cathartic trust, identification, and admiration of its subjects which the state requires if its political system is to function. This essay probes some of the problematics — of theory and of policy — confronting state authorities in contemporary Europe as they seek to achieve, sustain, and enhance their always vulnerable legitimacy.

This paper is reprinted with permission from *Political Science Quarterly*, volume 92, number 3, Fall 1977.

THE CONCEPT OF LEGITIMACY
IN CONTEMPORARY
POLITICAL THEORY

The study of the problem of legitimating political authority goes back
to Aristotle who said that political power elicits compliance by the use
of force, by the distribution of rewards, by education, or by some
combination of these three procedures. In modern social science
rhetoric, Aristotle's triad would be referred to, respectively, as coercive,
utilitarian, and normative techniques of rule. Plato, by analogizing the
state to the household and family, and then by equating the ruler's
authority with that of the father or, alternatively, of a physician (i.e. an
expert), missed the essence of the political bond and thereby deprived
himself of the chance to make a productive contribution to the analysis
of political legitimacy. The most influential (and by now classical)
modern discussion of the problem is Max Weber's elaboration of three
types of legitimating norms for political power: the traditional, the
charismatic, and the rational-legal. This paper proceeds on the assumption that the contemporary European political systems, both Communist and non-Communist, are too advanced and developed for
Weber's traditional and charismatic legitimations to play more than
auxiliary roles, and that the central type for them must be the rational-
legal one.

In contemporary political science, the discussion of the problem was
explicitly reopened by Seymour Martin Lipset with his distinction
between the effectiveness of political systems, which is judged by
instrumental criteria and relates to their performance (often, nowadays,
their performance in achieving modernization goals), and their legitimacy, which is an evaluative criterion and refers to a perception by
their publics of their appropriateness and a belief by these publics that
the regimes of such systems have a right to exercise political authority
in their given domains. Depending on historical circumstances,
effectiveness and legitimacy (as well as their negations) may
characterize virtually any form of political organization, and the
stability of political institutions both in normal times and in crises
depends on their effectiveness and on their legitimacy.[1]

Of course, these two axes, effectiveness and legitimacy, can be
distinguished for analytical and heuristic purposes only. In real political
life they are not only relevant to each other, but interact organically. A
perception on the part of its public that a system is legitimate can

compensate — for astonishingly extended periods of time — for erroneous, inefficient, and ineffective performance (thus proving Locke
rather than Hobbes the shrewder in assessing the likelihood and fre-
quency of revolutions under certain conditions). Indeed, subjects and
citizens who perceive a system as legitimate will even acquiesce in
actions by it against their interests. Similarly, a high level of effectiveness in meeting the public's needs and interests will purchase at least
some legitimacy for an initially illegitimate, revolutionary political
system. Finally, even a traditionally fully legitimate system is subject to
erosion and delegitimation over the long run if it becomes chronically
incompetent or ineffective. In this sense, legitimacy, like Ernest
Renan's democracy, has to be re-earned constantly ('le plébiscite de
tous les jours')[2] and no system stands still, forever legitimate, without
being effective.

Indeed, some contemporary social scientists have even proceeded
from this recognition of the organic nexus between legitimacy and
effectiveness to argue that the former is merely a dependent function of
the latter, and that the task of government is to educate public opinion
to accept this sequence.[3] In other words, technology and science,
translated into effectiveness and affluence, are to fill the void left by
the waning of traditional ideologies of legitimation. Not only academic
theorists but also ruling regimes sometimes subscribe to this seemingly
attractive solution to their dilemmas of eroding legitimacy. Hence we
have 'goulash socialism' (i.e. the effort to buy public support through
improved living standards and relative affluence) in East Central Europe
and the sanctioned cult of rampant consumerism in the West. But for
political regimes this is essentially a shallow and even desperate
perspective because such a pseudo-ideology, which holds legitimacy to
be a mere function of effectiveness, will leave them naked and without
principled authority if their efficiency declines.

Effectiveness as a short cut to legitimacy proves to be lame on
political as well as administrative grounds. First of all, regimes and
governments, even those of developed and advanced societies, are rarely
as effective (at any rate in providing human and humane services) as is
implied: garbage piles up, the environment is polluted, muggers control
the parks and streets, schools perpetuate illiteracy, etc. even when the
production of commodities remains relatively efficient. But there also
comes a time when that commodity production itself can no longer be
effectively organized without the system achieving a margin of legitimacy derived from a source transcending efficient production. Thus,

today in Gierek's Poland, the regime has difficulty providing goulash
socialism because the public will not work hard enough to achieve it
unless the regime first grants those human-rights reforms which, in turn,
would further undermine the frayed ideological claims of the Communist monoparty. Thus, the attempted circle of effectiveness-
legitimacy-effectiveness is difficult to close, precisely because the
regime lacks sufficient initial legitimacy to achieve the effectiveness in
production necessary to its own further ('surplus'?) legitimation. The
gap in the would-be circle is probably due to the current influence of
the intelligentsia on the proletariat, which contrasts with the compart-
mentalized political segregation of intellectuals from workers at the
time of the brief crisis which ousted Gomulka in 1970. By themselves,
workers might indeed be sufficiently impressed by sheer material
productivity to award legitimacy to a system that achieves it, but the
professional intelligentsia, in the East as well as in the West, remains
committed to extra-materialistic normative values. Knowing this,
prudent regimes have usually sought to isolate intellectuals and workers
from each other, especially in times of impending crisis, and have often
succeeded: for example, France in 1968, USA in 1968-72, Poland in
1970, Yugoslavia in 1971, and the USSR periodically.

More subtle and sophisticated than the school that suggests productive efficiency suffices to generate legitimacy, is the positivist-
systemic school which argues that the political system is so autonomous
that it creates its own legitimacy simply through longevity, clarity,
economy, and enforcement-capability in administration, without reference to normative principles beyond itself or to an independently
critical public.[4] This school, in turn, is criticized by Marxist and radical
ideologists who caution that a political system is likely to prove
unstable if its subjects' compliance stems only from habit, calculation,
or sentiment without the reinforcement of legitimating principles which
antedate the political system itself. They warn that when such a system,
having succeeded in debunking all former transcendental legitimating
ideologies, will eventually find itself delegitimated through erosion of
its own performance and hence of the public's compliance it will, for all
its modern scientific rhetoric, find no normative restraints within itself
against the temptation to resort to coercion and repression.[5]

That these critics of political positivism and systems theory and
jurisprudential decisionism are likely to be correct in their insistence on
the continuing need and significance of non-technocratic, normative
legitimating principles, is suggested by the observation that astute rulers

and regimes generally treat challenges to their legitimating principles as ultimately more serious than other kinds of challenge. Only such principles, apparently, are believed to be capable of eliciting sustained, voluntary obedience to political authority, because they alone confer on that authority an aura of rightfulness. Thus, Charles II knew what he was about when he had the public hangman burn Hobbes's *Leviathan* despite that tome's ostensible defence of strong and comprehensive executive power, for Charles appreciated that the book's doctrine was compatible with any de facto regime, including Cromwell's, and that its twinned appeals to effectiveness as conveying legitimacy upon the sovereign and to interest as providing the sole basis for the obedience of the subject were fundamentaly subversive of his own extra-systemic claims to kingship by divine right. Furthermore, in highly ideologized political systems, challenges to the ruler's content-interpretation of the legitimating principles are treated as grave heresies. Thus, Brezhnev perceives Roy Medvedev's neo-Leninist critique of the Soviet regime 'from within' Marxism as no less corrosive than the 'external' Slavophile and liberal delegitimations of Alexander Solzhenitsyn and Andrei Sakharov, respectively. And all three regarded as far more serious challenges than M. A. Birman's criticism of the system's economic-administrative effectiveness.

LEGITIMACY IN COMMUNIST EUROPE

It is often alleged these days that for its operational (as contrasted to its rhetorical) ideology, the Soviet regime has, of late, substituted Russian nationalism for Marxism-Leninism. Even if this observation were correct, such a change would still evidence that regime's awareness of the need for legitimating principles which precede and transcend the political system itself and are not generated merely by its technocratic and administrative performance. But the observation itself is erroneous or at best, vastly exaggerated. Russian nationalism is undoubtedly of growing importance as a commitment of the Soviet *apparat* but by itself fails to legitimate the political monopoly of that apparat, for the Party has no unique claim to incarnate it. Hence the continuing need by the Party and its cadres for Marxist-Leninist doctrinal legitimation. It appears that the Soviet Party elite — in contrast to those of several

Communist regimes in East Central Europe — has succeeded in harnessing this Marxist-Leninist doctrinal legitimation together with nationalism in a manner adequate to give that elite subjective confidence in its own ongoing legitimacy.[6]

Discussions of legitimacy and legitimation risk irrelevancy if they overlook this crucial dimension of a ruling elite's own sense of its legitimacy and focus exclusively on the other dimension of the public's or the masses' perception of that elite's legitimacy. Indeed, it has been suggested that the masses intervene in history in a revolutionary manner only after becoming aware of an elite's loss of confidence in the legitimacy of its own domination.[7] Surely this is precisely the pattern accounting for the several East Central European eruptions in East Germany in 1953, Hungary and Poland in 1956, Czechoslovakia in 1968, Poland again in 1970 and 1976 and, perhaps, Yugoslavia in 1971. In the most recent of these bouts of mass effervescence, the Polish food-price riots of June 1976, the regime had felt so unsure of itself and its legitimacy and had, in consequence, so isolated itself in a defensive posture, that it plugged up the potential feedback pipelines from the public. Had these pipes remained open, they would have conveyed signals that might have alerted the regime to the intolerability of its proposed price-policy innovations.

Closer examination of the sequence of the East Central European legitimacy crises chronologically itemized in the preceding paragraph, suggests a secular change within that sequence of the issues at stake. Certain structural fundamentals of Communist systems modeled on the Soviet pattern, such as nationalized industry and collectivized agriculture, which had still been controversial and challenged in the 1950s, had apparently become more legitimate and accepted by the 1960s and 1970s. On the other hand, the Party apparat's monopoly of power, curbing of human rights, and restrictions on dissent appear to have become progressively delegitimated, even within the elites, as evidenced by their increasing oscillation between dogmatism and opportunism, with their resultant cynicism and anxiety. Hence the heavy task that faces these regimes is to legitimate, or relegitimate, themselves in the eyes of their own elites as well as in the eyes of their publics in conditions of relatively advanced economic capacities and relatively matured social systems, i.e. in conditions that render both terroristic and charismatic rule obsolete and in which socialism in the minimalistic sense of non-capitalism is no longer at issue.

To the extent that the economic structures of socialism (as defined in East Central Europe) have matured and been widely accepted, it becomes increasingly implausible for the Party apparats to claim to be the surrogate for the dictatorship of the proletariat defending its achievements against the calculated counterattacks of the reactionary classes. Nor does a 'Khrushchevite' rationalization – that the Party supervises the performance of the economy – convince, since it begs two questions: Why is the Party apparat more competent than the technical intelligentsia to perform this monitoring function? And, how can the Party's élan and sense of mission, i.e. its perception of its own legitimacy, survive relegation to such a secondary and rather routinized responsibility? Finally, in conditions of international détente (assuming, for the moment, that détente in one form or another will remain operative over the next decade), an alleged Party mission as watchdog against international subversion will also sound increasingly hollow and can only be asserted intermittently, at best.

In the multiethnic states of Czechoslovakia and Yugoslavia the monoparty above-the-competing-interests may still have a credible legitimating role to play in containing, directing, regulating, or adjudicating the politicization of ethnicity. (Indeed, were the Soviet Party's apparat less overwhelmingly identified with Russian nationalism in its multiethnic state, it could perform such a function in the Soviet Union as well.) Though the military institution can also play a supraethnic role symbolically, it is not well equipped to perform such an integrating function politically. Hence the Party can here have an authentic legitimating and legitimacy-conferring task to perform. But in such relatively monoethnic states as Poland and Hungary, the Party's search for such a task is even more troubled than in the multiethnic ones.

If the ruling Communist parties were to try to transform themselves more generally into the adjudicators of all the interests in a heterogeneous, pluralistic society characterized by participatory institutions, they would not only risk their Leninist self-image but also the reality of their authority. They might then either be sucked into that competition of social interests which they were supposedly adjudicating, thus sacrificing their autonomous guidance-and-direction function, and/or they would need to hold in reserve some rather clumsy levers for last ditch interventions when the competition of plural interests threatens to get out of control – witness, for example, Tito's belated over-intervention in Croatia in December 1971. In short, the trends of the mid-1970s reconfirm Richard Lowenthal's earlier observation that the European Communist regimes are impaled on a dilemma, one horn of which is the need to adapt to a mature industrial society, and the other is the need to relegitimate their power monopoly.[8]

LEGITIMACY IN
NON-COMMUNIST EUROPE

This essay has so far made no explicit distinction between such terms as 'authorities', 'regime', 'political system', and 'state' in discussing the repositories and generators of legitimacy. Such discriminations become particularly helpful when turning to an analysis of the legitimacy problem in non-Communist European societies. Indeed, the failure to make such distinctions has misled even the usually judicious Richard Rose into a tendentious lapse. In an otherwise astute essay on the subject of legitimacy, he alleges the disappearance of Estonia, Latvia, and Lithuania as independent states in 1940 to have been an extreme example of legitimacy repudiated.[9]

Now while it may well be that the governments and perhaps even the constitutional structures of these three Baltic countries had lost legitimacy during the difficult decade of the 1930s, it is emphatically not the case that their status as independent sovereign states had been repudiated by their citizens or elites.[10] Their independence was terminated by coercive Soviet annexation under the terms of the Hitler-Stalin Pact of 23 August, 1939, and not as the product of internal delegitimation. This episode is a sad reflection on the legitimacy (in a general, moral, sense) of the international system, not on the legitimacy (in this essay's more political sense) of these states in the eyes of their own publics.

In his discussion of political support-inputs into systems, David Easton has distinguished three objects of such support: the community (for example, 'France' as a state); the regime (i.e. the prevailing ideological values, constitutional rules, and authoritative structures of the political game); and the authorities (the government of the day and other occupants of formal political authority roles).[11] This classification can also be productively applied to the analysis of legitimacy. When, for example, nineteenth-century French republican-secularists, royalist-clericalists, and Bonapartist-imperialists were ceaselessly seeking to delegitimate each others' regimes and authorities, none of them ever questioned (indeed, all vividly affirmed) the legitimacy of a unitary

French state. In other words, the legitimacy of the political community
per se was not at issue.

Applying this typology to contemporary Western Europe suggests
that in at least one, very serious, dimension, the challenge to the
legitimacy of several of its states is today potentially more serious than
it was, and at least as serious (though in a different dimension) as in the
East European countries. With the possible exceptions of the GDR, the
USSR, and Yugoslavia (and even here some hostile wishful thinking
may be at play), the other Communist states do not appear to be
targets of domestic repudiations and delegitimations as state entities.
Even the most vehemently anti-regime and anti-governmental Poles,
Hungarians, Romanians, etc. affirm the desirability and legitimacy of
the Polish, Hungarian, Romanian, etc. states, even as they long for
different political systems. By contrast, the Basque, Breton, Flemish,
Scottish, Québécois and other nationalistic movements in the Western
world appear to be intent on delegitimating the historic Spanish,
French, Belgian, British, Canadian, etc. states as political communities
per se. Thus, we appear to be witnessing an historically ironic reversal
of the situation between two World Wars when it was the states of
Eastern Europe that were wracked by delegitimating secessionist and
militant ethnic movements while those of the West appeared to be
solidly legitimate nation-states. The change in Eastern Europe is largely
a product of the considerable demographic simplification imposed
during and after World War II: the Nazi extermination of Jews and
Gypsies; the flight, expulsion, and exchange of other nationalities; and
the redrawing of some frontiers. In the West, on the other hand, many
long-dormant ethnic and national groups have recently reawakened to
self-consciousness and political activism. Yet, just as the current travails
of regime-legitimation in Eastern Europe have an economic dimension,
so too are the would-be delegitimations of some Western states based in
substantial part of resentment and alienation over discriminatory modes
in the structural incorporation of certain ethnic regions into the metropolitan economies.[12] Furthermore, the current Western anti-state
nationalisms, though indeed supported by such traditional elites as the
local clergy and humanistic intelligentsia, increasingly draw the endorsement of the modern industrial elite and the technocratic intelligentsia,
and — perhaps most interestingly — are for the time being tilting toward
the general poltical Left in a problematical but potentially potent
association. They therefore appear to be delegitimating the regimes and
authorities as well as the states into which they are currently incor-

porated and it would be deceptive to dismiss them as merely parochial and reactionary *frondes.*

Despite the rise and potency of several newer twentieth-century 'isms', nationalism, or politicized ethnic consciousness, remains Europe's (and the world's) major ideological legitimator and delegitimator of states, regimes, and governments. A state's legitimacy depends heavily on the population's perception of the political system as reflecting its ethnic and cultural identity. Indeed, most people would rather be ruled poorly by their own ethnic brethren than well by aliens, occupiers, and colonizers. Entrepreneurial political elites, in turn, seek to mobilize this sentiment in order to achieve statehood for their nation or to forge a nation from the population of the state. (The French are said to have been welded into a nation by their centralized late medieval state, whereas the Italian nation preceded and created the modern Italian state.) Often, of course, competing elites will race each other to realize the one or the other possible pattern. Thus, it is valid to ask but impossible to answer comprehensively whether the Québécois, Scots, Flemings, Croations, or Ukrainians will achieve independent statehood before organic Canadian, British, Belgian, Yugoslav, or Soviet nations are molded − or whether the latter process will carry the day. (We omit any listing of developing countries undergoing the same dialectical tensions.)

No type of society or political system is today immune from the burgeoning pressure of ethnic nationalism, with its possible legitimating or delegitimating effects. Communist and non-Communist, old and new, advanced and developing, centralistic and federalistic states must all respond to the pressures of this ascendant ideology. The conventional academic wisdom used to claim that modernization and development would defuse and dissolve this allegedly primordial sentiment of ethnicity or, at a minimum, would relegate it to a species of folkloristic trivia. But today we must recognize that it is rather this conventional academic wisdom which has been reduced to triviality by the power of this ubiquitous and growing phenomenon of ethnic consciousness and assertiveness. Even urbanization, contrary to all expectations, intensifies it. Marxists have failed to come to intellectual terms with this movement which cuts across and negates their preferred, and supposedly more rational, class solidarities, while Liberals, in turn, are rendered uncomfortable by ethnic insistence that ascriptive group-solidarity obligations have priority over individualistic choice-preferences.

Though ethnic political consciousness is today geographically universal, it has not been historically universal. In the ancient and medieval worlds rather few peoples resented or rejected rule by ethnic strangers, and as recently as 1688 and 1714 the British repudiated a native dynasty and replaced it with foreign ones – and this at a time when their sovereign was not yet a figurehead and still exercised extensive political and administrative powers. But by the mid-nineteenth century, these same British refused to confer on their queen's husband, Albert, the honorific title of king-consort (which she had requested) precisely because he was a foreigner.

What had happened between the early eighteenth and the mid-nineteenth centuries is that the Lockeian concept of popular sovereignty as against rulers (a concept which had been ethnically indifferent) had become transformed into the Mazzinian doctrine of the self-determination of peoples qua ethnic communities. The engine of this transformation had been the French Revolution and the subsequent Napoleonic Wars, which had changed the notion of 'the people' from an a-ethnic agglomeration of autonomous individuals into a national community of ethnic brothers. *Fraternité*, which had orginally been a cosmopolitan appeal, became a nationalistic rallying cry.

In the course of the nineteenth century, European politics was thus transformed from a series of dynastic issues – the War of the Spanish Succession, the War of the Austrian Succession, etc. – into a series of national 'questions' – the Polish Question, the Irish Question, etc. World War I and the resultant Paris peace treaties supposedly resolved many (but scarcely all) of these so-called national questions within Europe, but the demonstration-effect of the creation of a number of new national (or supposedly national) states on that continent predictably whetted the appetites of the Asian and African subject-peoples of Europe's colonial empires for their own states. Their demands, in turn, were largely granted after World War II.[13]

Neither in Europe nor elsewhere are most of the states that were created in this century in response to these nationalistic pressures true nation-states in the sense of incorporating within their borders all members of – but no more than – a single ethnic community. The facts of human demography are simply too intricate and convoluted to allow for such a neat and clean map of state borders exactly congruent with ethnic boundaries. Most of the world's states are multiethnic and yet the moral force of the norm of national self-determination remains extraordinarily potent. Indeed, it is today the world's major legitimating and delegitimating ideology for political authority.

INDICES OF LEGITIMATION
AND DELEGITIMATION

Does the concept of legitimacy have predictive utility? It is easy to be wise after the event and to find, say, in 1918 or 1959 that the Russian Tsarist or French fourth republican regimes had earlier exhausted their legitimacy. But can one identify and possibly even measure indicators which might signal in advance that legitimacy is eroding below (or accumulating well above) some danger line? The political sociologist, Reinhard Bendix, has likened political legitimacy to the confidence that a bank's depositors have in its soundness – a confidence that allows the bank to re-invest the depositors' savings elsewhere for extended periods on the secure assumption that they will not all decide to withdraw all their deposits simultaneously.[14] In other words, political legitimacy, like the bank's credit, is seen as an implicit mandate from the public (depositors) to the regime and authorities (managers) to rule (invest) in an unexpected manner. But are there readable storm signals which would warn regimes that a legitimacy crisis (run on deposits) is impending before it bursts on them? And who, ultimately, are the significant publics? A massive flight of capital from a country is a probable signal that the propertied classes no longer impute high legitimacy to its regime. But modern states resort to various devices to prohibit, prevent, stem, and mask such a flight of capital.

To pursue, for a moment, the bank-confidence analogy: every time a depositor withdraws a part of his deposit, he tests his implicit assumption that the bank is reliable. Should he have difficulty in making a valid withdrawal because the bank lacks the necessary reserves to cover it, his confidence would immediately vanish and he would take his business elsewhere. But in political life such tests are less frequently arranged, more difficult to interpret, and less likely to be immediately decisive in the event of a negative experience. Most citizens, most of the time, avoid testing a regime's authority. Similarly, most regimes, most of the time, avoid subjecting their publics to extraordinary, innovative, or unnecessary tests of support. Indeed, the political scientist's difficulty in assessing any extent regime's legitimacy gradient results precisely from this fact that in conventional political and administrative life regimes and publics 'collude' in eschewing explicit, clear, readable test-signals. Furthermore, even a moderatly negative political episode is not likely to prove decisive as a test of legitimacy. The citizen who deeply resents his particular tax assessment or his supposedly unfair traffic fine will not necessarily withdraw his confidence in the system's nor the government's legitimacy in the manner of the rebuffed depositor.

Authentic crises, on the other hand, will put that confidence to an acute test. Such crises may be general — war (especially a lost war), or personal — profound moral objections to a policy. A regime that masters such crises further enhances its legitimacy and, what is even more important, further strengthens the implicit bonds which hold the political community itself together. A regime that fails the test sacrifices a certain quantum of legitimacy. Thus, the storm signals that might furnish predictive evidence about a regime's or a system's margin of legitimacy are to be observed in significant crises that fall short of an ultimate crisis; for example, its performance in a depression, a natural disaster, a war, in the face of extensive tax or draft evasion or administrative corruption. Nevertheless, these storm signals are still wanting in predictive reliability about the legitimacy margin of any particular extant regime. But their very itemization suggests that it is not so much the failure to master any one crisis that will result in precipitous delegitimation, but rather a string of failures in the face of a series of such challenges extending over time. Legitimacy, after all, is not a binary quality that is either present or absent, but an incremental one that can be amplified or squandered. The Russian Tsarist regime's loss of the war against Germany between 1914 and 1917, for example, was but the last of a long train of sequential crisis-failures. So, too, the interwar royal Yugoslav regime and the postwar Fourth Republic in France had long records of failure before they were finally delegitimized by, respectively, the German invasion of 1941 and the Algerian insurrection of the late 1950s. And in all these and similar cases, the failures were not only those of effectiveness but also failures to fulfill public expectations of normative principles, such as benevolence, supraethnicity, and equality.

The evidence to be evaluated in making a current or anticipatory assessment of a system's or a regime's or a government's legitimacy is, as Richard Rose has indicated, public support and public compliance.[15] But these two indicators are ambiguous and not easy to relate to each other. When the French bourgeois and peasant publics manifest low levels of compliance with the tax laws, they are probably not signaling a transfer of support from the current regime to an alternative one, but rather appear to be restating a venerable French judgement about the tolerability of any regime's authority over family property. Alternatively, high levels of compliance may reflect coercion, calculation, habit, apathy, or affection rather than authentic political support based on the imputation of legitimacy. Many regimes, furthermore, seem pragmatically (perhaps myopically) willing to settle for such a trade-off. One is reminded here of Caligula's alleged aphorism: 'Let them hate me as long as they fear me', which indicated a readiness to be content with compliance secured through coercion, and of Kadar's authenticated maxim that 'he who is not against us is with us', which signaled his disposition to interpret apathy as support. But would we construe either of these conditions as presumptive evidence of reliable legitimacy for a future crisis-contingency? Our answer is bound to be qualified. On the one hand, though personally erratic, mediocre, or gray, such rulers can and do borrow institutional legitimacy from the offices and structures which they occupy and which sustain them. On the other hand, being formal and rather abstract, legitimacy narrowly derived from a system may not suffice to carry a government through a thoroughgoing crisis.

PUBLICS AND ELITES

Whose support and compliance are significant? Our previous use of the term 'public' has so far screened the fact that in any political system there are many publics with different political engagements, values, intensities, and weights. These publics elicit different levels of concern on the part of the regime as it strives to maintain legitimacy in their several judgements. Also, as mentioned earlier, one kind of public may be more inclined to award legitimacy to a regime in return for utilitarian gratifications, while another public will show greater concern for normative principles. Again, it is easy retrospectively but difficult prospectively to identify which specific publics are strategically critical to a regime's legitimacy. Even an astute observer of the American scene of the 1950s would have been unlikely to identify students as the coming delegitimators of the 1960s. Alternatively, Gomulka, believing that in the Poland of the 1960s the peasants were crucial to the authority of his government, coddled them – only to be ousted by the workers whose support he has stipulatively taken for granted and whose capacity and readiness to delegitimate him he had consequently under-rated and misjudged. We can, however, here reiterate the earlier suggestion that those publics which are parts of the elite or of the dominant social categories are more crucial than others in that their defection and their loss of a sense of legitimacy in their own domination is likely to prove generally delegitimating because of its multiplier-and-demonstration effect. In other words, in assessing the legitimacy of a power-wielder, we must distinguish between the perceptions of other powerholders (including, to a certain extent, other regimes in the international system as well as domestic elites) and the perceptions of those (the proverbial masses) over whom power is exercised. Only in exceptional circumstances are the perceptions of this second category likely to prove decisive. History and contemporary life abound in examples of governments thoroughly unpopular with, and morally repudiated by, the masses nevertheless surviving by virtue of having preserved their legitimacy in the judgement of other power clusters, such as the armed forces, the bureaucracy, the national bank, or a multi-national corporation. Alternatively, some popular governments fall because they are deemed illegitimate by such auxiliary power centers. Indeed, one austere definition of legitimacy would claim that governmental power is legitimate precisely and only to the extent that it can draw on reserves of power located in other power centers – implicitly on terms acceptable to those other centers.[16] But this again does not specifically predict (though it generally suggests) when this condition will or will not be met, i.e. when the other (elite) centers will lend their authority to legitimate a government. When, for example, will an army assent or decline to disperse demonstrations – or, indeed, decide to oust the government? When will a bureaucracy or a judiciary precipitate the delegitimation of a government?

In practice these particular questions appear to be less acute in today's mature European states than in the developing ones of the so-called Third and Fourth Worlds. (Nazi Germany has already illustrated the reluctance of the military and civil services to organize the delegitimation of an ideological movement-party in a developed society.) Nevertheless, the general proposition that, at the margin, the legitimacy of regimes and governments is conferred more by elites than by masses, does appear to apply to contemporary Europe, West and

East. And its corollary is also plausible: that truly critical delegitimation of a regime begins with the moral and psychological defection of
elites, whose very defection, or loss of a sense of legitimacy in their
own domination, communicates to the masses the onset of a general
crisis. And this capacity to delegitimate belongs, in the long run, as
much to social, intellectual, and religious elites as to the more specifically political contending counter-elites.

CONCLUSION

We close with at least as many questions as answers and with the
traditional scholarly refrain that the problem merits further study. To
revert to the opening theme: though rulers, governments, and regimes
correctly view their legitimacy as essential and mobilize symbolic,
substantive, and ideological political resources to enhance it,[17] they
nevertheless suffer today from its widespread erosion — in Europe no
less seriously than elsewhere. Furthermore, in a somewhat perverse
acknowledgement of legitimacy's cardinal importance, they often seek
to delegitimate each other across interstate and interideological
frontiers and yet, in today's Europe, they also occasionally grope to
halt this process as presumably irrational in the long run. Note here the
ambivalences of the three 'Helsinki baskets': the inviolability of
Europe's post-World War II frontiers; economic, scientific, technological, and environmental cooperation; human rights and cultural cooperation. More than any other basis of support, legitimacy permits the
containment of social cleavages and political conflicts before, and lest,
they rend the community or the system asunder. Thus, both the
authorities and the society benefit from ample legitimacy. The former,
because they can then make difficult and controversial allocation
decisions at lowest cost and with the widest margin of support, even
from those who disagree with them in particular instances; the latter,
because it is then assured that its values will be sustained and possibly
even augmented.[18] Where legitimacy has been gravely eroded, regimes
and governments are obliged to devote so much energy to defending
their authority, that they cannot use it productively — to their own
detriment and the community's loss. The most generous output of
material benefits, the most demonstrative mobilization of sheer power,
the most dexterous manipulation of affective identifications (in short,

even maximal effectiveness) will not fully substitute for normative legitimacy. Let the Europeans — both East and West — take note.

NOTES

Prepared for the Conference on Legitimation and Delegitimation of European Regimes, held 22-24 April, 1977, at the CUNY Graduate Center in New York City under the general sponsorship of the Committee on Political Sociology of the International Sociology and Political Science Associations.

1. Seymour Martin Lipset, *Political Man,* New York: Doubleday, 1959, ch. III.

2. Ernest Renan, *Qu'est-ce qu'une nation?* Paris, 1882, quoted by Hannah Arendt, *The Origins of Totalitarianism,* Cleveland: Meridian Books, 1958, p. 125.

3. Thus, Carl Friedrich, not a partisan of this school, notes its propensity to believe and to suggest that 'the ruler who improves the standard of living will be considered legitimate'. Carl J. Friedrich, *Man and His Government,* New York: McGraw-Hill, 1963, p. 243. For the argument that legitimation is a form of 'reinforcement learning', see Richard M. Merelman, 'Learning and Legitimacy', *American Political Science Review,* LX (3) (September 1966): 548-61.

4. For example, Niklas Luhman, as cited in Jürgen Habermas, *Legitimation Crisis,* Boston: Beacon, 1975, Part III, ch. 5.

5. For example, see Jürgen Habermas, *Legitimation Crisis,* Boston: Beacon, 1975, *passim.*; Claus Mueller, *The Politics of Communication,* New York: Oxford University Press, 1973, ch. 4; John H. Schaar, 'Legitimacy in the Modern State', in Philip Green and Sanford Levinson, eds., *Power and Community,* New York: Random House, 1969, pp. 276-327.

6. Seweryn Bialer, 'The Soviet Political Elite and Internal Developments in the USSR', in William E. Griffith, ed., *The Soviet Empire: Expansion and Détente,* Lexington, Mass.: Lexington Books, 1976, *passim* but especially pp. 45-51.

7. Paul Kecskemeti, *The Unexpected Revolution,* Stanford: Stanford University Press, 1961.

8. Richard Lowenthal, 'On "Established" Communist Party Regimes', *Studies in Comparative Communism* VII (4) (Winter 1974): 356.

9. Richard Rose, 'Dynamic Tendencies in the Authority of Regimes', *World Politics,* XXI (4) (July 1969): 610.

10. Joseph Rothschild, *East Central Europe Between the Two World Wars,* Seattle: University of Washington Press, 1974, ch. 9.

11. David Easton, *A Systems Analysis of Political Life,* New York: John Wiley and Sons, 1965, chs. 11, 12, 13.

12. For examples, see Michael Hechter, *Internal Colonialism: The Celtic Fringe in British National Development, 1536-1966,* Berkeley: University of California Press, 1975; and Milton M. da Silva, 'Modernization and Ethnic Conflict: The Case of the Basques', *Comparative Politics,* VII (2) (January 1975): 227-51.

13. The three preceding paragraphs draw on Walker Connor, 'The Politics of Ethnonationalism', *Journal of International Affairs* XXVII (1) (1973): 1-21.

14. Reinhard Bendix, *Nation-Building and Citizenship,* New York: Doubleday Anchor, 1969, pp. 24-25.

15. Richard Rose, 'Dynamic Tendencies in the Authority of Regimes', *World Politics* XXI (4) (July 1969): 606-7.

16. Arthur L. Stinchcombe, *Constructing Social Theories,* New York: Harcourt, Brace, and World, 1968, pp. 160-62.

17. Note, for example, that though Communist regimes ostensibly claim to derive their legitimacy from the laws of historical development, they also seek to draw on the supplementary legitimating bonus of (albeit rigged) elections. Hitler also occasionally organized plebiscites to supplement the 'laws' of racial biology as his legitimation bases. Napoleon was particularly versatile in utilizing plebiscites, coronation, marriage to a Habsburg, and a concordat with the papacy as legitimating symbols.

18. Cf. Peter G. Stillman, 'The Concept of Legitimacy', *Polity,* VII (1) (Fall 1974): 43.

4

THE LEGITIMACY BIAS:
Conservative Man in Market and State

Robert E. Lane
Yale University, USA

I. INTRODUCTION

In a market society there are two main 'governments', i.e. two authoritative regulators of behavior that elicit compliance: the market, whose main agencies are now principally business corporations, and the state, with its multiple levels and branches equipped with coercive powers. While the reference to the state is easily understood, some explication of the market may be in order. All societies include some aspects of market control, but we may consider a society more marketized to the extent that (1) transactions (exchange of goods and services for money) are widespread and frequent; (2) social control and coordination are achieved through transactions; (3) the principle of substitutability is maximized, i.e. values (tastes, people, goods, services) are easily and frequently substituted for each other, e.g. capital for labor, one kind of labor for another; (4) coordination of transactions is achieved through price mechanisms;[1] and (5) there is no regnant center of control, political and economic authorities are separate, coordination is achieved through multiple decision centers on the principle of unit gain informed by a price-rich information network, and regulated by feedback (consumer demand) in a cybernetic-like process.

A system is regarded as legitimate when the claims to rightful power by its leaders, the procedures which they employ, and the outcomes of their acts are regarded as morally appropriate; to grant legitimacy is to engage in an act of moral evaluation.[2] Legitimacy may be treated as an empirical question or as a philosophical one; the empirical approach permits objective answers. What fraction of the public holds, with what degree of intensity, an opinion treating the economic or political system as illegitimate? But, of course, it suffers from the moral and analytical defect that any system whose leaders can persuade the public of its legitimacy becomes, ipso facto, legitimate. The philosophical approach permits a critic to apply his own criteria to a regime quite irrespective of public opinion, but says nothing about the actual status of support for the system. Here we shall be focusing on the empirical question, but in order to explain problems of delegitimation, we shall include some of the moral philosophical critiques which, if they were persuasive, might lead to empirical delegitimation.

The *process* of granting or withholding legitimacy to a system always involves both an objective and a subjective term. Like all judgements or perceptions, it is conditioned both by the properties of the target object and the properties of the individual or set of individuals who is making the judgement. Thus, in assessing the resistances to delegitimation, we will be concerned with the values, the competences, and learned behaviors of the relevant population — in this case, for the most part, the American public. In speaking primarily of this process of evaluation, we imply no necessary system consequences of widespread feelings that the system is illegitimate; no doubt systems work better when legitimized, but they may survive cynicism, contempt, resignation.

This paper seeks to explicate some of the psychological difficulties in delegitimation: why, in the face of multiple defects in both the market and in contemporary democratic (or other) regimes, the tendencies toward withholding legitimacy are minimal. In the following section the paper illustrates some of the recent criticisms of market and state legitimacy; then it reports on properties of modern society (illustrated by the American case) that would make populations receptive to these criticisms. Third, on the basis of survey evidence, it argues that while the American public reveals increased system dissatisfaction, it does not seriously question the legitimacy of marke or state. The remainder of the paper suggests why, at least in the United States and probably in other Western societies, these conditions and arguments do not persuade, do not, in fact, lead to a crisis of legitimacy.

II. CURRENT CLAIMS OF ILLEGITIMACY
AND THEIR RECEPTION

The market

Because of its reliance on self-interest and its justification of inequality (or, rather, inability to justify any particular income distribution), the market, more than the state, has recently depended for its legitimacy more upon performance than upon its ontological claims. The following selected allegations of illegitimacy, therefore, give more attention to the value consequences of the market than to property and contract rights which originally justified the power of market agencies.

(1) To start with the Marxists, they claim that the market justifies the expropriation from labor of the rewards that are appropriately (by the labor theory of value) theirs; encourages a division of labor that alienates the laborer from his product, himself, his fellow man, his human qualities; destroys non-economic non-material values; disrupts family life; controls government in the interest of the owning class; inhibits self-fulfillment; and encourages competition instead of a more natural and felicitous cooperation among men, finally pitting social class against class culminating in the demise of the market economy.

(2) Many economists have joined in critiques undercutting the usual justifications of the market: E. J. Mishan argues that the modern mass market is incapable of allocating many goods (such as privacy and quiet) to those with minority demands for those goods and encourages an economic growth devoid of human satisfactions; J. K. Galbraith states that producer sovereignty has taken the place of consumer sovereignty and that the market economy starves the demand for public goods; Tibor Scitovsky finds that five-fifths of the sum of total human satisfaction escape the market mechanism; Robert Heilbroner believes the business civilization is declining because it overemphasizes pecuniary values at the expense of others and treats work solely as a means; and E. F. Schumacher faults the market for treating the world's capital goods as income and for its costly and value destroying gigantism.[3]

(3) The manner in which the market treats work and leisure has been criticized by two sociologists from two different directions: Daniel Bell arguing that the consumer culture encouraged by the market has substituted hedonistic narcissism and instant gratification

for the work ethic that the economy needs to survive, while Philip
Slater (and the drama critic, Walter Kerr) argues that the work ethic
prevents us from enjoying leisure culture.[4]

(4) A variety of psycho-social critics believe that the market
destroys personality, the best known being Erich Fromm's claim that
market capitalism creates a protean 'marketing orientation' characterized by efforts to shape oneself into whatever form is most saleable; it
influences people to think of themselves as 'things', destroys warm
interpersonal relationships, and deprives men of the belief that they are
the author of their own acts.[5] Marcuse argues that people in successful
market societies internalize the prevailing technical ideology, thus
losing objectivity and pursuing socially molded wants rather than life-
enriching needs;[6] similarly, William H. Whyte, Jr. holds that life in the
big corporations creates the 'organization man' marked by the delivery
of his conscience into the hands of the organization.[7]

(5) More conservatively, two market defenders believe that the
market has unjustifiably lost its legitimacy: Joseph Schumpeter,
because the entrepreneurs lost their will to accumulate capital under
the force of misguided criticism from the Left and the decline of the
lineal family, and Ernest van den Haag, because the invisibility of
market processes makes them 'morally unintelligible and psychologically desolate'.[8] Others have observed survey evidence of recent
increases in lost confidence in 'big business' and believe that government interference and misguided 'idealism' (or self-interest) have
empirically eroded what is philosophically legitimate.

This brief sampling of views, of course, does not do justice to the
full range of criticism, especially those dealing with the inequity of
market distribution, the inability of the market to solve the chronic
problem of job shortages, and more recently, of inflation, the ugliness
of the market civilization, the market emphasis on interpersonal
competition (rivalry) instead of cooperation, its tendencies to foster
alienation and anomie, and much more.

The democratic state

Unlike the radical critics of the market economy, the critics of the
democratic state (except for the unreconstructed communists and a
scattering of right wing fringe groups) rarely question its premises and
would not replace it with something else. Rather, they claim that the

original purposes have been perverted to serve 'illegitimate' ends, that it has been seized by business interests to serve their own purposes, that it is either too responsive or insufficiently responsive to popular demands, and that various supporting latter-day theories have misled analysts and practitioners regarding the likely outcomes of contemporary practice. Some of these may be briefly suggested as follows.

(1) Because the class structure of society and the economic power of the owning classes (power elite) gives to these owners the control of 'news' and opinion and hence agenda-formation, power over the financing of elections, control over investment and the withholding of investment (with its consequences to prosperity), hegemony over cultural, consciousness-forming institutions, and so forth, the possibilities of genuinely popular control of elections and hence of government are negligible. These views, of course, are Marxist, but they are also shared by other 'radicals', such as Jurgen Habermas, Anthony Giddens, and J. O'Connor among others.

(2) There are two lines of criticism directed at defenses of the political system which the critics regard as justifying a perversion of the democratic idea. Against the pluralist argument claiming that the play of organized interest satisfies the conditions of democracy, Theodore Lowi and Walter Dean Burnham argue that because this pluralist theory destroys the concept of (and possibility of achieving) a genuine public interest, and because it erodes the valued symbols of democratic legitimacy in the struggle for group interest, the concept and practice of interest group democracy contributes to a 'crisis of legitimacy'.[9] And against the argument that democracy is, at best, a competition among undemocratically chosen elites, T. B. Bottomore and others argue that this elite competition theory fails to accommodate the democratic principle that men should participate in decisions affecting their own lives.[10]

(3) Criticisms relying on the ineffectiveness of democratic governments to solve current pressing problems (energy, pollution, race relations, unemployment — inflation, income inequality), join with Lipset in believing that persistent ineffectiveness erodes legitimacy, whatever the constitutional status of the government.[11]

(4) Criticisms of several varieties are directed at the infringement by government on the rights or needs of their publics. The common business criticism of the government's infringement of the rights of property and contract represents one of these. More generally, Robert Nozick, arguing from first principles very like Herbert Spencer's,

believes that only 'the minimal state, limited to the narrow functions of protection against force, theft, fraud, enforcement of contracts, and so on, is justified'; otherwise the state violates the rights of individuals.[12] Robert Nisbet, believing that the emphasis on individuals is a mistake, argues that the government has destroyed society's capacity to give people a sense of community by usurping the functions of families, villages and neighborhoods, even trade unions.[13]

(5) In a more searching argument than the others, John Schaar argues that there is in fact and by right a legitimacy crisis due to three powerful underlying forces in modern society. (i) Because of an epistemological revolution, we now believe that truth, being man-made, can be as readily changed as a suit of clothes; there are no eternal truths to which one can appeal in assessing government, or government's claims to legitimacy. (ii) In our individualism, we have forgotten that ethical norms are group products; the existential doctrine that each creates his own values undermines group life and sets us all adrift without reliable moral rudders. And (iii) the rise of impersonal bureaucracy and of rationalistic efficiency norms has destroyed both the inclination and capacity for warm personal leadership, the kind of leadership (charisma?) that evokes loyalty. The themes of relativism, individualism, and impersonality in modernity deprive us of a sense that our government and its leaders are invested with power by virtue of some moral right.[14]

(6) In his *Legitimation Crisis*, Jurgen Habermas, considering both market and state to be mutually embraced in an advanced capitalist system, deals with both together. The state, overloaded with functions it cannot handle, hampered by an intractible class structure, a profit maximization ethos, and a culture eroding 'scientism', is unable to generate a political ethic that persuades or a value structure that does not depend upon the waning residues of the prebourgeois period. The market promises reward for merit but cannot deliver, undermines work and saving because they do not satisfy the growing needs for nonmaterial values, and loses its ethical appeal in a compassionless system of exchange values. Together, they offer a bourgeois ideology which includes no relief from guilt and no respite from affliction. As a consequence, human motives wither and the threat to the legitimacy of the two systems arises primarily from a motivational deficit.[15]

(7) Finally, as with the market critics, there are those who discover in survey and other sources evidence of a 'legitimacy crisis', whether or not philosophically justified.

A receptive population?

As pointed out earlier, the process of legitimation (and delegitimation) involves both the properties of the target system and of the persons evaluating it. The above deals with what are thought to be the system properties; here we turn to population characteristics. In traditional societies the question of legitimacy of economic, political (and religious) systems hardly occurs because of the embeddedness of the population in the system and the acceptance of religious rationales for the prevailing order. Thus, the first characteristic of modern populations which might make such arguments as the above persuasive is a general increase in consciousness, as described by the psychoanalysts, Allen Wheelis and Frederick Weiss,[16] and a particular consciousness of alternatives, or if not that, of the possibility of alternatives. Now it is the case that those cognitive properties which inform this consciousness, including cognitive complexity or hypothetical reasoning, increase both with education and, cross culturally, with degrees of modernization. The better educated and the more Westernized are generally better able to entertain counter-factual propositions; in Lerner's analysis they can imaginatively place themselves in the position of another; in Goodnow's words, they are better able to 'transform an event in their heads' without concrete manipulations.[17] For both of these reasons one might expect modern populations in Western market societies to be more receptive than others to questions of legitimacy of political and economic systems.

Furthermore, this capacity has a specifically moral expression in moral reasoning. According to the tests of moral reasoning developed by Lawrence Kohlberg, this moral capacity, based on an underlying cognitive capacity, is also improved by education and is higher in more modern societies. Its specific relevance here is that only those persons who are at the higher, 'post-conventional', states of moral reasoning can bring to bear on a given situation a set of moral principles which are independent of public opinion and official legal prescriptions. Thus, only these post-conventionals are able to question the legitimacy of an act, a law, or a system from a moral principle independent of the status quo. There is some slight evidence that the middle class sons of middle class fathers in the United States are more likely to be post-conventional than their fathers (but there is no similar evidence in the working class).[18]

The capacity to question legitimacy implies several other properties

which, likewise, seem to have experienced an historical increase. Con-
formists are not likely to question the legitimacy of a regime unless
they are lodged in a group where this questioning prevails. The documented decline of conformist preferences in the United States (as well
as Britain where the tendency was never so strong) thus releases persons
for such system interrogation.[19] And this is part of a general tendency
towards 'sociological release', a tendency to express opinions deviant
from those of family and peer groups.[20] Furthermore, the decline of
authoritarianism and the authoritarian family implies a decline in the
tendency to ingratiate oneself and obey the powerful, whether they be
officers of corporations or government.[21]

Add to these tendencies the concept of 'moral obsolescence', by
which we mean the tendencies to regard the moral prescriptions of
parents and other authorities as lacking in binding force, rooted in the
experience within a life time of knowledge obsolescence, technological
obsolescence, the obsolescence of child-rearing orthodoxies, and even,
perhaps, market-induced fashion obsolescence. Together these embrace
the concept of the 'generation gap'. Thus, whatever was legitimate for
the founding fathers and for one's own father has not the persuasive
power it once had. Under the influence of greater economic security in
childhood, children in Western nations have tended to develop what
Inglehart calls 'post-materialist values'[22] which provide standards for
judging market economies that are uncongenial to their own rationaliza-
tions and of polities that hold them to a higher standard of performance.

These standards of performance are themselves moralized. To be
inefficient or incompetent, particularly in positions of public trust, is a
moral defect; thus is the triumph of technique which Ellul so execrates,
converted, like the Protestant Ethic before it, into a moral matter
appropriate to legitimacy judgements. Furthermore, as many studies
have shown, while a sense of well-being is associated with higher income
in any one nation at any one time, the increase in national income does
not bring any commensurate increase in the sense of well-being for the
population; the judgement is relative to the standards set by relevant
others.[23] Thus, the objective performance of an economy does not
relieve it from adverse judgements based on material success. Finally,
the experience of increased income in the past creates rising expectations of greater income in the future; the economy, and those who
govern the state in which it thrives, generate sources of discontent by
their own success.

For these various reasons, therefore, one might have expected attributions of illegitimacy to increase in modern societies including the United States.

Evidence on 'the crisis of legitimacy'

Survey evidence reveals a decade long (1966-76) decline in confidence in the leadership of major social institutions and reports over 60 percent current (1974-76) support for such propositions as the following: 'quite a few people running the government in Washington are crooked'; 'the government in Washington is pretty much run by a few big interests'; 'what you think doesn't count any more'; 'the rich get richer and the poor get poorer'; 'most people with power try to take advantage of people like yourself'; 'the country ... is on the wrong track', and, compared to the view that our 'problems are no worse than at any other time', 58 percent believe we are 'in deep and serious trouble'.[24] Such evidence, and much more, may indeed suggest a legitimacy crisis, and not simply event specific, leadership specific, dissatisfaction. At the very least, Marcuse's 'happy consciousness' seems to be finished. But for a variety of reasons we must accept Everett C. Ladd's assessment: 'Available data surely do not sustain the argument that the US has experienced any sort of legitimacy crisis – or that the country is at the beginning of one.'

To qualify as a crisis of legitimacy, these critical views would have to (a) be directed at the system and not at the incumbents or policies; (b) be directed at the rationales or values underlying the system, and not merely serve to identify villains or even criticize system performance; (c) persist over some long duration and not be merely ephemeral; (d) be rooted in some structural property of the system such that a group, or set of groups, is systematically deprived of crucial values; and (e) enlist a sense of personal malaise related to system performance. The last point, it should be noted, is not a moral or logical requirement but a practical one: people contented with their own lives do not act upon or act out their beliefs in system inadequacy.

The first two criteria (attacks on the systems and their values), are under-cut by the fact that more than 80 percent of the public believes 'our country will be strong and prosperous again', and 'the American way of life is superior to that of any other country', and 63 percent agree that 'our government system should not be changed in any major

way'.[25] More revealing is the Gallup report showing that while a fairly
constant (1973-77) 25-30 percent of the population have 'little' or 'no
confidence' in big business, only 14 percent lack confidence in the 'free
enterprise' system which legitimates business. Furthermore, since more
people fear big government than big business (38-23 percent),[26] it
seems those with little confidence in business or free enterprise have
nowhere to turn. On the matter of the durability of these views, the
main survey data hardly span more than a decade. To remedy this
defect with respect to the economic system, we turn to Galambos's
content analysis of diverse periodicals for the period 1880-1940 revealing that negative references to big business rose in the populist period
from 1880 to *an all time high in 1898*, declined slowly from then on
until 1935, and more sharply in the next five years.[27] Extending this
with poll material for the years 1936, 1945 and 1950, John Morgan
reports 'the findings reported in these sources are consistent with the
content analyses . . . a summary of the polls summarizes the rest of [the
data] quite well . . .. Americans are overwhelmingly supportive of big
business. Across the 15 years of survey results . . . between 60 and 70
percent of the responses were clearly favorable toward business.' Since
this compares favorably with the 25-30 percent 'little or no confidence'
finding of Gallup in 1977, a century, rather than a decade, seems to
offer rather similar support for business, and by inference, the business
civilization which it represents. There is little doubt that positive
opinions towards the American democratic regime have the same or,
more likely, even more favorable profiles.

Whether the discontent with the American system reported earlier
reflects a structural deprivation of values for some segment of the
American society is unclear; the black population may represent such a
group, especially since its earlier faith in governmental redress has been
sharply eroded, but the changing complexion of youth values reveals
the inadequacy of dependence on structural sets carved out of the life
cycle. And, finally, the evidence that people report their own lives quite
in order, with optimistic references to their own futures, at the same
time that they look with dismay at the social system,[28] implies a lack
of behavioral disposition to act on any allegations of illegitimacy that
may accompany these social views.

In short, while circumstance and argument may support the
questioning of system legitimacy, the evidence shows that the American
public has not yet arrived at that point where the term 'legitimacy
crisis' is appropriate. To explain why is the business of the next two
sections.

III. RESISTANCE TO DELEGITIMATION

In many ways, as noted, the claims for legitimacy of market and state are complentary in a market society. But since they represent alternative ways of coordinating and directing social activities, they also conflict in particular areas. In a period when there is widespread dissatisfaction with the performance of both market and state, and widespread allegations among intellectuals, if not among the public, that each agent is, in some way, illegitimate, we must ask whether there are systemic forces at work favoring either agency or, perhaps, favoring both, perhaps, indeed, all established authority. Mostly on social psychological (the nature of man) grounds, I will argue that there are reasons to think, first, that the market is favored, and secondly that there are strong tendencies in the nature of man to support all established authority.

Before turning to the psychological arguments, and as a protection against appearing to overpsychologize the forces at work, let us first note certain features of advanced capitalism which also inhibit criticality.

(1) In the West the market system has greatly reduced poverty (but the United States lost ground in this area in the seventies), and democratic regimes have weathered multiple 'crises', including, in the United States, the endless prosecution of an unpopular and unsuccessful war and the removal of a president for malfeasance. Evaluations of performance, therefore, will necessarily be mixed.

(2) Structurally, the benefits accorded to the organized working class are considerable; it is the unorganized underclass of youth, minorities, and the less well educated who have the greatest grievances, but who also (now) are the least articulate and the least powerful.

(3) The 'legitimizers' *may* be the intellectuals (the economists and political philosophers, according to Keynes) but in a 'mass society' the mass media must serve as transmitters of their criticisms. While some believe the documented loss of confidence reported earlier stems in part from systemic media tendencies to focus on failures and the rise of journalistic 'adversary' positions,[29] the media, financed by advertising, privately owned, and fearful of giving offense, conveys primarily system supportive images and messages.

(4) All systems tend to 'reproduce themselves': the capitalist system, in part, by socializing the public to prefer commodities, which it produces in some abundance, rather than favorable 'social activity

contexts', which require collective non-market action.[30] But for most of human history it was the dearth of 'commodities', i.e. material resources, that defined poverty and misery. It is within the framework of these circumstances that the following psychological resistances to delegitimation occur.

Attribution of cause

Most causal inferences are ambiguous. Is the cause due to the actor or to the environment? Did I enjoy the movie because *it* was excellent or because *I* was in a good mood?[31] Are people poor because there are no jobs or because they do not seek jobs and work hard? This is relevant here for it seems to be the case that the different 'visibilities' of market operations and government operations create situations where defects in the economic system are attributed to deficiencies in the environment, with little blame attached, while deficiencies in government are attributed to actors, particular political leaders, agencies, or government in general. Where blame attaches, so also do allegations of illegitimacy.

Cybernetic feedback

While democracies and markets are both, in a sense, cybernetic agencies such that the acts of firms and administrations provide feedback from consumers and citizens, the market is much quicker to respond, has more visible criteria of 'success', and has more resources for relieving deficiencies in supplies to meet demands. This superior cybernetic quality means that, within its domain, it can satisfy its critics more rapidly. Furthermore, this cybernetic efficiency means that it can extend its domain, commercializing family norms, community relationships, leisure world ethics, even culture itself, infusing them with market values. In doing this, of course, the market deprives the public of grounds for criticizing these norms, values, and methods thus unconsciously embraced. A democratic government can assume the functions of other social units, as Nisbet points out, and can, to some extent, affect such values as equalitarianism, but it is not so efficient as the market in penetrating society with its value structure.

Equity and efficiency

If, at least in the minds of the American people, democratic government stands for justice and equity and the market stands for efficiency
and affluence, the tradeoff between the two that Okun poses in terms
of the market[32] can also be considered as a tradeoff regarding which
agency will be favored. What this means in the United States, but by no
means in the rest of the world where the agency-value links are not so
ordered, is that the less prosperous, suffering from what may seem to
many to be inequities,[33] will not flock to the standard of the government for the repair of these inequities but give some continued loyalty
to the 'unjust' market because of the even more desparate desire by the
poor for more 'affluence'.

Cost-benefit visibility

The visibility and immediacy of the relationship between cost and
benefit is much greater in the market than in government. In the
consumer market the person pays and receives specified contingent
benefits immediately (or after a slight delay), while in government the
person pays a generalized cost in the form of required taxes and
receives unspecified rewards in the form of security, public goods, or
often it seems to some, transfer payments to others. This has two
effects. The first is that it is easier to justify a cost when the benefit is
immediate and contingent on payment. A second is that one has a
greater sense of control over one's outcomes if they are visibly paired
with one's responses − a major contribution to a sense of controlling
one's own fate.[34] This latter sense of control is further enhanced by
the voluntary nature of the market payment in contrast to the coerced
tax payment. Both of these considerations represent increments of
gratification, and hence of outcome legitimacy, less available to the
government.

Trust in government and market:
see-saw or slide

Why should it not be the case that as the legitimacy of business
declines, the legitimacy of the government, as the only visible alterna-

tive, rises: the see-saw model? As noted above, recent history shows
that trust in government and business decline together: the slide model.
This is because of the insoluble link between the two in a modern
market society. Governmental trust declines because it is seen, in part,
as having been corrupted by business; in part because of its residual
fiduciary relationship to the public, making it accountable for market
outcomes; in part because, as mentioned above, the attribution process
points more frequently to government; and, in part, because of the
opaqueness of causes: where *does* the responsibility for inflation, or
unemployment, lie? This has the ironic effect of implicating government in every failure of the market; its utility as a market substitute is
then impaired.

Rewards and punishments

In popular perception, for some of the reasons given above, the market
distributes rewards while the state distributes punishments. This, in
itself, is a major market advantage. Furthermore, in learning theory,
rewards contingent on responses to stimuli create the probability that
the act producing the reward will be repeated. Punishment, or even the
threat of punishment, of course, has the opposite effect. But not only
the opposite effect; what punishment does is to create avoidance
behavior such that not only the act, but the field within which the act
took place, is avoided. Sometimes, moreover, the whole class of acts
related in a person's mind to the threat of punishment is avoided, for
the punishment tells you to avoid the punisher as well as the punishable
act. A coloration of positive hedonic tone is thus associated with the
market and a negative tone is associated with government, affecting
their respective legitimacies.[35]

IV. THE CONSERVATIVE
NATURE OF MAN

To fail to accord legitimacy, to delegitimate an established institution
or process, is an act that runs contrary to many 'natural' psychological
processes. The evolutionary programming of the human species (which

is much less conservative than other, more stimulus bound, species), the requirements of group living, the pattern-maintenance devices of cultures, the power of habit, i.e. learned responses, the very nature of cognition, all conspire to make us accept as legitimate that which is. In an era of change, we forget how strong the forces against change and challenge really are. In what follows I will outline a few of the psychological reasons why it takes extraordinary steps to think of an established form of government or economic institution as illegitimate. It is a biased account; there are other psychological forces at work, but cumulatively it may help us understand the legitimacy of the existential.

(1) The power of familiarity

The general rule is that 'the more frequently the stimuli are presented, the greater the liking and the positive evaluation of them'.[36] This is true for such varied stimuli as persons, art, English words and nonsense syllables, and groups to which one belongs. It is true in politics: in *The American Voter*, Angus Campbell and associates found that the longer one was associated with a party, a union, or a place, the more one identified with it.[37] Like all general rules, of course, this one competes with others: the variable preference, for example, for limited degrees of novelty and complexity and challenge. Furthermore, much research (some focused on race relations) reveals that the circumstances of this 'familiarity' make a substantial difference; it can, indeed, breed contempt — experimentally. Nevertheless, even with the exceptions, familiarity (or, as some say, familiarities — since there are many kinds) represents a powerful force making for loyalty to a known form of government and a known form of economic behavior. And, for obvious reasons, this is related to adult maturation and hence adult tendencies toward conservatism.

There may be physiological bases for the preference for the familiar. First, most kinds of life change, including benign ones (such as a promotion), create stress which is predictive of subsequent increased probability of illness.[38] Secondly, the human response to the unfamiliar is a matching response to test for danger: when the new stimuli are perceived, they are matched against 'neural models' in the cortex where, if they are perceived as similar to the stored models, the cortex informs the reticular activating system to 'hold its fire'.[39] If they are perceived as dissimilar, as in the case of challenging beliefs, they stimulate what is called 'the orientation response' followed by the preparation of the body for fight or flight, the 'adaptive reaction'. Since this sequence involves the dilation of the pupils, a momentarily more acute hearing, muscle tension, changes in the brain waves, a flow of blood from the extremities to the brain, changes in breathing and heart rate, palm sweat, and changes in blood and urine chemistry, such responses and reactions may be physiologically costly. The orientation response takes place many times a day, but when it occurs too often, according to Selye, there is bodily fatigue and, if extended too long, takes a heavy toll and, indeed, may become irreversible.[40]

The physiological response to challenge or even to the unfamiliar may easily be caricatured, but within the bounds of plausibility it offers one small reason why, in the interest of conservation of energy, serious challenge to the legitimacy of familiar institutions does not occur more often.

(2) The 'just world' hypothesis

Melvin Lerner argues that 'the person's concern with justice arises partly from learning and internalizing the societal norms. More important, however, the desire for justice is viewed as an extension of the more basic commitment to deserving one's own outcomes. This commitment to deserving appears to be the natural result of a familiar developmental process'.[41] This process, says Lerner, takes the form of a 'personal contract' with oneself to delay gratification and accept discipline on the assumption that this will be rewarded, and by extension one comes to believe that others, too, are appropriately rewarded and punished for their self-discipline or lack thereof. Any indication that others do not receive the appropriate reward or punishment for their own acts, threatens a person's own belief in the fruitfulness or morality of his own self-control and effort. There are various forms of 'justice' which the individual can accept under these circumstances but, however construed, the point to be made here is that perceptions of injustice in the world are threatening to the belief, carefully nurtured in socialization, that if one is self-denying (following the reality principle over the pleasure principle) appropriate outcomes will follow. Perhaps it was for this reason that in my Eastport interviews with working and lower middle class men, they expressed almost no resentment of the very rich, but considerable resentment of the poor living on welfare.[42] The rich had 'earned their rewards', those on welfare had not.

Furthermore, there is a least cost principle here, too. Equity theory research finds that for many self-perceived victims of inequity (bearing a disproportionate share of the costs of some enterprise, being exploited in some ways), it is easier to believe that the inequity was somehow deserved, or that the exploiter will suffer later punishment, or that his exploitation was somehow costly to the exploiter himself; in short, justifying the situation, rather than taking steps to rectify the wrong, or even, at times, to perceive the injustice.[43]

The just world hypothesis is more congenial to market allocation than to state allocation of rewards, for the market seems to fulfill the conditions set down in the original learning process: if I am self-denying and do what is 'right' I will be rewarded. As noted earlier, market rewards follow closely on such behavior in easily visible ways, whereas state rewards do not. In some such fashion the agency of justice, the state, is dissociated from the 'just world' and the market, which makes no great claim to some kinds of social justice, is embraced into that world. Moreover, it is important to note that the psychology of the just world is silent or negative on the question of outcome equality. For both government and market, the just world hypothesis helps to explain men's reluctance to impugn the legitimacy of either government or the controllers of the market, the great corporations, for this hypothesis supports the view that people get what they deserve.

(3) The attribution of cause: individual actor or system?

Returning to the psychological attribution of cause, mentioned earlier as favoring the market over the state, we may now see how the Western attributional process justifies the legitimacy of both. In the West generally, and in the United States in particular, there is a bias in favor of actor attribution: it is the implication of our individualism, our belief that individuals are and should be, and should certainly think of themselves as, masters of their own fates. The principle instrument for measuring whether or not people generally think of themselves as controlling events or as being controlled by them, is Rotter's measure of 'locus of control', indicating whether people believe that outcomes are contingent on their own efforts ('internals') or whether these outcomes are independent of their own efforts, i.e. dependent on luck, the acts of others, or of some vague entity like society ('externals').[44] While attribution of cause to either the actor or to the environment is substantially dependent on circumstances and, indeed, is quite easily manipulable, there is substantial evidence that internality/externality dispositions represent personality traits, applicable across situations and persistent over time.

The paradox, for our purposes, is that 'externals', those who blame the system for the deficiencies in their lives and may therefore impugn its legitimacy, are just exactly those who do not believe that they can do anything about it, since, by definition, they do not perceive events as contingent on their own efforts. There is some evidence that for the black population of the United States this is often the case.[45] On the other hand, those who blame themselves for, say, their economic failures or low status, exculpating 'the system' for these deficiencies, would tend to seek remedies through their own individual efforts.

(4) Competence and the illusion of control

The drive to master the environment, to control one's own destiny, the motivation behind the 'internality' discussed above, is said to be innate and, although easily discouraged, universal at birth.[46] To release that drive from various blockages, and to unlearn that 'learned helplessness' which circumstances may have taught, is the task of therapy. To find and express it, is the condition of happiness, autonomy, self-actualization. Animals who are subject to uncontrollable and inescapable shock do not then seek to escape from shock when they can do so; humans exposed to uncontrollable noise have decrements of later functioning and volunteer less often to help others; subjects who struggle with unsolvable problems do not learn to solve solvable ones later; inmates of institutions who have no say in the circumstances of their lives give up their small initiatives and sometimes give up their will to live, as well.[47] On the other hand, when humans are led to believe that they *can* control some aversive stimulus (such as loud unpredictable noise), even if they do not use that control (even if the unused control is a dummy switch), they do not suffer the symptoms of helplessness. It is the *belief in control* that prevents helplessness, not the aversive stimulus, nor even the exercise of control.[48]

These findings have a dramatic bearing on the problem of legitimacy of both democratic governments and of the market controlling corporations. The doctrines of popular sovereignty and of consumer sovereignty foster a belief in people's capacity to control the events in their lives; the operations of the ballot and of shopping reinforce these beliefs. Regardless of the actual workings of elections and markets, these operations represent the buttons giving the members of society the belief (or illusion) of control that permits them to believe in their own 'competence', their own control over their environments. The opaqueness of the actual control mechanisms does not afford them information on the degree of actual control exercised, but neither does it permit *rapid* disillusionment; although, in the long run, persistent disillusionment would teach something else — perhaps apathy. In the short run, at least, the belief in control is fostered by ballot and market, and the legitimacy of the regimes and markets thought to be subject to controls of these kinds is reinforced.

(5) The 'agentic state' and the legitimacy of authority

In his well-known experiments Milgram has demonstrated that most ordinary, decent, even humane people will, when so instructed by an appropriate authority figure, give damaging, potentially lethal shocks to unknown persons, not out of any feelings of aggression, nor from any sense of threat to themselves, but simply because they are told to do so. Milgram argues that evolutionary processes have programmed in mankind capacities for both autonomous action, where the individual takes responsibility for what he does, and obedience to authority, where the collectivity is served by unified control and individual obedience. Most people obediently give up responsibility for their own acts ('agentic state') when the source of a request is accorded legitimacy, something we accord easily, perhaps as the consequence of daily experience where legitimate teachers, employers, traffic policemen, doctors instruct or order us to do, on the whole, reasonable things.[49] Thus, the agentic habit, the unquestioning obedience in our daily lives to these authority figures, leads us to generalize this easy attribution of legitimacy to other situations and to forget to question the basis and the consequences of obedience. The agentic capacity is overtrained; the autonomous capacity is underutilized. And without serious competitors to the authority of the state or the authority of private property, we accord them legitimacy without thought.

(6) Conformity, positivity, acquiescence

Under conditions of group pressure, people tend to deny the clear
evidence of their senses (visual and auditory) and go along with the
group, although this varies according to national culture: the French,
for example, being more independent of group pressure than the
Norwegians.[50] Furthermore, when confronted with truly ambiguous
stimuli (the illusory movement of a point of light in a darkened room),
people tend to accept norms established by the reports of others, a
situation which has some correspondence with abstract statements
about governmental performance in complex situations. Finally,
although, as reported above, there is evidence of some secular decline in
Americans' tendency to be concerned about their 'popularity', com-
parisons with the British and the Russians reveal that, as Tocqueville
said, Americans are unusually sensitive to public opinion.[51] Since there
is a tendency in all publics to exaggerate the prevalence of majority
opinion and underestimate the prevalence of minority opinion (a
phenomenon called 'pluralistic ignorance'), this American sensitivity
and apparent desire to conform will serve to support perceived conventional majoritarian opinion, something which clearly includes the
endorsement of the legitimacy of prevailing regimes and economic
practices. There is a parallel here with Milgram's 'obedience to
authority', for the individual is here relinquishing his own autonomous
judgement to the control of others, in this case not a particular
authority, but rather to a group.

Of uncertain weight in this argument on the conservative nature of
man is the finding that cognitive processes favor positive, as contrasted
to negative, statements. In tests of learning, storing, and solving conjunction and disjunction problems, 'the use of negatives in the
description led to much longer storage time . . . . The subjects appeared
to convert each negative into its positive counterpart . . . . This
confirms many studies which suggest that subjects prefer to carry
information in its positive form and that converting a negative requires
time'.[52] Although, of course, delegitimizing statements may be made in
positive form, it is likely that most subjects carry around in their heads
a set of homilies about government and private property in their
positive forms. A faint, positivity bias may be the residual trace of

evolutionary processes programmed in the human brain.

So far as I know, this positivity bias has not been related to what has been called the 'acquiescence set', but there may be a relationship. There are two conditions for variations of an acquiescent tendency to agree: one is less education, implying less cognitive training and capacity; the other is greater emotionality, even among the better educated, involving less capacity for the delayed gratification implied in deliberative processes.[53] A tendency to agree derived from either source is, of course, by no means pathological, and it is the case that modernity, with its higher education and training in delayed gratification, tends to decrease acquiescence. But the presence in society of such predispositions, especially among those who are deprived, imposes obstacles to the criticality, the 'negation' that might lead to delegitimating thoughts.

Societies do change; we have seen important value changes in our own life-times, the public is more critical of both market and state than it has been for some time, the intellectuals' critique of the legitimacy of these agencies of control may have waned but it will not disappear; there are, indeed, contradictions in the economic order which a self-regulating market cannot easily solve. But the forces according legitimacy to both market and state, especially the market, are strong — and some of them have to do with the nature of man, himself.

NOTES

This paper owes much to the discussion in the faculty seminar on The Market Oriented Society and Personality, sponsored by the Institution for Social and Policy Analysis, Yale University. I would also like to express my thanks to James Fishkin and Thomas Pangle for their helpful reviews of an earlier draft, excusing them from responsibility for the statements in this one.

1. This formulation is from C. E. Lindblom, 'The Market Variable(s) in the Study of Market Effects on Personality', ISPS, Yale, September 1976.

2. 'Legitimacy refers to the extent that a polity is regarded by its members as worthy of support . . .'. The sense of moral fitness is central . . .'. Harry Eckstein, *The Evaluation of Political Performance: Problems and Dimensions*, Beverly Hills, California: Sage Publications, 1971, p. 50. James Fishkin argues that such definitions as this, indeed virtually all present definitions, are defective

in that they inadvertently legitimate tyranny. 'Tyranny and Legitimacy', Working Paper 794, Institution for Social and Policy Analysis, Yale University, 1977.

3. E. J. Mishan, *The Costs of Economic Growth*, Harmondsworth, England: Penguin, 1969; John Kenneth Galbraith, *The Affluent Society*, 2nd edn., Harmondsworth, England: Penguin, 1969; Tibor Scitovsky, *The Joyless Economy*, New York: Oxford University Press, 1976; E. F. Schumacher, *Small is Beautiful: Economics as if People Mattered*, New York: Harper Torchbook, 1973.

4. Daniel Bell, *The Cultural Contradictions of Capitalism*, New York: Basic Books, 1976; Philip E. Slater, *The Pursuit of Loneliness: American Culture at the Breaking Point*, Boston: Beacon Press, 1970.

5. Erich Fromm, *Man for Himself*, New York: Rinehart, 1947; and *The Sane Society*, New York: Rinehart, 1955.

6. Herbert Marcuse, *One Dimensional Man*, Boston: Beacon Press, 1964.

7. William H. Whyte, Jr, *The Organization Man*, Garden City, N.Y.: Doubleday/Anchor, 1957.

8. Joseph A. Schumpeter, *Capitalism, Socialism and Democracy*, London: George Allen & Unwin, 1950, p. 161; Ernest van den Haag, 'Economics is Not Enough: Notes on the Anticapitalist Spirit', *The Public Interest*, 45 (Fall 1976): 110.

9. Theodore J. Lowi, *The End of Liberalism*, New York: Norton, 1969; Walter Dean Burnham, 'Crisis of American Political Legitimacy', *Society* 10 (November/December 1972): 24-31.

10. T. B. Bottomore, 'The Insufficiency of Elite Competition', reprinted from his *Elites and Society*, in Henry S. Kariel, ed., *Frontiers of Democratic Theory*, New York: Random House, 1970, pp. 127-39.

11. See Seymour M. Lipset, *Political Man*, Garden City, N.Y.: Doubleday/Anchor, 1963, pp. 64-70. This is the basis of Eckstein's argument on performance; see note 2 above.

12. Robert Nozick, *Anarchy, State, and Utopia*, New York: Basic Books, 1974; the quotation is from p. ix.

13. Robert A. Nisbet, *Community and Power*, New York: Galaxy/Oxford, 1962. At various times the book has been called *The Quest for Community*.

14. John H. Schaar, 'Legitimacy in the Modern State', in Philip Green and Sanford Levinson, eds., *Power and Community*, New York: Random House/Pantheon, 1970, pp. 294-309.

15. Jurgen Habermas, *Legitimation Crisis*, transl. by Thomas McCarthy, Boston: Beacon Press, 1973, pp. 68-92.

16. Allen Wheelis, *The Quest for Identity*, New York: Norton, 1958; Frederick A. Weiss, 'Self-Alienation: Dynamics and Therapy', reprinted from *American Journal of Psychoanalysis* by Eric and Mary Josephson, in their *Man Alone*, New York: Dell, 1962, pp. 463-79.

17. Daniel Lerner, *The Passing of Traditional Society*, New York: Free Press, 1958; Jacqueline Goodnow, 'Cultural Variations in Cognitive Skills', in Jerome Hellmuth, ed., *Cognitive Studies*, Vol. 1, New York: Brunner/Mazel, 1970, p. 245.

18. Lawrence Kohlberg and R. Kramer, 'Continuities and Discontinuities in Childhood and Adult Moral Development', *Human Development* 12 (1969): 93-120.

19. Otis Dudley Duncan, Howard Schuman and Beverly Duncan, *Social Change in a Metropolitan Community*, New York: Russell Sage, 1973, pp. 39-44.

20. Vern L. Bengsten, 'Generation and Family Effects in Value Socialization', *American Sociological Review* 40 (June 1975): 358-71.

21. Nevitt Sanford, 'Authoritarian Personality in Contemporary Perspective', in Jeanne N. Knutson, ed., *Handbook of Political Psychology*, San Francisco: Jossey-Bass, 1973, pp. 139-70.

22. Ronald Inglehart, 'The Silent Revolution in Europe: Intergenerational Changes in Post-Industrial Societies', *American Political Science Review* LXV (1971): 991-1017.

23. Ronald Inglehart, 'Values, Objective Needs and Subjective Satisfaction Among Western Publics', *Comparative Political Studies* 9 (January 1977): pp. 429-58; Otis Dudley Duncan, 'Does Money Buy Happiness?' *Social Indicators Research* 2 (1975): 267-74.

24. Everett Carll Ladd, Jr, 'The Matter of Public Confidence: Inadequate Data and Untested Theories', paper presented to meeting of the American Association for Public Opinion Research, May 1977. A condensed version is available in Ladd's, 'The Polls: The Question of Confidence', *Public Opinion Quarterly* 40 (Winter 1976-77): 544-52. The quotation below is from the article, p. 552.

25. E. C. Ladd, 'The Matter of Public Confidence', op. cit.

26. *The Gallup Opinion Index*, Report no. 140 (March 1977): 11, 15.

27. L. Galambos, *The Public Image of Big Business in America, 1880-1940*, Baltimore: Johns Hopkins University Press, 1975. I have here relied on the reanalysis of Galambos's data by John Morgan, in his 'Popular Support for the Corporate Ethic: The Outline and Content of a Belief System', Yale University, 1977. The quotation below is from Morgan, unpaged.

28. Daniel Yankelovich, 'The Status of Ressentiment in America', *Social Research* 42 (Winter 1975): 767-68.

29. Paul H. Weaver, 'The New Journalism and the Old', *The Public Interest* 35 (Spring 1974): 67-88.

30. Herbert Gintis, 'Consumer Behavior and the Concept of Sovereignty: Explanations of Social Decay', *American Economic Review* LXII (May 1972): 267-78.

31. See, in addition to much current work, the classic article by Harold Kelley, 'Attribution Theory in Social Psychology', *Nebraska Symposium on Motivation 1967*, Lincoln: University of Nebraska Press, 1967, pp. 192-238.

32. Arthur M. Okun, *Equality and Efficiency: The Big Tradeoff*, Washington, D.C.: The Brookings Institution, 1975.

33. See for example, Lee Rainwater, *What Money Buys*, New York: Basic Books, 1974, p. 176.

34. See, for a review of experimental work on the theory underlying these statements, Herbert M. Lefcourt, *Locus of Control: Current Trends in Theory and Research*, New York: Wiley/Halsted, 1976.

35. For an application, critique, and defense of the learning theory, or behavior modification theory, underlying these statements, see Harvey Wheeler, ed., *Beyond the Punitive Society*, San Francisco: Freeman, 1973.

36. William J. McGuire, 'The Nature of Attitudes and Attitude Change', in Gardner Lidzey and Eliot Aronson, eds., *Handbook of Social Psychology*, Vol. III, Reading, Mass: Addison-Wesley, 1969, p. 191.

37. Angus Campbell, Philip E. Converse, Warren E. Miller and Donald E. Stokes, *The American Voter*, New York: Wiley, 1960, pp. 326-27.

38. For empirical research following the pioneering work of Thomas H. Holmes, see Barbara S. Dohrenwend and Bruce P. Dohrenwend, eds., *Stressful Life Events*, New York: Wiley, 1974.

39. Alvin Toffler offers a brief summary of these processes in *Future Shock*, New York: Bantam, 1971. A similar account, divorced from the concepts of orientation response and adaptive reaction, but focusing on cognitive control, may be found in David C. Glass and Jerome E. Singer, *Urban Stress*, New York: Academic Press, 1972, pp. 7-12.

40. Hans Selye, *The Stress of Life*, New York: McGraw-Hill, 1956.

41. Melvin Lerner, 'Social Psychology of Justice and Interpersonal Attraction', in Ted L. Huston, ed., *Foundations of Interpersonal Attraction*, New York: Academic Press, 1974, p. 331.

42. Robert E. Lane, *Political Ideology: Why the Common Man Believes What He Does*, New York: Free Press, 1962, pp. 57-81.

43. For a recent review of equity theory and research, see Elaine Walster, Ellen Berscheid and G. William Walster, 'New Directions in Equity Research', *Journal of Personality and Social Psychology* 25 (1973): 151-76; on the particular justification theory above, see p. 166.

44. Julian B. Rotter, 'Generalized Expectations for Internal and External Control of Reinforcement', *Psychological Monographs* 80 (1966): 1 Whole no. 609. See also Lefcourt, *Locus of Control*, op. cit.

45. Daniel Yankelovich, *The New Morality: A Profile of American Youth in the 70s*, New York: McGraw-Hill, 1974, p. 134; *Gallup Opinion Index*, Report no. 134 (September 1976), pp. 19-29; Gerald Gurin and Patricia Gurin, 'Personal Efficacy and the Ideology of Individual Responsibility', in Burkhard Strumpel, ed., *Economic Means for Human Needs*, Ann Arbor, Mich.: Institute for Social Research, 1976, pp. 134-39.

46. Robert W. White, 'Motivation Reconsidered: the Concept of Competence', *Psychological Review* 66 (1959): 297-333; Edward L. Deci, *Intrinsic Motivation*, New York: Plenum, 1975.

47. Martin E. P. Seligman, *Helplessness*, San Francisco: Freeman, 1975.

48. Ibid., pp. 45-56; also Glass and Singer, *Urban Stress*, op. cit.

49. Stanley Milgram, *Obedience to Authority*, New York: Harper & Row, 1974.

50. Stanley Milgram, 'Nationality and Conformity', *Scientific American* 205 (6) (1961): 45-51.

51. Maurice L. Farber, 'English and Americans: Values in the Socialization Process', *Journal of Psychology* 36 (1953): 243-50; Eugenia Hanfman, 'Social Perception in Russian Displaced Persons and an American Comparison Group', *Psychiatry* 20 (1957): 135-36; Alexis De Tocqueville, in Phillip Bradley, ed., *Democracy in America*, Vol. II, New York: Knopf, 1945, pp. 10-11.

52. Michael I. Posner, *Cognition: An Introduction*, Glenview, Ill.: Scott Foresman, 1973, p. 116.

53. A. Couch and K. Keniston, 'Yeasayers and Naysayers: Agreeing Response Sets as a Personality Variable', *Journal of Abnormal and Social Psychology* 60 (1960): 151-74; 'Agreeing Response Set and Social Desirability', *Journal of*

Abnormal and Social Psychology 62 (1961): 175-79. Further research along the same lines may be found in Douglas P. Crowne and David Marlowe, *The Approval Motive*, New York: Wiley, 1964.

5

THE DELEGITIMATION OF OLD AND THE LEGITIMATION OF NEW SOCIAL RELATIONS IN LATE CAPITALIST SOCIETIES

Branko Horvat
University of Zagreb, Yugoslavia

Legitimacy involves the capacity of the system to engender and maintain the belief that the existing institutions are the most appropriate ones for society.[1] Institutions will be considered appropriate if, ceteris paribus, they satisfy the needs of the members of that society. Thus, a theory of needs may be a convenient starting point for our analysis of legitimacy.

A 'micro' theory of needs, such as that elaborated by Maslow which is concerned with individuals, cannot serve our purpose. We need a 'macro' theory that will treat persons not as individuals, but as members of the society. Individual needs and social needs, clearly, are closely related; society is composed of individuals. But one must not commit the fallacy of composition and identify the two. Individual needs are best examined in a laboratory; social needs by studying historical development.

In the text that follows I am concerned not with legitimacy as such, but with the dynamic process of legitimation and delegitimation. If a new legitimacy is to be created, the old one must be destroyed. One can observe how this happens. One can also engage in a purposeful design of guiding and speeding up the process. The latter represents my primary concern. In Marxian sociology this is known as the process of transition between two social systems.

HISTORICALLY OBSERVED
SOCIETAL NEEDS

We can identify four categories of needs structured in a hierarchy.

(1) Since physiological needs have a survival quality, neither an individual nor a society can exist if they are not satisfied. At the societal level this category is enlarged to include all *physical needs* such as food, clothing and shelter. (These correspond to Maslow's first level stage of 'safety needs'.)

(2) Once basic physical needs are relatively satisfied, a category of need arises which we may call *cultural needs*. People, at first, are concerned with their bodies; next, they become concerned with their minds. Education, entertainment, art and science fall under this heading. Health should be included here as well. At the lowest stage, health is often traded for increases in material comforts. It is only after a certain minimum level of living is achieved that health as such becomes of primary concern. (This category corresponds to Maslow's 'hygiene' needs.)

(3) The first two stages make for the level of living. The next two stages make for the quality of life. In a relatively affluent society people become increasingly concerned with what are called political liberties. Political needs (freedom of speech, conscience, assembly, etc.) correspond to Maslow's third level for needs self-esteem.

(4) Finally, in an affluent and politically liberated society, it is not sufficient to simply survive, enjoy life and be recognized as a separate and formally equal member of the group; it is also necessary to live one's own self-determined and authentic life. This *need for authenticity* and *self-determination* corresponds to Maslow's self-actualization need. It includes affective needs, since personal life cannot be authentic if solidarity, love, friendship, etc. are thwarted or alienated.

Stages (1) and (4) are the same at both individual and societal levels; stages (2) and (3) are not. Besides, the historical evidence is not straightforward. The periodization above corresponds to the development of *etatism*. In capitalist development, political liberties were established before the cultural needs of the broad masses of population were satisfied. The explanation for this historical indeterminacy is not difficult to find.

The precondition for the development of capitalism was the establishment of a free market. This, in turn, required that feudalism's political restrictions be removed, and that political freedoms be made available for the bourgeoisie, as well as for the aristocracy. On the other hand, the proletariat could not improve its position vis-à-vis the bourgeoisie unless political freedoms were extended to all members of the society, regardless of their origin and their ownership of property. In this way the class struggle generated political democracy while the satisfaction of cultural needs remained only rudimentary.

Consider now a different historical situation in which, owing to a revolution, economic growth is substantially accelerated and the benefits are spread fairly evenly throughout the society. People now will tend to be more concerned with improvements in the level of living than with politics. This explains the social stability of etatism. It is, of course, unlikely that the absence of political democracy can be preserved for long without overt political repression. But the repression is not a *differentia specifica* of etatism. It exists in capitalism as well, where it takes the form of economic repression. On occasions when the oppressed refuse to tolerate the continuation of economic exploitation, economic repression is immediately replaced by political repression.

As the consumption and cultural levels of the population increase, it becomes less possible to prevent a full development of political democracy in an etatist environment. Similarly, material affluence and political democracy lead to a gradual satisfaction of cultural needs (free education at all levels, health insurance, setting up of museums, art galleries, etc.). In this way, both systems converge to a state in which the relative satisfaction of material, cultural and political needs will generate pressures for radical social changes in the direction of self-determination.

Needs are satisfied by work. This is true not only in the trivial sense that work produces goods and services for consumption. It is also true in a more important sense — that work is an essential human activity. Thus, there will be some correlation between the types of needs satisfaction and the types of work. In the first three needs satisfaction stages, work is merely instrumental and, consequently, alienated. One sells one's labor power and works in order to achieve something else. Work as such is a pain, a cost, something to be avoided. In the fourth needs satisfaction stage, the situation radically changes: work becomes an enjoyment, a need, an end in itself. Let us take a somewhat closer look at this process.

Work is a complex activity with several dimensions. The development of capitalism and etatism is accompanied by a decomposition of work along its various dimensions. The totality is broken up into components, the components become independent and the process results in alienation. The labor of an artisan or a peasant is an undifferentiated whole. The first step in the process is to separate the producer from the means of production. This is also the most difficult step. It has extended over centuries. In Britain, it implied enclosures; in the Soviet Union, collectivization. It meant transforming human beings into appendages of machines, into a factor of production along with other factors such as capital and land. Labor was reduced to pure and simple manual labor; workers ,were reduced to 'hired hands'. The producers refused to work, resisted, and tried to combine in order to control their destinies. The owners knew better.

> Combination among workers was visited with brutal punishment, flogging, prison and banishment were the penalties for strikes. Workers were bound for long terms of service, often extending over several years, and were hounded down like military deserters if they left their employment.
> There was frequently forced recruitment of labor for privileged establishments of all kinds, and parents who did not send their children into industry were threatened with heavy fines.[2]

These methods, characteristic of Europe during the sixteenth to the eighteenth centuries, reappeared in the European colonies in the nineteenth and twentieth centuries.

The separation of the producer from his means of production meant not only a differentiation of labor into free and hired, but also its decomposition into manual and non-manual. The latter was retained by the owner for himself. Economic development and the ensuing division of labor pushed the decomposition one step further. The owner began to hire persons with the expertise necessary to cope with various production problems in an undertaking the complexity of which was growing. In this way hired manual labor was supplemented by hired mental labor. The owner retained only entrepreneurship, i.e. the overall control and supervision, for himself. Eventually, the supreme supervisory labor was also hired, and the owner remained as an owner, pure and simple.

This process of decomposition that generated several partial workers resulted in at least three important consequences. First, the sequence of decomposition – manual labor, hired mental and hired supervisory labor – is at the same time the order of socio-economic positions or social strata in contemporary class societies: manual workers occupy the lowest position, business and political bosses the highest.

Secondly, however paradoxical it may seem, up to a point the various strata have a common interest in preserving the existing system. For the ruling stratum, that is obvious. That manual workers, on the other hand, still find themselves in the region of lower needs satisfaction is quite compatible with the existing social system. In the United States this is reflected in the conservative attitudes of the unions which are primarily oriented toward improvements in their material well-being. In the Soviet Union, intellectuals receive little support from the workers in pressing for political freedoms.

Thirdly, pure-and-simple ownership — either private or state — is devoid of the productive function and becomes growth-inhibiting, which renders it dysfunctional. Functionless or dysfunctional institutions sooner or later are replaced by those that are positively productive. On the other hand, pure-and-simple labor i.e. alienated labor, cannot be tolerated once the lower basic needs have been relatively satisfied. Thus, the next evolutionary step can only consist of reversing the past trends. The decomposition of labor has reached its ultimate limits. What one can expect in the future is a reintegration on a new basis. This new basis can only consist of self-determination.

SEARCHING FOR A GENERAL
STRATEGY OF TRANSITION

How is this reintegration of producers and the means of production, of various components of labor, to come about? Which is the social force that will carry it out? The traditional answer was that this social force was the proletariat. History shows, however, that the proletariat does not transcend its trade union consciousness, i.e. that it remains within the confines of the system of decomposed and alienated labor. This is particularly true if the system leaves sufficient room for the gratification of lower basic needs. Two solutions for the problem have been offered.

The first one is Lenin's. Consistent with his idea of the working class not being able to produce socialist consciousness by its own efforts, he urged the creation of a disciplined party of political activists, headed by revolutionary intellectuals, that could lead and educate workers and would rule by dictatorial methods until socialist consciousness was established. This strategy proved technically efficient, but socially self-defeating. It generated etatism, not socialism.

The second strategy is to look for another revolutionary force outside the proletariat. This force is found in students, radical intellectuals and exploited minority groups in developed countries, and in peasants in undeveloped countries. Leaving the problem of peasants aside, the second strategy is well represented by the work of Herbert Marcuse:

> By virtue of its basic position in the production process, by virtue of its numerical weight and the weight exploitation, the working class is still the historical agent of revolution; by value of its sharing the stabilizing needs of the system, it has become a conservative, even counterrevolutionary force. Objectively, 'in itself,' it is not.[3]

While workers are becoming conservative, small and weakly-organized groups of militant intellegentsia, cut loose from the middle class and the ghetto population and similarly cut loose from the organized working class 'by virtue of their consciousness and their needs function as potential catalysts of rebellion within majorities to which, by their class origin, they belong'.[4]

Elaborating this idea to its final consequences, Marcuse ends in an impasse:

> ... the established democracy still provided the only legitimate framework for change and must therefore be defended against all attempts on the Right and the Centre to restrict this framework, but at the same time, preservation of the established democracy preserves the *status quo* and the containment of change. Another aspect of the same ambiguity: radical change depends on a mass basis, but every step in the struggle for radical change isolates the opposition from the masses and provokes intensified repression ... thus further diminishing the prospects for radical change ... Thus, the radical is guilty – either for surrendering to the power of the *status quo,* or of violating the Law and Order of the *status quo.*[5]

Unlike Lenin's, Marcuse's strategy has not proved successful and, clearly, never will.

Where do we go from here? Is socialist transformation intrinsically impossible, as is squaring a circle? If a particular solution fails, it is always a good rule to look first for the reasons for the failure. Since the working class represents one-half of the population, an exploited half at that, no socialist transformation is possible without the working class. Both Lenin and Marcuse would agree with this proposition and it is, in fact, generally accepted. Here, however, the agreement also ends. Where Lenin and the Old Left err (not withstanding all stated claim to the contrary) is in treating the proletariat as an object of change that has to be taught and led. In fact, the emancipation of the working class must be achieved, not by inspired leaders or an elite party, but by the workers themselves and this in the most real sense of the word. Where Marcuse and the New Left err is in a simplified dichotomising of reality: either Law and Order or a radical change. Why not use Law and Order *for* the change?

A historical parallel will clarify the issue. Suppose we find ourselves in a feudal society and seek to speed up capitalist transformation. What do we do? The most sensible thing to do is to discover the fundamental capitalist institution — the one that essentially governs the system — and try to transplant it into the feudal environment. The institution we are looking for is clearly a universal market, i.e. a free market for both products and factors. The transplantation, of course, has its problems and the environment may reject the transplant. But, suppose we succeed? The institution will gradually corrode the feudal structure from the inside, and the structure will begin to crumble. If everything can be bought and sold, then feudal estates and aristocratic titles will soon be offered for sale, and lords will soon prefer to receive monetary rents from free tenants rather than labor services from their serfs.

The fundamental institution of socialism is self-management. If universal self-management (in both market and non-market sectors) is introduced to either capitalist or etatist societies, it will gradually resolve the old production relations. Eventually the disintegrating system will have to be replaced by something more compatible. By fighting for a continuous extension of participation until it reaches full self-management, workers learn in their daily lives how to control their destiny; how to overcome fragmentation and decomposition of labor; how to achieve meaningful social equality; how to destroy antiquated hierarchies. They do that without the tutorship of omniscient leaders. They prepare themselves for self-determination. And they use Law and Order for exactly that purpose. Self-management clearly cannot be established overnight. But neither was the capitalist market. And just as, however gradual or irregular, the development of the market could not be anticapitalist, the growth of participation from its primitive forms of joint consultation toward fully-fledged self-management cannot be antisocialist, in spite of the attempts to misuse it for the preservation of the status quo.

TRANSITION IN DEVELOPED
CAPITALIST COUNTRIES

As Marx wrote: 'The carrying of Universal suffrage in England
would ... be a far more socialistic measure than anything which has
been honoured with that name on the Continent. Its inevitable result,
here [in England], is *the* political supremacy of the working class'.[6]
Exactly forty years later his friend and collaborator, Friedrich Engels,
remarked in a letter: 'During forty years Marx and myself have been
tirelessly repeating that the democratic republic for us is the only
political form in which the struggle between the working class and the
class of capitalists may first become universal and then be completed
together with the decisive victory of the proletariat.'[7]

Today, a century later, all developed capitalist countries have long
ago established universal suffrage. Most of them are republics; those
that are not are sometimes more democratic than those that are. In
England and Germany, the two countries referred to by our authors,
workers represent the majority of the population. In both countries
labor parties are in power and have been so several times in the past. In
some other countries social-democratic parties have held political power
for many years. And yet, in none of them has socialism been
established; neither can it be expected to happen very soon. Both
violent revolutions and peaceful and piecemeal reforms have failed to
produce socialism so far.

It is not difficult to uncover some of the reasons for that. Capitalist
development has been fast enough to enable all classes to share — albeit
unequally — in the benefits. The ruling class have been able to grant
substantial political and economic concessions, while yet retaining the
reins of political and economic power. The workers have been concerned with the lower levels of needs satisfaction, and failed to develop
effective socialist consciousness. Workers' organizations, trade unions
and parties, to a large extent have been integrated into the system and
failed to produce a viable radical alternative. In the struggle for survival,
unions and labor parties were forced to build bureaucratic structures
which enhanced their power, but greatly reduced their socialist
potentials. In a word, the society was not ripe for socialism.

Yet, Marx and Engels were undoubtedly right when they asserted
that under political democracy the conditions for a socialist transformation are most favorable. We now have to investigate how to exploit
these conditions effectively. We may proceed in stages, first by studying

the two fundamental preconditions for a social change, and then considering the available instruments and, finally, designing two institutional changes.

THE SATISFACTION OF NEEDS CRISIS

Whenever a discrepancy develops between the forces of production and the relations of production, sooner or later the latter will be adjusted. In late capitalist society this discrepancy is reflected in the failure of the system to satisfy certain fundamental needs. Observing the prolonged misery of the working class, the nineteenth-century socialists believed that the system's failure to improve the material level of living would generate an increasing discontent which would eventually result in a revolutionary explosion. This belief proved to be unjustified. It was replaced by another belief, connected with the obvious contradiction between the social nature of production and private appropriation. Observing periodic slumps, many socialists came to believe that capitalism would become increasingly unable to harmonize supply and demand; that business cycles would become more violent; that unemployment would increase; that further accumulation would become impossible, and, at some point, the system would break down (Z. Boudin, F. Sternberg, and, though with a different explanation, H. Grossman). This did not happen either. The theory of *Zusammenbruch* proved false. The system managed to raise the level of living substantially, even to reduce the inequality in income distribution. Unemployment and business cycles, though not eliminated, were brought under partial control. The rate of growth and accumulation, if anything, increased.

The third widespread belief concerned the colonies. Colonies, it was argued, were indispensable for the normal functioning of capitalism, because they provided outlets for capital and commodity exports (Rosa Luxembourg). Imperialism, as it were, resulted from this necessity to secure ever-expanding markets. Without them capitalism could not survive. After World War II colonial empires disintegrated; former colonies won their independency, and capitalism survived, with trade expanding faster than ever before. In general, it was not in consumption, or in the barriers to accumulation, or in the structure of the markets where the system failed to satisfy needs; it was in the work process itself.

In 1969 the Survey Research Center at the University of Michigan conducted a revealing survey of more than 1,500 American workers. At that time, the population of the United States enjoyed the highest level of living in the world. The survey found that one of every four workers under thirty felt dissatisfied with his work. This percentage was identical for both blue-collar and white-collar workers under thirty. The percentage of discontented workers was the same for all levels of education. Of the eight-top-ranked aspects of work, six were related to the content of the worker's job. Good pay only ranked fifth; after interesting work, enough help and equipment to get the job done, enough information to get the job done and enough authority to do the job.[8] This survey was undertaken after it became apparent that work discontent resulted in serious production disruptions, such as wildcat strikes, high labor turnover, absenteeism, poor quality of output, slow-downs, and outright sabotage.

> The young worker . . . says he hates the job, particularly the monotonous factory job. At times he hates it so much that he deliberately will throw a monkey wrench in the machinery, or turn to drugs to escape boredom. To him, whether the job is better than it used to be or pays more and gives benefits is beside the point.[9]

Obviously, the affluent educated worker is no longer prepared to consider his work as purely instrumental for something else. He wants to engage in *meaningful* work. 'The prospect of tightening up bolts every two minutes for eight hours for thirty years doesn't lift the human spirit.' The young worker feels 'he's not master of his own destiny. He's going to run away from it every time he gets a chance. That is why there's an absentee problem.'[10]

The worker is no longer satisfied with the collective bargaining which treats him as a 'pay category'. Neither will he tolerate being 'moved' from one job to another, or being 'put to work' on a machine as if he were a piece of a tool, without participating in the respective decisions. The system encounters an unresolvable contradiction. Unemployment does not discipline workers any longer; it creates dangerous political ferment. Secure employment, on the other hand, generates the will to control one's own destiny.

Better education and further increases in the level of living will strengthen these attitudes. So will changes in family life brought about by the equalization of the status of women. When a man is the only bread-winner, he will endure many hardships, if only to support his family. He will seek his personal fulfillment through his family. 'As long as the money comes in, and as long as the family provider is not threatened, most men will go along . . . with the work routine, however arduos it is. If, however, the man's role as breadwinner grows less vital, the whole fragile bargain threatens to break down.'[11] In this respect the employment of women and the free education of children cause a profound change. The marital partners share the financial responsibilities while social insurance and public education make savings for old age, medical treatment and tuition fees unnecessary. The social relations and the conditions of work, the quality of life, emerge as the most important life concern.

While workers are becoming more sensitive to how they are treated, the employers are becoming more vulnerable. For them work discontent is a serious danger. Slaves and serfs can operate only the simplest and crudest machines. More sophisticated machinery, invented during the industrial revolution, required free wage labor. Similarly, the highly capital-intensive plants and automated lines of late capitalist society require a new kind of labor force. The entire assembly line comes to a standstill if one member of the crew is missing. Great damage, out of any proportion to the wage cost, can be caused by poor work in a continuous-process plant. Major savings in production costs are no longer to be found in cutting the worker's wages. They come from improving yields, reducing waste and avoiding shut-downs. If the modern forces of production are to function properly, workers must be responsible and reliable. For that, they must be content with their jobs. That is why the employers — regardless of their individual or class preferences — must find remedies for work discontent. And, in fact, they are rather busy experimenting with all sorts of solutions suggested by the hired experts. In the United States special legislation has been introduced to provide for 'research for solutions to the problem of elimination among American workers and to provide for pilot projects and provide technical assistance to find ways to deal with that problem . . .'.[12]

If work is to become less monotonous and boring, then jobs should be rotated, enriched and enlarged; jobs must be upgraded so as to promise workers a way of transcending dead-end jobs; isolated subordinates should be replaced by autonomous work groups; autocratic management by participative management. The 'scientific' Taylorist organization of work, in which complex operations are broken into elementary motions and workers are asked to perform these motions like trained cattle, is abandoned and the trend is reversed. Fragments are reintegrated. The assembly line in a car factory is broken into separate teams. Billing clerks in a telephone company are given complete responsibility for specific accounts, rather than for performing a single operation on each account. Piece work is replaced by team work, and work teams are given specific autonomy in work design. Workers are given the authority to control assembly of the product, and the assignment of jobs along the assembly lines. Hourly wages are replaced by weekly salaries. Insulting status differences are eliminated. The amenities for blue-collar workers are equalized with those of the white-collar workers.

All these measures have generated measureable productivity gains; work discipline was improved, supervisory and management costs were reduced. They have also contributed to an improvement of working conditions and to the humanization of work.

It is good to see capitalists competing in improving working conditions, different as that is from what happened during Marx's time when the sweating system, long working day and low wages, were the sources of high profit. But current improvements do not even touch the main source of trouble, the autocratic hierarchy within the productive establishment. The work remains alienated, the worker discontented and the production system is in constant jeopardy.

Since work is existentially important, the discontent with work leads to a discontent with life. The Michigan Survey shows that very neatly. Those who have negative attitudes toward work have also negative attitudes toward life. In both respects the self-employed report least dissatisfaction. Clearly, this is due to the independence they enjoy; to the possibility, however small, of self-determination. But the percentage of self-employed is constantly dwindling. The work and life dissatisfactions are increasing. The society is becoming ripe for a change. The change will not be caused by material poverty, but by the failure of the system to satisfy the higher, historically determined needs. 'That is, the chief accusation against capitalism is no longer than it cannot produce the goods necessary for a decent standard of living, but that it fails to create the fundamental conditions for human freedom and self-expression. It does not permit, at any level, individual self-determination . . . .'[13]

THE LEGITIMACY CRISIS

In 1919, the first turbulent post-war year, William Straker, The Northumberland Miners Agent, expressed the following views to the Sankey Commission on the Nationalization of the Mines:

> In the past workmen have thought that if they could secure higher wages and conditions they would be content. Employers have thought that if they granted those things workers ought to be contented. Wages and conditions have improved; but the discontent and unrest have not disappeared. Many good people have come to the conclusion that working people are so unreasonable that it is useless trying to satisfy them. The fact is that the unrest is deeper than pounds, shillings, and pence, necessary as they are. The root of the matter is the straining of the spirit of man to be free.[14]

Yet, there could be no producer of freedom for the mines in Britain, the most liberal of all capitalist states. Strikers were defeated, mines remained in private hands, employers' autocracy was re-established. It is only now, half a century later, that this freedom has come to be generally considered as a fundamental human need. That, of course, must have far-reaching consequences concerning the legitimacy of the existing order.

If an order fails to satisfy certain fundamental needs, its legitimacy will be questioned. If an increasing number of people are dissatisfied with work and life, the institutions cannot be the most appropriate ones. And if the institutions fail to function properly, the value configuration of the community must have changed. This, in fact, is the crucial point. For an increasing number of individuals the existing social arrangements cease to be justified. They feel that a change is possible. And if it is possible, it ought to be undertaken.

Some fundamental values — such as freedom, democracy, and equality of opportunity — may not change, but they gradually acquire a new content and a different interpretation. Consider the concept of democracy: can a society be democratic if the democracy applies only to political life and stops at the factory gate? Behind the gate democratic fights are suspended, and a repressive autocracy is established. Why should such a duality be justified, i.e. tolerated? In 1965 the organ of the German business interests, *Industriekurier*, wrote: 'The democratisation of economy is as meaningless as the democratisation of schools, barracks or prisons.'[15] A century ago such a pronouncement would not have caused much disagreement. Today it does not indicate that economic democracy is impossible, but rather that corporations are organized like barracks or prisons. And that simply is not acceptable any longer.

Similar reasoning applies to other values mentioned above. Taking a job with a firm no longer appears as a mere free contract. If the firm is organized like a barracks or a prison, then the wage contract implies surrendering one's own personal freedom. Closely related is the treatment of property. It may remain sacrosanct; yet one may refuse to justify the use of property for the appropriation and disposal of the labor of others. The latter resembles slavery, and so wage slavery becomes a socially meaningful concept. Democracy and wage slavery are obviously not compatible. As for the equality of opportunity between rich and poor, or between weak and powerful, it sounds like a coarse joke, not like a serious proposition.

The erosion of legitimacy is always accompanied by an erosion of moral standards in public life. A new term, the 'credibility gap', has come to be used to describe one aspect of this phenomenon. Attrocities of the French military machine in Algeria and American genocide in Vietnam produced deep moral crises in these two countries. The Watergate affair, the ITT subversion in Chile, and the world-wide Lockheed corruption affair are some examples of the credibility gap.

It is not difficult to indicate the inherent contradictions of the system. Business authoritarianism tends to be extended into political authoritarianism which, of course, means the death of democracy. The costs of armaments and repression destroy the rationality of the economic calculus. Free business initiative destroys ecological balance and, on the world scale, prevents development of poor countries. The list can be extended at will.

No social order can be changed if it succeeds in preserving its legitimacy. That is why the erosion of capitalist legitimacy is of fundamental importance for a socialist transformation. It proceeds spontaneously, as in the cases described above. It can also be speeded up. To do that is the revolutionary mission of the intellectuals. On that point Lenin and Kautsky also agree. A study of revolutions reveals that the desertion of intellectuals preceeds successful revolutions.[16] The intellectuals question the legitimacy of the old order, reinterpret the values and create new consciousness. They explore the alternatives and work out possible solutions. There is no revolutionary movement without revolutionary theory, said Lenin.

Not every attack on the established values will undermine the system's legitimacy. It may even strengthen it. Consider the following set of conservative bourgeois values as juxtaposed to the values of the hippy counterculture:

Bourgeois	Hippy
Conservative	Rebel
Hard work	Leisure
Achieving	No purpose
Decent, straight	Shocking
Growth	Stagnation

Although the hippy also has a case, the naive negation of established social values can only generate strong resistance. The old values will be defended and the pseudo-radical critique will be dismissed as silly. For some, hard work may mean the 'Puritan ethnic', as well as work for the community. Work, being an existential activity, has been valued by all societies; leisure is certainly not a substitute, but a complement to it. What one would like to do is to increase the spontaneity and creativity of work, not to abolish it. Achieving may be alienating, when oriented to money and to power accumulation, but it also may mean perfecting one's art and good craftsmanship. Lack of purpose is certainly not a humanizing alternative. Stupid and hypocritical conventions of the 'straight' bourgeois society cannot be fought by frivolity and obscenity, but can by genuine decency. Finally, the damaging effects of growth cannot be eliminated by stagnation, but can by socially-controlled growth.

This brief excursion into pseudo-radicalism suggests the following simple rule: there is no need to deny historical continuity in cultural development. Socialism does not represent a mere negation but rather a new — if you wish, dialectic — synthesis. Thus, free initiative, responsibility, individual freedom, competition, democracy, and other old values ought to be included in the list of radical political slogans and be appropriately reinterpreted. For instance:

- free initiative of associated producers, not monopoly control by a corporate oligarchy;
- free men in free society, not wage slavery and the rule of plutocracy and bureaucracy;
- genuine democracy of full participation, not a fake democracy for bosses;
- self-management, not managerial authoritarianism;
- equality of opportunity, not class stratification;
- self-government, not party machinery;

- competition for a good life, not in exploitation or killing;
- respect for individual personality, not for the possession of property or power;
- culture of fully developed individuals, not primitivism of crippled money makers or office holders;
- production for better living, not for destruction;
- expansion of useful output, not of waste and pollution; and
- greater efficiency, not unemployment and waste of resources.

In the 1976 German elections the conservative opposition fought against the ruling Social Democrats under the slogan: *Freiheit oder Sozialismus* (Freedom or Socialism). This Freiheit was not meant to be exactly the same as freedom in this present book. But the mere fact that conservatives could mobilize votes under such a slogan, and almost win, indicated that something was wrong with traditional socialism. Its two main variants, social democracy and communism, failed to destroy the legitimacy of the bourgeois order. Bourgeois revolutions produced certain essential individual liberties. The socialist revolution needs neither to deny them nor oppose them; it should *transcend* bourgeois freedom. If freedom is really to be meaningful, it implies control of the existential conditions of one's own life. In this essential sense, freedom can be attained better in socialism than in any other alternative system. Thus, the strongest ideological weapon of bourgeois society can be turned against it, and used for a powerful attack on its legitimacy. The twenty-ninth thesis, announced at the Paris Sorbonne on the turbulent days of 13-14 June 1968, proclaimed: 'The bourgeois revolution was legal, the proletarian revolution was economic. Ours will be social and cultural so that man can become that what he is.'[17]

THE SOCIALIZATION OF
PRODUCTIVE CAPITAL

That capitalism is a social system based on the ownership of capital, of course, is banal observation. But it directs attention to one important fact: the *ideological* justification of the familiar organizational-distributional formula: workers receive profits (interest) on their capital and exercise control. To individuals reared in a capitalist environment, this formula belongs to the category of natural rights and self-evident truths. However, if the ideological backing is removed, if the legitimacy of the system is questioned, the formula suddenly appears quite arbitrary.

Why should not workers also participate in profits and in the decision-making? The nineteenth-century argument was that the owner waited and abstained from consumption; therefore, he must be compensated by profits (interests). A comparison of consumption levels of owners and workers makes this argument rather dubious. Currently, the standard argument is that the owner bears risk and has to be compensated for that.[18] Yet the worker bears risk as well: he can lose his job. In fact, his risk is comparatively greater. The owner can spread his risks by acquiring a diversified portfolio of shares, while the worker has only one labor power and one job.[19] As for control over the labor, that was a matter of a 'free' wage contract. As long as the other party was weak, management's prerogatives could not be touched. When the power relations changed, these become negotiable as well; so command and control ceased to be the natural rights of owners.

The issue will not be resolved by theoretical means; it is the changes in social relations that matter in such cases. Two ideological changes can be observed. The worker is becoming a partner in the production process — a co-entrepreneur. Consequently, it is right and proper for the worker to participate in profits and in decision-making. On the other hand, the system automatically generates a concentration of wealth[20] and power, which is at odds with the stated ideals of democracy. Democratic control can be established by means of participation in management and deconcentration of productive wealth. The latter implies some sort of profit sharing. We thus again reach the same conclusion.

The discussion of and experimentation with profit sharing is as old as capitalism. Profit sharing has been recommended as a device that will make workers loyal to the firm, provide work incentives and keep out trade unions. What is new in the current development is an insistence on the *right* to share in profits, a replacement of cash payments by a *distribution of shares* and, finally, the establishment of *collective trust funds* rather than individual appropriation of shares. If a part of profits is paid out in cash, it represents an addition to wages and that is the end of the story. If it is paid out in shares to individual workers, these shares can be sold; in any case, an increase in the minuscule number of shareholders does not change anything in the control of industry.

Collective ownership, however, makes for a radical change. It means socialization of the means of production without nationalization or expropriation. Coupled with workers' management, it means social ownership without the interference of the state. Although participation in management and socialization are independent, to a certain extent it is obvious that only social ownership makes fully-fledged labor management socially possible. By using a certain percentage of profits to buy shares in the firms, the firms are gradually expropriated and the old owners, or their representatives in the management, lose the power of decision-making. Thus, the market mechanism itself, the old rules of the game, are used to destroy old property relationships. This then makes for the final delegitimation of the old system.

NOTES

1. S. M. Lipset, *Political Man*, New York: Doubleday, 1963, p. 64.
2. M. Dobb, *Studies in the Development of Capitalism*, New York: International Publishers, 1963, pp. 234-35. Stalinist collectivisation was not essentially different.
3. H. Marcuse, An Essay on Liberation, Harmondsworth: Penguin, 1972, p. 25. Another representative writer is Norman Birnbaum: 'As for the proletariat, it is neither in its culture nor in its politics a harbinger of the future or a revolutionary force. Today's avant-garde in industrial societies will be found amongst the young, particularly students (that is to say, those without immediate responsibilities or bondages to the existing order), and amongst intellectuals, those with a certain freedom from routine and a certain proclivity to employ their critical faculties' (*The Crisis of Industrial Society*, London, Oxford Univ. Press, 1969, p. 94).
4. H. Marcuse, *op. cit.*, p. 57.
5. *Ibid.*, pp. 71-73.
6. K. Marx: 'The Chartists', *New York Daily Tribune*, 25th August, 1852.
7. The letter to Turati, 6th February, 1892.
8. N. Q. Herrick, 'Who's Unhappy at Work and Why', *Manpower*, (Jan. 1972), 3-7. Similar were the findings of a Canadian study a few years later. It turned out that 'the single most important consideration in the minds of Canadians proved to be interesting work' and 'that aspects of work such as having sufficient information and authority outweigh the importance of extrinsic features such as salary or comfortable surroundings' (M. Burstein et al., *Canadian Work Values: Findings of a Work Ethnic Survey and a Job Satisfaction Survey*, Ottawa; Information Canada, 1975, pp. 29, 30).

9. As reported by H. Johnson and N. Kotz in the *Washington Post*, 16th April, 1972.

10. Walter Reuther, president of the United Automobile Workers Union, in a television interview, a few weeks before his death, quoted from R. Edwards, N. Reich and T. Weisskop, *The Capitalist System*, Englewood Cliffs, Prentice Hall, 1972, p. 259.

11. D. Yankelovich, 'Changing Attitudes Toward Work', *Dialogue*, no. 4 (1974): 12.

12. Cf. H. Wachtel: 'Class Consciousness and Stratification in the Labor Process,' in R. Edwards et al., *Labor Market Segmentation*, Lexington, Mass. Health & Co., 1977, p. 112.

13. R. Aronson and J. C. Cowley, 'The New Left in the United States', in R. Miliband and I. Saville, eds., *Socialist Register*, London: 1967, p. 84.

14. Evidence to the Sankey Commission on the Nationalization of the Mines, 1919.

15. On 7 October, 1965; once again on 6 November, 1968. Quoted from F. Deppe et al, *Kritika saodlučivanja*, Beograd, Komunist, 1974, p. 183.

16. Something of the kind seems to have happened in Sweden after 1965. 'From that time there appeared an increased criticism towards social structure and policy in Sweden. Most established institutions got their part. The critical theme concerned very much industrial relations and the exploitation of the rank and file. Employers, unions and bureaucrats were made responsible for the unsatisfactory conditions. Several novels were published showing the damaging effect of working conditions, piece-work, hard-working rules, inhuman supervision, etc. Journalists, film producers and theatrical groups tried to elucidate the exploitive relations. Through mass media they spread to a large proportion of the people. Even popular culture in its different manifestations transmitted some of the ideas. It is hard to deny the effect of these ideas' (E. Dahlström 'Efficiency, Satisfaction and Democracy in Work', mimeographed paper for the Dubrovnik conference on self-management, Jan. 1977, p. 18). In 1975 Meidner's Report (see note 19, below) appeared. A year later a trade union congress gave strong support to requests for self-management. In the same year the Social Democrats were defeated after having held power for almost a half century. That can be taken as a sign of too little, rather than too much, genuine socialism.

17. As quoted by M. Marković 'Nova ljevica i kulturna revolucija', *Praxis* (1970): 943.

18. The more sophisticated version of the argument is the widely accepted theory of the American economist Frank Knight, who argued that an entrepreneur bears uninsurable risks called uncertainty.

19. As was argued by the Swedish trade union economist Rudolf Meidner, in the debate on the Wage Earner Funds (*Ekonomisk debatt* (Jan. 1976): 78).

20. In the United Kingdom, 6 percent of population own 75 percent of total personal wealth and represent 92 percent of tax payers who own shares (J. E. Meade, *Efficiency and the Ownership of Property*, London: Allen & Unwin, 1964, p. 27). In the United States, 1.6 percent of the total adult population in 1953, who each had $60,000 or more in total assets, owned 82 percent of all corporate stock, all state and local government bonds, and from 10 to 33 percent of each other type of personal property; 1 percent of the adult population

received 40 percent of the total property income; 2.3 percent of households own about 80 percent of the national productive capital (R. J. Lampman, *The Share of Top Wealth-Holders in National Wealth: 1922-1956, National Bureau of Econ. Research*, Princeton: Princeton University Press, 1962, pp. 23, 195, 108). In Sweden 1 percent of tax payers own one-half of personal wealth (R. Meidner et al., *Lontagarfonderna*, Stockholm: Tiden, 1976, pp. 38, 43).

6

LEGITIMACY, HEGEMONY AND DOMINATION:
Gramsci – With and Versus Lenin

Franco Ferrarotti
University of Rome, Italy

Forty year after his death in a fascist jail, and thirty years after the defeat and collapse of fascism and the re-establishment of a democratic regime in Italy, Antonio Gramsci is finally coming into his own and is being recognized as one of the most important European intellectuals of this Century. Why? How can one explain the extraordinary revival of interest in the philosophical and political thinking of Gramsci during recent years? The man was primarily a political leader and party organizer. He died prematurely when he was barely 48. He never wrote anything systematic. And yet, his *Prison Notebooks* have already achieved the status of a classic.

There are at least two sets of reasons. These reasons reflect the problems that Gramsci saw for his own time and those we perceive for ours.

In the first place, there is the instrinsic value of Gramsci's writings. From his early articles in the *Grido del Popolo* and in the *Città Futura* just before World War I to the *Ordine Nuovo* and the founding of the Communist Party of Italy, and to the last entries in his prison journal, one detects in his writing a fundamentally coherent revolutionary spirit which reflects creatively the political and intellectual climate that the young Sardinian student found in Turin, the only Italian city at that time in which a modern capitalistic system of production was making headway on a grand scale.

Quite probably young Gramsci came to Turin from Cagliari already a convinced socialist. But he certainly was not in agreement with the established elite at the top of the party, which was rather positivistic and evolutionary; wavering in a sad confusion between Marx on the one hand, and Darwin and Spencer on the other; passively waiting for a socialist society and a proletarian revolution, as if these were chronological inevitabilities instead of historial tasks. Young Gramsci and his student friends, Umberto Terracini, Palmiro Togliatti, Ottavio Pastore and Angelo Tasca, to mention only a few, were deeply influenced by Croce's historicism and generally by neo-Hegelian idealism; by pragmatism in the sense of a need to test ideas through action; by Bergson and his notion of 'elan vital', and by Georges Sorel and his idea of violence as a regenerating force in society. Theirs was a peculiarly voluntaristic Marxism. Their attitude was definitely anti-positivistic. The right historical occasion for the working class to achieve power had to be created, that is, consciously planned and implemented.

From the immediately political point of view, the two major influences on this young socialist group were the then-editor of *Avanti* Benito Mussolini, considered at that time a representative figure of a left-wing Marxist revisionism, and Gaetano Salvemini, historian, famous for his vitriolic criticism of the national policies of Giovanni Giolitti. In their eyes, Giolitti was the perfect figurehead of *Italietta*, that is, the little Italy of the first decade of the century, satisfied with modest day-to-day policies, neutral as far as the relationship among the big European powers was concerned, trying to make ends meet by striking some sort of viable compromise between the demands of a growing industrial working class and an insecure, shortsighted bourgeoisie.

Giolitti's program was too prosaic for the young revolutionary socialists in Turin. As Gramsci wrote in an article in the *Grido del Popolo*, 31 October, 1914:

The present historical moment is very serious – its consequences can be very grave indeed . . . . Let's act in such a way as to solve most of the issues that the past has left untouched, helping mankind to get again on its way without allowing so much sadness and injustice to block the road and a new similar catastrophe to darken its future . . . . [socialists] have been caught by surprise by events . . . . The comfortable position of absolute neutrality [vis-a-vis World War I] should not make us forget the tragic nature of this moment nor induce us even for a second to indulge in an excessively naive contemplation and a buddhistic renunciation of our rights . . . . Revolutionists who conceive history as a creation of their own spirit, made of an uninterrupted series of breaks as regards the other passive and active forces in society, and work for the most favorable conditions for the final break [the revolution] should not be satisfied with the provisional formula of absolute neutrality.

Leaving aside the rhetoric which at that time was in the air and which is echoed time and again by such diverse writers as Marinetti, Prezzolini, Papini, and Piero Gobetti, we have here a clear expression of that voluntarism which was bound to remain as an essential ingredient of Gramsci's Marxism. Later, when the socialist interventionists had been expelled from the Socialist Party (among them Mussolini) and when, through *Ordine Nuovo*, an ideological battle was waged against the right-wing reformists, also in the name of the Bolshevik revolution, a second feature of Gramsci's thinking surfaced: a keen sensitivity to the feelings of grass-roots militants, and to the idea and practise of the revolutionary movement as a process of a direct democracy, based on a network of workers' councils, deeply rooted in the substance of every-day life and in the reality of the workplace. Although the *Manuscripts* of the young Marx, as well as the *Gundrisse* were still unpublished, Gramsci was able to detect the notion of a 'global revolution' — economic and political, but at the same time moral and intellectual — as a guiding criterion for a true revolutionary change and not merely a reformistic institutional readjustment.

As regards the Russian revolution, his insight was extraordinary. He saw very clearly the function of Lenin, when Lenin was being sought for imprisonment by the Kerensky government in early July 1917, and many Bolshevik journals were suppressed; and on 5 January, 1918, when the Bolsheviks were already settled in power, Gramsci wrote an article for *Avanti*, 'La rivoluzione contro *il Capitale*' (The revolution against *Das Kapital*) which demonstrates how far his conception of revolution was from being mechanistic and his idea of Marxism from being doctrinaire. Gramsci's main contention was that the Bolshevik revolution disproved any deterministic interpretation of Marxism: 'the social will of the Russian people' proved more decisive than any 'law' of the capitalist mode of production. Contrary to Marx's expectation and prediction, in backward Russia the socialist revolution took place sooner than in the developed capitalist countries of Western Europe.

It is true, however, that Gramsci knew very little about the actual conditions in Russia at the time of the Revolution. Moreover, his knowledge of the thinking of Lenin was far from complete. As Togliatti has admitted, he did not know the early Marxist work by Lenin, *The Development of Capitalism in Russia,* nor had he read *What is to be Done?*, *State and Revolution*, or the other major philosophical and political books. He was familiar only with the writings of Lenin that dealt with immediate political problems. It is no wonder then that

Gramsci would project onto the Russian state of affairs his own private notion of a revolution from below as an act of supreme historical consciousness and, at the same time, as an example of popular inventiveness.

In Gramsci this was no moralistic rhetoric. Especially at the time of *Ordine Nuovo*, it was a reasoned reflection of an actual political experience which carried the mark of a profound originality and implied a new conception of the State and a new, original notion of legitimacy as stemming from a consensus directly connected with the everyday experience of factory life. Finally, in his *Prison Notebooks*, despite the terrible sufferings and limitations imposed by a fascist jail systems, Gramsci tested the main points of his philosophical and political theoretical framework against a whole series of intellectual trends and traditions.

The language and the style of Gramsci became increasingly sober. They lost their former sentimental nature that was probably derived from a humanistic education divorced from any scientific training. He was especially empathetic in his articles as a young socialist journalist but, little by little, his language became sufficiently functional and at times it succeeded in making irrationalism and the exercise of reason coincide.

The second set of reasons that explains the renewed interest in Gramsci is of a different order and concerns the present-day political situation in Italy and in the rest of Europe Gramsci saw himself as a Leninist. The irony is that Gramsci now comes back as a major political and philosophical figure because he is regarded as the representative of a Marxist way of thinking that goes well beyond and, eventually, even against Lenin. I submit that today the interest in Gramsci is directly proportional to the need for a democratic legitimation of communist parties in Western Europe.

Eurocommunism has found in Gramsci a prophet as well as a political leader. During the past three years the political scenario of Western Europe, especially of Italy, France, Spain and, to some extent, Portugal, has changed dramatically. Communist parties are rapidly approaching participation in government. Their contribution to the stabilization of an otherwise shaky democratic situation is already essential. For these parties a new legitimation in democratic terms is badly needed. Gramsci's thinking, which is basically historicistic and voluntaristic, seems to fit this need quite adequately. His conception of politics as an expression of historical consciousness, i.e. as an activity and at the same time a legitimating instrument in so far as it rests on a constantly renovated popular consensus, meets the present-day demands of the political and social system.

Even in Gramsci's terms, legitimacy is not a static state of things, but a process. It is not a general concept in that there is no metaphysic of legitimacy, but is a situation that is linked with the specific features of a given historical phase of development. In this perspective, Gramsci seems to connect himself with the Italian elitist school and makes the most of Machiavelli's lesson. The Marxian idea that illegitimate violence is nothing but the historical midwife of a legitimate new political order is here completed with the Machiavellian notion that at the bottom of any legitimate regime or principality there is an act of illegitimate violence: Romulus killing Remus.

Legitimacy, then, is not grounded in some metahistorical principle of natural law, nor is it logically possible to derive it from some supposedly innate traits of 'human nature'. Men do not have a nature, but have a history. That is to say, the 'nature' of human nature cannot be identified, much less understood, unless the historical *milieu* is taken into consideration. This notion of milieu has always remained somewhat vague among the theoreticians of historicism. One point, however, is quite clear: human nature is not an independent variable and does not enjoy any kind of priority. There is not, therefore, such a thing as a human essence − set apart, separate and aloof, untouched, as it were, by the course of historical development. There has been a broad convergence toward agreement among the majority of present-day scholars of law, philosophy and political science on this point. In a sense, it is correct to maintain that all of them are the 'grandchildren of Machiavelli', as Leo Strauss would put it. In his judgement, the renunciation of a definite metahistorical notion of human nature necessarily implies the notion of 'values' and the reduction of qualitative evaluations to quantitative factual statements. In this respect, Strauss seems quite certain that Machiavelli would qualify as a full-time 'teacher of evil' (see, in particular, his *Natural Law and History* and *Thoughts on Machiavelli*).

Fear of a regression toward dogmatism, however, has been so deep-seated and sweeping among present-day scholars as to have built historicism into a new orthodoxy. It has been widely held that legitimacy can only be a product of history and accidental circumstances, and not the necessary consequence of an eternal principle. Thus, legitimacy is seen as the problematic, a fluid, unstable result of contrasting social forces in a specific historical situation as defined by the average social awareness of a given community.

Having accepted these presuppositions, it is no wonder that Gramsci entertained so much admiration for Croce. He did not seem aware of how profoundly and essentially idealist Croce's approach to history is, just as he did not seem to have a realistic assessment of the negative import connected with the Crocean reform of Hegel's dialectic. By introducing a 'dialectic of distincts' as a corrective device to the Hegelian dialectic of the 'opposed', Croce was, in fact, diluting the inner tensions and contradictions of social and political life and of the power relations among divergent economic interests. The very idea of social class and the Marxian image of society as a dichotomic reality were undermined. Gramsci felt that Croce's concept of history as 'ethical-political history', embodying events and meanings, and therefore conveying the whole of meaningful human experience, was a decisive explanatory and operational category. Of course, Gramsci was quite conscious that it was still a 'speculative', or 'idealistic', not a materialistic, category but his extraordinary admiration remained. Gramsci wrote:

> It is necessary to state that Croce's historiographic thinking, even in its most recent phases, deserves to be studied and meditated with attention . . . . For the philosophy of praxis [Marxism], the speculative method itself is no futility but it has been the carrier of 'instrumental' values that the philosophy of praxis has incorporated [e.g. the dialectic]. Croce's thought should then be praised as an instrumental value; thus one may say that it has called attention to the study of cultural and intellectual realities as elements of political domination, to the function of great intellectuals in the life of States, to the moment of hegemony and of consensus as a necessary form of the concrete historical bloc. Ethical-political history is therefore one of the canons for historical interpretation to be kept always in mind in the examination and exploration of historical development if one aims at integral history and not at partial or extrinsic histories.[1]

This is no mere formal concession, I suspect, to a dominant intellectual figure of his time. The construction by Gramsci of Marxism as 'absolute historicism' is perfectly consistent with his overall evaluation of Croce's philosophical position. Gramsci always felt that, outside of the historicistic outlook, Marxism tends to become abstract and 'mechanistic'.

It is rather startling that Gramsci did not see the danger in reducing historical materialism to a pure and simple 'method of historiographic analysis', devoid of any specific content, as Croce had done in a rather definitive way in his *Materalismo storico ed economia marxistica.* The fact is, Gramsci was primarily concerned with the danger of proposing a narrow-minded interpretation of Marxism in terms of naive *economism*, as the positivistically-oriented socialists of his early youth had done, and he feared the political consequences in terms of reformist passivity, if the socialist revolution were seen as a result of the impersonal 'laws' and 'objective' contradictions of the capitalistic mode of production. What he liked in Croce was the strong commonsense perception of the importance attached to individual, 'subjective' initiative. In this respect, again quite incredibly, Gramsci went so far as to compare Croce with Lenin. in both of them he saw at least a glimpse of what he called the principle of social 'hegemony'.

This humanistic subjectivism, typical of Gramsci, and perhaps connected with his essentially literary education (as it is for Togliatti), has remained a permanent feature of Italian Marxism, and of Western Marxism in general. This peculiar kind of Marxism is still strangely reluctant today to accept the empirical social sciences and has only sporadic connections with economics. Its orientation is basically literary and philosophical (see my comments in 'Betrachtungen über Marxismum in Italien' in *Koelner Zeitschrift für Soziologie and Sozial-Psychologie,* 1967). It has been aptly pointed out that, although Gramsci was perhaps the last representative of Western Marxism who could face the basic issues of class struggle in Europe in their broadest terms, he has nothing to say about the capitalistic economy as such, nor did he analyze the 'laws' of the capitalistic mode of production. For years, while in prison, he was in close contact with Piero Sraffa, the economist, but in this case personal friendship was not accompanied by any intellectual exchange or communication.[2]

One might suspect tha the divorce between science and philosophy which had been expounded and conceptually justified, especially by the Italian neo-Hegelian idealists such as Gentile and Croce, resulted in a gross devaluation of science, and of the social sciences in particular. In the end, these were regarded as totally deprived of any cognitive value in the proper sense and were seen as mere 'inferior means on intellectual life', which may have had an impoverishing effect on Western Marxism. What is gained, in terms of voluntaristic initiative and a feeling for the value of a not yet institutionalized spontaneity, is perhaps more reminiscent of Fichte than of Bergson or Sorel and is likely to be lost when we require a sober verification of any aspiring 'revolutionary' anticipation.

Especially in Italy, Marxism has thus remained the province of professors of literature and the humanities who have never shown any inclination to deal with the natural or social sciences. If one also considers that most Marxist intellectuals, with the exception of Gramsci himself, were of urban middle-class origins and that, with the advent to power of fascism any sustained relationship with the working class was precluded, it is not difficult to understand the theoretical, practical, and existential reasons for the progressive impoverishment of a debate that, at the beginning of the century, seemed full of hope and closely connected with the actual experiences and struggles of the 'laboring classes', as they were then called. After Gramsci, Marxism becomes professorial, essentially academic and highly theoretical. Needless to say, this is a far cry from the attitude of its founders.[3]

Gramsci's 'organic' link, i.e. his ideological and also existential link with the working class and its everyday problems, is a fact. It is true, however, that he holds a conception of 'historical development' which is still 'global' and 'theological'. History, for Gramsci as for Lenin, is holistic, an unfolding dynamic reality with one single emerging meaning which is to be understood, spelled out, and 'obeyed', as it were, rather than implemented on a practical, day-to-day basis by each social group or class through the necessary mediation of its 'organic intellectuals' acting as its official interpreters. But the historical task of these intellectuals is not merely one of mediation in the narrow, legalistic sense. Organic intellectuals are actually the authorized elaborators of the needs, and therefore the makers, of the legitimacy, in its universalistic meaning, of the social and political movement from below and for the economic, material interests expressed by the movement, and upon which the movement counts for its survival and final victory.

This sounds rather Leninistic, at least in the sense that for Lenin, too, the popular masses could not speak or fight for themselves in the first person. They were, inevitably, in need of an active revolutionary minority that would have to guide them, lest the masses confine their demands to a pure-and-simple trade-union level, i.e. to a 'bread-and-butter' policy', incapable by itself of conceiving and effecting a radical transformation of the existing social structure and of the prevailing system of power relations.

According to Lenin, the revolutionary party is nothing but the 'conscious and organized vanguard of the working class'. In this connection, a crucial one because it directly concerns the very concept of social revolution, we hear in Gramsci a different tone. It is true that

Gramsci remains essentially *totus politicus*, i.e. a man of action devoted to political initiatives in order to seize political power for the revolutionary party on behalf of the underlying masses. But the organic intellectuals he writes about are also interested in something else. It seems that there is in them an emphasis on 'civil society', on the importance of a substantially legitimate representation of general interests, and on a broad social consensus which is clearly absent in Lenin.

I detect in Gramsci a concern for 'civil society' in its broadest sense, and for legitimate political action. Despite his Marxian allegiance, I do not feel that Gramsci would accept the formula: *Macht macht das Recht,* although he obviously accepts the principle set forth in the Preface to the *Introduction to a Critique of Political Economy*, that *Sein macht das Denken.* He indicates that the revolutionary party is the new Machiavelli's Prince. It is well known that Machiavelli can be regarded as a teacher of evil, as Leo Strauss argues, because Machiavelli equates ethics with any successful enterprise. But Gramsci's historically situated reading of the same works reveals to him that Machiavelli's apparent amoral approach to the study of political reality was, in fact, based on the substantial legitimacy of his attempt to bring about the unity of Italy.

It is evident that the organic intellectuals of Gramsci are not in the least anarchistically inclined, nor are they sensitive to any conspiratorial plotting in the *Commune* or to Blanqui's insurrectionist tradition. I do not agree with Louis Althusser when he maintains that Gramsci chose to use the formula 'social hegemony' instead of the more traditional one concerning the 'dictatorship of the proletariat', merely to evade the censorial strictures of the jail system. I think there is something more here than a linguistic trick to avoid censorship. Gramsci's organic intellectuals are, naturally, interested in the seizure of power, but they are also, if not primarily, interested in securing and confirming a broad cultural dominance over the general society, including the proletariat and its actual or potential allies. The notion of 'historic bloc', in this perspective, is revealing and important.

The very role that Gramsci assigns to the 'workers' councils' indicates a genuine concern for some sort of 'legitimation from below'. The experience and direct contact at the time of World War I with the Turinese workers at Fiat were crucial for Gramsci. He would never entertain a notion of grass-roots workers' organizations as a purely instrumental device for something else, even if this something else were the workers' State. Marx never wrote much about the State and there is no comprehensive Marxian theory of the State. The comments by Lenin in *State and Revolution* are scanty and naive. The notion that any worker can be a bureaucrat, and vice versa, has shown itself as historically doctrinaire and untenable in practice.

According to some commentators, notably Norberto Bobbio,[4] the main departure of Gramsci from orthodox Marxism must be traced to the idea of 'civil society'. Both Marx and Gramsci admittedly derive this idea from Hegel, but while for Marx civil society was identical with social and economic structure, for Gramsci, they believe, the concept of civil society belonged to the sphere of the 'superstructure'. In this way, the concept of civil society is no longer concerned with the material basis of any society, i.e. with the global reality of the material production relationships, whereby any given historical society takes care of itself and provides the means for its survival and perpetuation. Gramsci is presented as the theorist of civil society in such general cultural and ideological terms as to obliterate the overall importance of the economic aspects of the structure of society and to slip out of contac with the original Marxist tradition. His notion of civil society is thus impoverished and reduced to its purely intellectual connotations. The whole of Gramsci's experience of *Ordine Nuovo* is also misinterpreted and buried.

I feel that Gramsci perhaps departs from Lenin, but not from Marx. For Lenin, force, even in its most violent and extreme manifestations, is to be accepted as a normal means of political activity. It is the prerequisit of legitimacy. We have already mentioned that for Gramsci, too, legitimacy is not a metaphor nor a metaphysical concept. Legitimacy is man-made. It is historical and political. It can be regarded as a limit-concept (a *Grenbegriff*) in the sense that is never fully conquered nor completely and for ever achieved. It is a problematic process. But it rests, basically, on the economic interests and the needs of the masses, not as interpreted and brought to the working class from outside by the bourgeois intellectuals, but as these needs are directly expressed and lived through by the workers at the plant and community level.

The only Marxist thinker and militant who seems to be on the same wavelength as Gramsci is Rosa Luxemburg. Gramsci called her book *The General Strike, the Party and the Trade Unions,* 'one of the most significant documents of the theory of programmed war as applied to the political art' (Antonio Gramsci, *Note sul Machiavelli*, p. 65). Gramsci criticizes Luxemburg's 'spontaneism' and 'primitive economic determinism', but the idea of a large-scale grass-roots workers' participation is a shared value.

In Lenin the aspirations and needs of the rank and file are by definition subordinate to the strategic and tactical exigencies of the revolutionary party. This party is dogmatic and centralized. It is based on a total, monolithic obedience to the top leadership. Grass-roots participation is nonsense. According to Lenin, workers' consciousness, if not filtered through the party leadership directives, is only group-, not class-consciousness. It reverts inevitably to petty bourgeois attitudes and values. The trade unions are mass organizations, while the party must be a selective elite organization. Hence, union activities must be geared to the guiding function of the party. No self-government at the local level can be permitted. As for the relationship between unions and the party, Lenin does not admit any kind of neutrality.

This policy comes from a distant past. Lenin wrote in 1908 that 'all our party has recognized that in the trade unions it is necessary to work not with a spirit of neutrality, but with the spirit of a closer and closer bond with the social-democratic party .... Social democrats must organize within the trade unions compact cells, and whenever this is not legally possible, illegal, clandestine cells must be organized (*Proletarij*, no. 22, 4 March, 1908). Later, Lenin seemed ready to attribute to unions a pedagogic function as regards the working class masses, but they were always to be in an ancillary position vis-à--vis the party and its top leadership. Especially in 'Function and Task of Labor Unions in the Conditions of the New Political Economy', Lenin went to great pains to explain in detail how the unions should 'educate the masses': 'unions should work for a quick reconciliation whenever attritions and conflicts arise between single groups of workers in a given factory and State organizations'.[5] State prerogatives and general interest as defined by the central political power must have absolute priority on any workers' claim coming from below. Any such claim seems to be considered be definition 'disruptive' and 'illegitimate'.

The reactions of Plekhanov, Martov, Trotsky, Vera Zasulich, and especially Rosa Luxemburg, were understandably negative. Lenin's conception of the party constituted, in the words of Luxemburg, 'a pitiless centralism which posits as a principle, on one hand, the selection and organization of a separate body of active militants confronting the unorganized mass surrounding them, and, on the other, a severe discipline, in the name of which the ruling centers of the party intervene directly and in an authoritarian manner in all the internal matters of the local party organizations'.[6]

Trotsky's criticism was even more pungent. He accused Lenin of sectarian and intransigent jacobinism; of tending to substitute for the proletariat, radical intellectuals coming from the bourgeoisie; of thus transforming the dictatorship of the proletariat into a bureaucratic dictatorship *over and against* the proletariat; he warned that the absolute priority assigned to the organization would necessarily lead to the absolute power of the dictator. More specifically, he warned that the party would be replaced by the organization of the party; the organization by the Central Committee, and finally the Central Committee by the dictator.

This sequence is a good piece of reasoning in terms of sociology of organization. The final outcome was certainly not the deliberate intention of Lenin. It was largely an unanticipated consequence. I do not think that Lenin ever developed a comprehensive and coherent theory of the party. He was first of all a man of action. He used ideas as weapons without paying too much attention to formal coherence. His revolutionary spirit would lead him to the most drastic pragmatism: ideas and theories would be good or bad, true or false according to whether they would ultimately 'function' or not. He viewed the role of intellectuals in the same way, it seems to me. They were to be used at the slightly higher level than the masses, but without too much pathos. One must build with the bricks at hand; that is, if one wanted seriously to build. And Lenin was most certainly a deadly serious builder.

But Lenin's emphasis was almost exclusively an organizational efficiency. He spoke and acted like a genuine manager of the revolution. As in the classic tradition of entrepreneurship, there was no fit between thought and action. Like a naturally predatory animal, he sought political power as the early entrepreneur sought profit maximization — ruthlessly and amorally. He could not afford the luxury of being bothered by moral or intellectual scruples nor by theoretical 'idle curiosity'.

With the typical pedantry of a frustrated didactic vocation, Togliatti managed to gather various fragments from Lenin's work, especially from *What Is To Be Done?*, in order to offer a Leninist theory of the party. But Lenin cared so little about the purely theoretical aspects of his political struggle that a whole series of theories of the party can be found in his writings, depending on the specific historical circumstances. Contrary to what L. Kolakowski seems to maintain in a recent paper (presented in Venice at the meeting on 'Dissent', November 1977) in which he defends the view that the whole of Leninism can be understood and easily mastered simply by a careful reading of the first seven issues of 'Iskrà'., A. Carlo has demonstrated that, as far as party organization is concerned, Lenin did not present a single theory but rather 'a series of complex and contradictory positions'.[7] Carlo maintains, on the basis of a study of Lenin's *Collected Works,* that there is an early conception, rather inclined toward economic determinism, at the turn of the century, the phase of *What Is To Be Done?* on which Togliatti has capitalized; a variety of positions according to expediency between 1905 and 1919; and, finally, a tendency toward bureaucratic supremacy which is visible in *Left-Wing Communism: an Infantile Disorder,* and which is quite convenient for present-day collectivistic regimes of Eastern Europe and the Soviet Union itself as a pseudo-theoretical justification post factum.

While Lenin's emphasis is on efficiency and organization, and therefore of discipline and obedience under the label of 'democratic centralism', Gramsci's emphasis is on a broad social consensus linked with an 'intellectual and moral reformation' which should give cultural as well as political hegemony to the proletariat as to the new 'general' class, capable of expressing those universal values of justice, freedom, and equality which have been historically betrayed by the bourgeoisie. For Lenin the most urgent and important task of the revolutionary party is the conquest of central political power irrespective of methods, provided they work, i.e. provided they are successful. The problem of legitimacy comes up later, at a different stage, once the central power is solidly seized and secured. For Gramsci, on the contrary, the seizure of central power and the development of a generalized social consensus at the grass roots of society are not two separate phases of the revolutionary process. The two moments must be simultaneous in order to achieve a true revolution instead of a mere transition from one elite despotism to another, from capitalist exploitation and alienation to collectivistic bureaucratic domination.

The very concept of revolution is here involved. The problem does not seem to be, as many critics maintain, in the Machiavellian indifference to means in connection with the goals to be achieved. Rather, the problem is that the instruments chosen to achieve the goal condition and change the goal itself. This seems to me the dividing point between Lenin and Gramsci. The latter appears to be more and more conscious of the danger that out of the proletarian revolution against capitalist class domination, a new class of oligarchic bureaucrats might rise in the very name of the proletariat. What in his last years was for Lenin an anxious premonition about the despotic traits of Stalin's character, becomes in Gramsci a conscious theoretical effort to build an integrated theory of revolution as a global process involving simultaneously culture, structure, and personality.

I have tried to show[8] that both Lenin and Gramsci, not to mention other revolutionaries such as Karl Korsch and Rosa Luxemburg, have had the historical merit of trying to open the road toward a post-bourgeois type of democracy. Whereas Max Weber could not see any way out of the dilemma facing the democratic regimes of his time — falling into the pseudo-democratic game of *camarilla* or entrusting all the power to a Führer endowed with a special charisma — Lenin and Gramsci sought a solution through the broadening of the social basis of power, by advocating the transition from a purely formal bourgeois democracy, conceived as a set of legal procedures irrespective of social and economic contents, to a substantive democracy in which legal or purely formal rights would be guranteed practical implementation through economic equality.

This goal is common to Lenin and Gramsci. My contention is that the basic differentiating point between Lenin and Gramsci concerns the conception of such a transition, i.e. how to reach that goal. Most commentators are mesmerized by the common goal; they tend to blur the qualitative difference that has to do with substance and not only the mood and climate of thought or with the peculiarities of the specific historical situation. I would not agree with Massimo L. Salvadori that 'both Gramsci and Lenin and Trotsky asserted, together with the "freedom of thought" of the masses and of intellectuals, the task of the revolutionary party to "keep in line", through ideological directives and militant actions, artistic and scientific expressions which in their implications would give rise to conservative or reactionary trends'.[9]

We will see later that the role of intellectuals is qualitatively different in Lenin and in Gramsci — so different in fact as to be opposite. Here we are concerned with their overall positions which do not seem to differ only on occasional grounds. It is true that the convergence between the two great revolutionaries concerns important aspects of their work. Both Lenin and Gramsci believed in the revolutionary method of class struggle; both were voluntaristic; that is, they did not expect revolution to come about as a natural, spontaneous product of an automatic evolution of historical circumstances. Revolution was for both of them an historical task, the result of consciously planned human effort. The practical implementation of such a task was not mysterious or 'charismatic'; it did not require an 'irruption of grace' from above; it required the presence and the initiative of a specific instrument, the revolutionary party.

Here we have a difference between Lenin and Gramsci, perhaps a clear-cut contradiction, as regards the internal structure and functioning of the party and the relationship between the party and the masses. We have already clarified that the party was for Lenin instrumental with respect to the revolution to be effected. For Gramsci, too, the party was an instrument, but an instrument of a very special kind. It was an instrument for the revolutionary transition to socialism and, *at the same time,* it had already to be, *hic et nunc,* a prefiguration, an anticipation, concrete although necessarily circumscribed, of the socialist post-capitalist society to be built. While in Lenin the principal question was the seizure of central power, for Gramsci the fundamental question consisted in guaranteeing the making of the revolutionary process as an everyday struggle which aimed at the conquest of power but which at the same time *socialized, at the local level, power itself in all its forms and instances,* from factory to neighborhoods, through a constant erosion of capitalist power prerogatives and a slow, but continuous, change of power relations in favor of the exploited majority of the underlying population. In Gramsci the conquest of power and the legitimation process were the two faces of the same unfolding reality. What in Lenin is a unilinear sequence of a *prius* and a *post,* in Gramsci presents itself as a self-constituting 'contextuality'.

It is easy to understand now why the role of intellectuals is so different in the thinking of Lenin and Gramsci, and why the concept of 'social hegemony' is so crucial for Gramsci while in Lenin it seldom, if ever, surfaces. The criterion of contextuality of political victory and of intellectual and social reformation is in Gramsci the basic presupposition which makes regressive developments and a return to bourgeois bureaucratization *after* the advent to power on the part of the masses logically and virtually impossible. Between Lenin and Stalin there is an essential, necessary continuity which does not exist between Lenin and Gramsci. It has been aptly observed that

> Stalin's conception of Marxist theory is . . . his justification for the character and organization of the Bolshevik party as opposed to Marxist parties of the Western type. Because the party is the embodiment of 'scientific' truth, and because that truth is uncompromisingly revolutionary . . . the party must be

'monolithic', a centrally controlled army under strict military discipline, tolerating no other parties except for temporary reasons of expediency, hunting down and destroying compromisers – all who are disposed to take the edge off the revolutionary drive, to let things move more gradually – both in society at large and within its own ranks. The same claim to infallible 'science' lies at the base of Stalin's theory of the party purge . . . . A procedure that to Western minds is a sign and a further cause of weakness is for Stalin a means to strength because strength derives ultimately, nor from numbers, but from 'knowledge' which harnesses revolution to the laws of history: the purge eliminates those whose allegiance to this 'knowledge' and the program based on it, is dubious.[10]

The dogmatic political consequences of such a 'scientistic' standpoint need but a passing mention. It might simply be considered naive if, in the case of Lenin and Stalin, it were not tragic. It is interesting to observe that Gramsci does not write about the 'science of politics' – he was perhaps too much of a historicist for that – he simply refers to the 'art of politics' which in the Italian conventional wisdom amounts to defining politics as 'the art of what is possible'.

An indirect, but convincing, confirmation of Lenin's still mechanistic and acritical conception of science, technology, and organization has been offered by Paul Piccone. The myth of science becomes in Lenin, according to Piccone, the presupposition for the acceptance of science, and of technology as applied science, as essentially 'neutral', therefore susceptible of socialist use. The example of 'Taylorism' adequately illustrates this point. Lenin admired Taylorism as a great 'technical achievement', unfortunately combined with the refined brutality of capitalistic exploitation. There was no awareness in Lenin of the intrinsic negative features of Taylorism as a system of work organization based on the refusal to recognize the humanity of human beings, considered and treated as if they were passive instruments instead of active agents. Piccone writes:

All would be well, according to Lenin, once the Taylor system were brought unter socialist management. How the brutality would be eliminated remains a moot point since efficiency and brutality are inextricably connected, it is understandable why the Russian revolution ultimately capitulated by reintroducing new relations of domination.[11]

In 'Americanismo e fordismo', Gramsci took a more sophisticated position. Lenin was enchanted by the 'miracle' of advanced technology. Gramsci saw through it and evaluated its repercussions on all the major aspects of the global society. In particular, above and beyond technology, he paid close attention to the 'inner', human repercussions of 'scientific management' which in the end essentially amounts to a more rigorous form of capitalist exploitation. Piccone is right when he points out that 'neither Gramsci nor Lenin was familiar with the Marxian theme of alienation, since the *Manuscripts* and the *Grundgrisse* were unknown to them'.[1][2]

However, if it is true that Lenin mechanically transposed Taylorism into the party and into the Bolshevik State using, or through a curious self-deception thinking that he could use, Taylorism to build socialism instead of speeding up capital accumulation and profit maximization for capitalists, Gramsci, on the other hand, conscious of the degradation of human beings to the level of mechanical robots, nevertheless seemed to believe that 'machine discipline' and technically advanced work would contribute to the education of a new type of proletariat. When he describes the rationalizing effects of the machine discipline, as regards the elimination of animistic habits of mind, and about the increasing weight of the cause-effect nexus in everyday discourse, he sounds quite Veblenian; he risks sharing Veblen's illusion about the 'soviets of engineers'.

I might add that Lenin's and Stalin's deep-seated 'scientism' does not only affect industrial workers in mass production, in so far as it makes a social and political hero of Stakhanov. It explains, or at least it sheds light on, their use of intellectuals for manipulatory purposes.

It must be granted that in a cursory examination of his writings, Gramsci might seem to have the same general conception as Lenin in regard to the intellectuals, their position in society, and their role in the revolutionary process. Lenin, however, no matter how violent his criticism of gradualistic reformism and abstract extremism, agrees in this respect with Karl Kautsky on one side, and György Lukàcs, on the other. Following a tradition of thought that sems to be typically middle-European, the intelligentsia attain in these authors the level and function of a levitic self-appointed elite group. This restricted group is supposed to bring from the outside to the working masses that revolutionary spirit and consciousness which the masses would not be able to develop by themselves. In the sociological literature this notion is certainly connected with Karl Mannheim's idea of the intellectual as a *freischwebend* social agent, detached from any petty, or material, class interest, and only busy, like some other sort of Holy Spirit, elaborating and transmitting the proper *Zeitgeist*.

No doubt this concept is a clear psychological projection and self-justification for those bourgeois intellectuals, beginning with Marx and Engels, who have chosen the proletarian revolution as their personal destiny. They are in every respect the gatekeepers of socialist revolution. To use the words of Kautsky, neither the forms nor the time of revolution are exactly predictable, although the social struggles in the meantime are bound to become more and more extended and severe; at any rate, it is necessary, according to Kautsky (who sees eye-to-eye with Lenin on this topic) to distrust any kind of 'spontaneism' from below because the construction of socialism is essentially a 'scientific' enterprise.

Nothing could be farther from Gramsci's theoretical position and general sentiment. He writes about the 'organization of culture and of intellectuals' and his concept of intellectual freedom has little, if anything, to do with the traditional romantic concept of the intellectual as a lonely *Steppenwolf* in Hesse's meaning of the term, nor does he conceive of the intellectual as an individualistic explorer of the final truth. Gramsci does not think of intellectuals as a separate social stratum or specialized body. 'All men are intellectuals', he asserts. In other words, all men are potentially capable of understanding and directing their destiny, if only the division of labor, especially the barrier between mental and physical labor, and the class division of society could be overcome.

To achieve this genuine unity of mankind, i.e. in order to go beyond capitalistic exploitation, based on the 'commoditification' of human labor, and to restore the human polity as a community, a fusion between theory and practice has to be implemented and a general moral reformation of society must be effected in concomitance with the elimination of private property and a radical transformation of all the major social institutions.

In Gramsci's thinking there is no room for such a figure as a 'pure' intellectual. Anybody professionally interested in intellectual problems is bound to become 'abstract' and is himself a victim of the capitalist division of labor. *Gramsci's intellectual is a specialist plus a policy-maker. He sees and conceptually dominates the interconnections of the social.* He understands the contradictions of capitalism, but he also knows that purely verbal mediations are a fraud. The objective contradictions of capitalism cannot be solved on a purely intellectual level; they must be solved through a revolutionary transformation of society. 'Pure intellectuals' are for Gramsci 'pure asses'. For this reason it is erroneous to maintain that Gramsci gives priority to the 'structure', as most New Left commentators would have it, or to 'culture'. It is true that the whole question of the relationship between *Unterbau* and *Ueberbau* comes to the fore again. But that does not mean that Gramsci gives priority to the *Unterbau* or to *Culture* as such. As a genuine dialectical thinker, he sees both elements, or levels, inextricably interconnected, or, to put it more precisely, 'interwoven'.

In this respect interpretations of Gramsci by analysts such as N. Bobbio and M. L. Salvadori appear to be biased in an anti-materialistic and especially in an anti-economic sense. They demonstrate the typical attitude of liberal-minded democrats who can bring themselves up to the border of socialism without entering it. Their idea that who ever believes that society is divided into two spheres or layers, as it were (structure and overstructure) and that society is therefore a dichotomic reality is by this very fact a Marxist, is clearly untenable. For example, 'I consider Marxist theories all those that in some way do accept the fundamental dichotomy between structure and overstructure'.[13] Many social scientists, for instance, would agree that society is made up of two basically different strata, but they certainly would not be regarded, nor would they consider themselves, as Marxists.

As I have mentioned earlier, that which makes a social theory distinctively Marxist is the emphasis on the dialectical relationship between the two levels. Now the question is: which level is going to have priority? Or, can one speak of a definite priority? From a purely theoretical point of view, no clear-cut priority can be assigned to one level as against the other. In fact, if the 'economic' (structural) level is given priority, then the relapse into a vulgar Marxism, or a mechanistic kind of economic determinism, or a metaphysical version of materialism, is inevitable. On the other hand, priority of the 'overstructure' necessarily implies the surrender to subjectivistic idealism.

I think Gramsci avoids both pitfalls. Usually, the themes of party, revolution, and hegemony are treated as separate topics, but in Gramsci they are closely related. Granted that for analytic purposes distinctions should be made, one should not lose sight of the peculiar Gramscian tendency to see things as dialectically belonging to the same global reality. The party is not only an instrument for revolution, as in Lenin. It does not only work for a different — economic, political, cultural, and moral — society. It is now already, at the microcosmic level, the prefiguration of such society. The revolution is a break from formal, routinized legitimacy, but in the name of a higher legitimacy to come. Revolution is no chronological fatality; it is no 'promised land'. Either it is already here, *hic et nunc*, anticipated in the quality of everyday life and internal human relationships *within the party*, or it is bound to fail, i.e. it is bound to reproduce, once power is seized, the alienating bureaucratic and exploitative features of bourgeois society.

From a practical political point of view, one would indicate the structural level as the starting base to make a clean departure from any purely moral-intellectual, and in fact moralistic, 'reforms' which would generally amount to a pure and simple reinforcement of the capitalist system of production and of bourgeois society. But obviously much would depend on the specific historic circumstances. Nothing would be further from Marxism than a timeless and spaceless doctrinaire recipe.

Should we then conclude that Gramsci is no different from Lenin and that, as Togliatti once remarked, his work is a mere footnote to the accomplishments of the Russian giant? For a comprehensive answer to these questions, one should carefully examine also the 'international point of view' of Lenin and Gramsci, and compare the two positions,. This will be done extensively in another work, but it is worth observing here that Gramsci, while agreeing with Trotsky regarding the danger of bureaucratic involution, criticizes rather severely his 'internationalism [which is] . . . vague and purely ideological (in the negative sense)' (A. Gramsci, *Note sul Machiavelli*, p. 115). On the other hand, Gramsci was not enough of an economist critically to appreciate Lenin's ideas about 'imperialism as the last stage of capitalism' and to evaluate their shortcomings as tested against the most recent changes in capitalism itself from accumulation-geared capitalism into a mass-consumption capitalism.

In short, Lenin's model accounts for late nineteenth/early twentieth century imperialistic policies, but it does not fit contemporary 'imperialism'. As regards contemporary capitalism, one notices a broad, if reticent, theoretical convergence and a certain amount of division of labor among present-day economists. Advanced bourgeois economists focus on 'economic development'; Marxist economists, on the other hand, deal with the issue of 'uneven development' and 'monopoly capital' (Emmanuel, Baran, Sweezy, C. Furtado and A. Gunder Frank) and their interconnections with capitalistic development. All the neo-Marxist models seem to confirm the obsolescence of Lenin's theory of imperialism. Instead, they look for new perspectives based on the profit-salary relationship and the new equilibrium in class struggle upon which it rests.

Gramsci's ideas about working class solidarity and internationalism are clearly expressed and should be specified. Gramsci accepts the substance of Stalin's principle of 'socialism in one single country'. He comments:

> Certainly, the development is toward internationalism but the starting point must be national and it is from this national starting point that the movement must begin. The perspective, however, is and cannot be anything else but international . . . . It is therefore necessary to study exactly the combination of national forces that the international class shall have to lead and develop according to international perspective and directives . . . . The concept of hegemony is the concept around which the national exigencies converge (Gramsci, *Note sul Machiavelli*, p. 114).

The question of hegemony and of its elaborators, the intellectuals, emerges again quite conspicuously. As compared with Lenin, this is a far cry from a pure and simple 'footnote'. It is an original, important contribution to Marxist thinking in the second half of the twentieth century. This is clearly recognized also by Togliatti's followers. As far as the concept of hegemony if concerned, 'there is a difference in meaning between Gramsci and Lenin, because Gramsci, when he talks about hegemony, at times refers to the leading ability; at other times he means the leading ability and the domination. On the contrary, Lenin, by the term hegemony, almost always means the dominating function.'[14]

The role of intellectuals is for Gramsci of paramount importance even though he rejects the idea of intellectuals as a separate elite. Intellectuals are, for Gramsci, decisively important because they provide the cultural and moral leadership without which the revolutionary process cannot develop or depend on generalized social consensus, and therefore becomes necessarily bureaucratic and brutally dictatorial. This means that, for Gramsci while it is true that any society can be explained and is in the last analysis determined by its economic structure, it is also true that no society can be *reduced* to its economic base. There is a *relative* autonomy of the cultural, or 'overstructural' or 'meta-economic', dimension in any society, which it is the function of the intellectuals to elaborate and spread in order to ensure the orderly development of that society above and against capitalistic contradictions, toward the new socialist society.

This should not be interpreted as an idyllic way to socialism. Gramsci was conscious of the importance of force and violence in the historical process. He simply refused to consider violence as an automatic generator of new values and new, socialist, social relationships.

Moreover, according to Gramsci, who in this connection disagreed with both Lenin and Trotsky, the 'military moment', i.e. the systematic use of violence, was not an absolute *prius*, but rather a last resort, an *extrema ratio*. For Gramsci it was clear that the proletariat had to become politically and culturally 'hegemonic' *before* it could positively seize power. Through the priority recognized to the phase of social and cultural hegemony, the proletariat would have, as it were, an historical guarantee that the revolution woul; be a profound economic and cultural transformation, reaching the depths of a given society and not just a passing *émeute*, an isolated revolt which would inevitably invite an even stronger reaction on the part of the declining bourgeoisie.

Genuine social, political and moral progress was, therefore, for Gramsci a dialectical complex of conservation and innovation. A true revolution was an organic process of growth; therefore, it could not have success on a *tabula rasa*. The past could not be liquidated as a whole; the collective memory could not be destroyed. There were, according to Gramsci, values in the past which shouldbe preserved and enhanced by the revolution. However, what would be preserved of the historical past could not be determined in advance; it would be the result of the very revolutionary process and no individual or leadership group could decide about that a priori.

We are now in a position to clarify Gramsci's thinking with regard to *domination, hegemony,* and *legitimacy.*

According to Gramsci, the supremacy, or the domineering position, or the 'ruling function', of a social group manifests itself in two ways: (a) as a 'domination' and (b) as an 'intellectual and moral leadership'. The domination aspect of a social group, or social class, concerns primarily its social 'enemies'; i.e. those rival groups, or classes, whose interests are so sectorial as to be contradictory to the 'general interest' as represented by the working class, or proletariat.

The 'hegemonic function' concerns, on the contrary, those groups, or classes, which do not contradict the 'general interest' and with which political alliances and compromises can be worked out on the road to power. When central political power is finally achieved, the two functions will still be there, that is to say, the workers' party will still have to rule with force when and if necessary, but *at the same time* will have to 'lead', i.e. to exercise an influence, moral as well as broadly cultural, on the civil society which does not coincide with and is not reducible to the formally codified political institutions.

It is important to observe that for Gramsci there is no basis for legitimation of a proletarian dictatorship unless social hegemony over the society at large already exists. Pure force, for Gramsci, is unacceptable.

To Gramsci, the historical maturity and ability of a revolutionary leadership is measured by its success in mustering sufficient democratic consensus to isolate in a minority position the 'social enemies' and, at the same time, in raising the workers' party out of the political 'ghetto' into a position of social prominence and prestige as a prerequisite for the advent to power and the political implementation of a new legitimacy.

NOTES

1. A. Gramsci, *Il materialismo storico*, new abridged edn, Rome, 1975, p. 219, translation by France Ferrarotti.

2. P. Anderson, *Considerations on Western Marxism,* London, 1976, ch. IV.

3. For the existential ties between Marx and Engels, on the one hand, and the working class on the other, see a recent study by Goran Therborn, 'The Working Class and the Birth of Marxism', Italian translation in *Comunita* 178 (August 1977): 129.

4. Norberto Bobbio, *Gramsci e la concezione della societa civile,* Milano, 1976, p. 27.

5. V. Lenin, *On Unions,* Italian edn, Rome, 1948, pp. 62-91.

6. Rosa Luxemburg, *Organizational Problems of Russian Social-democracy,* Italian edn, Rome, 1959, p. 38.

7. A. Carlo, 'Lenin and the Party', *Telos* 17 (Fall 1973): 40.

8. Franco Ferrarotti, 'Introduction', in *Sociology of Power*, Bari, 1972.

9. Massimo L. Salvadori, 'Politica, potere e cultura nel pensiero di Gramsci', *Revista di storia contemporanea* 1 (1972): 29.

10. Historicus, 'Stalin on Revolution', *Foreign Affairs* (January 1949): 23.

11. P. Piccone, 'Gramsci's Marxism: Beyond Lenin and Togliatti', *Theory and Society* 3 (4) (Winter 1976): 499.

12. Ibid., p. 500.

13. Bobbio, op. cit., p. 45.

14. L. Gruppi, *Il concetto di egemonia in Gramsci,* Rome, 1977, p. 21.

II

CASE STUDIES AND
SPECIFIC PROBLEMS

7

POWER CIRCLES AND LEGITIMACY IN DEVELOPED SOCIETIES

Charles Kadushin
Graduate School, City University of New York, USA

Though we often like to pretend that theorizing is a serious enterprise which should remain unaffected by common parlance and ordinary usage, most of us nevertheless tend to think in formulations not unlike those used in TV 'cops-and-robbers' series. There are good guys and bad guys, heavys and heroes. But we are getting modern. The good guys are now harder to recognize, and often come with rather strange attributes. For the purposes of this Conference, I suppose legitimation is a 'good guy' and so is 'integration'.

I am about to propose that these 'good guys' go hand in glove with some traditional bad fellows: power elites and national establishments. An integrated, legitimate elite must and does exist only as a single national power establishment. Among American liberals, the notion that there is a single national establishment is usually held to be deplorable. Americans of a Left persuasion tend to affirm that such a situation exists, but that it is bad. Liberals tend to deny that there is a single national establishment and instead assert that we are pluralistically governed, that some people and some institutions are important on a given set of issues, but that a different set of people and institutions are key power-holders on other sets of issues. I shall argue that Leftists are correct in the fact of such an establishment but wrong in deploring its consequences. The liberals are wrong in their view of the facts, but right in their notion that national decision-making systems tend to accommodate persons of vastly differing views. In fact, the more differing views that are represented, the more legitimate the elite.

Furthermore, I shall show that it is likely not only that the United States has a single national power establishment, but that most other countries do too. If they do not, then it is likely that the elites are neither integrated nor legitimate. Naturally, the converse is not necessarily the case: just because an elite is single does not mean that it is legitimate nor that it is necessarily integrated with the rest of the national institutions. But this means that the elite is non-representative.

These are rather broad claims and to prove them I shall have to backtrack a bit and introduce some jargon of my own, hopefully a set of concepts somewhat removed from the world of TV cops and robbers. I shall start first with the problem of establishments and only then attack the issue of legitimacy. Both matters are quite thorny. The concepts that have to to do with establishments are derived from a relatively new field in social science — network theory — and I will suggest that the only way to settle the issues around the theory and fact of national establishments is to recast them in network terms. I even have some data: two European small countries — very different in nature — Norway and Yugoslavia. And then, for contrast, especially for an American audience — the United States. Australia serves as the fourth example.

Let me begin with some concepts. For our purposes a network is a set of relationships between social units. The something that passes between the units is called a 'flow'. More than one type of flow may connect the same units. Some of the types of flows that have been studied by network researchers are objects (the famous Kula ring for example), labor and the exchange of services, affect, regard and evaluation (the usual flows studied in the sociometric tradition); knowledge and information (the flows studied by students of so-called 'invisible colleges' and those interested in the diffusion of innovations); prescription and opinion (the aspect of network studies identified with Lazarsfeld in terms of 'opinion leaders'); and finally, influence and power — the flows which concern us in the study of elites and legitimacy.

In general, the laws which govern the flow of objects between units may not be the same as those which apply to the flow of information. And most important for us, the laws pertaining to flows of power and influence are definitely not the same as those which apply to the flow of affect. That is, the connections formed between people who see each other because they like one another are quite different from those formed by people who interact with one another because they seek to influence each other or wish to allocate resources based on their relative positions of power. Despite this difference, some of our first and 'natural' assumptions about interaction in power relations and the development of cliques stem from the research experience of the sociometry of small groups and organizations. Needless to say, these assumptions are more often than not wrong. But more about this shortly.

An important feature of network analysis is that it deals both with relations between formally instituted roles and organizations, i.e. those relationships which are governed by law or by accepted and clear social custom, as well as with relationships that are called informal and which are not governed by clear laws or social customs. In particular, in network analysis we seek to trace the correspondence, if any, between the formal and informal networks. By now it should be evident why network analysis is so amenable to a discussion of some of the traditional questions in the analysis of political power. The formal government structure is rarely unitary and certainly does not presume to structure a national establishment. Even in one-party states, the primacy of the party is not necessarily based on constitutional arrangements.

I said we were interested in relations of power and influence between different social units. I have not specified what are the units. Both individuals and organizations are potential units for network analysis. In the present case we are going to talk about individuals, but they are persons whose relationships we trace because they hold key positions. Thus, in part we are talking about networks which link different organizations and institutional areas.[1]   I will therefore concentrate on *interstitial* relations, i.e. relations between organizations, institutions and sectors. Though relations *within* legislative bodies will not be ignored, for example, my main goal will be to trace relations between the legislature and other sectors such as labor, economic managers, parties, and the like. The nature and extent of these relations will show the extent of elite integration.

I have just outlined several features of network analysis that locate our present interests: relations between large national level units which emphasize the flow of power and influence whether or not these relations are governed by rule of law. I now want to add one more dimension – that of visibility. Perhaps the most puzzling and most exciting aspect of network analysis is that it unmasks invisible structures. In modern jargon, this is called 'demystification'. The kind of visibility I have in mind is the visibility of the entire system, not merely the adjacent relationships which are obviously known to the participants in a network. Just as there are latent functions, so there are latent networks which function perfectly well even though the participants may have no clear idea of the total shape or character of the network in which they are a part.

Visibility is always relative. The shape of a so-called Mafia network is less visible to me than to some of the more powerful chieftains within the organization. But in general, because we all live embedded within social systems, we can only see the person next to us. If we have unusual vision, then we see the person next to the person next to us. And this is the case, too, with power networks. Since the days of Lincoln Steffins, wielders of power when apprised of the shape and consequences of networks of which they were a part have consistently first denied that the network exists and then, when confronted with the evidence, exhibited considerable shock.

Finally, there is the question of legitimacy which we will have to explore here. If networks are invisible, does this necessarily affect their legitimacy? Is the Mafia network invisible *because* it is not legitimate, or are both a consequence of some other, third factor? In the case of national establishments, there seems a paradox. The network is mainly invisible, yet it is this very invisibility which gives it the flexibility and the inclusiveness which lends it legitimacy.

We should also introduce the notion of a circle. These are the dense parts of networks caused by the repeated interaction of units with common interests or common problems to solve. Unlike groups, and in common with networks, circles permit interaction at a distance; that is, corporate chief executive officer X can put pressure on White House staff member Z whom he does not know, through Senator Y, whom he does know personally. Circles tend to bend back upon themselves (hence the name) rather than form an infinite regress, as do networks.

While circles have a dense core, they do not have a systematic set of leaders in the sense that groups do. Since they are not groups in any usual sense, the notion of a formal cabal is also inappropriate and indeed misleading to a proper understanding of most national systems of power and influence. Furthermore, as we said, the entire shape of a circle is usually invisible even to the participants. Finally, circles in general (and there are all kinds of circles such as cultural circles, ethnic circles and more) tend to operate in situations in which 'external economies' are important, i.e. in situations in which the presence of other producers and other factors makes a product easier to put together. By locating next to one another, high-fashion garment producers, for example, are able to draw upon each other's resources, upon common fabric and accessory supplies, and the like, very quickly. The 'products' of business and politics also cannot be assembled without ready and quick access of power figures to one another.

Now to the issues surrounding the presence or absence of establishments, power elites or ruling classes. These matters have been much debated, at least in the United States, by so-called pluralists or elitists. There are four issues which I shall perforce review in some order, though in fact they operate simultaneously. The first issue is whether there is anything at all that can be said to be a national power system. In network terms this translates into the number of circles and the degree of density of any circles that are found in a network of national leaders. A single dense region is required by most power elite theories. In contrast, a pluralist system implies that there are several different clusters. Some pluralists also seem to imply that the clusters are not as dense as claimed by power elite theorists, but neither theory is very precise on this point.

A second, and related, issue is whether elites exercise power over all issues, including so-called 'non-decisions', or whether some elites are confined to power or influence over single issues. In network terms this is translated into the content of flows between any two points and whether more than one type of flow exists between the points.

The third issue mixes the basis of power together with the mode of recruitment to the elite. Does business and economic power control the elite; is it a class elite, an ideological elite, or an organizational elite? In network terms, the issue has to do with the pegs upon which a network or circle is draped. That is, what is there in terms of other features of society that facilitate or hinder relations among the elite. Thus, old boy or new girl networks mean that those who have been in the same clubs or the same schools or the same revolution at the same time have access to each other that outsiders might not have.

The fourth issue is who, in fact, is brought into the circles of power. Since all circles have unclear boundaries, whether or not a given person or unit is considered part of the national elite is determined by the number and nature of connections with others in the elite network. Despite some logical problems, this is an intentionally circular argument.

In network terms a strongly defined national establishment is one in which there is a single dense region — a 'power circle'. Furthermore, and this addresses the second issue in the power elite controversy, the units which compose the circle are linked together in the same way over a very wide range of flows. In the extreme, the same organizations and the same people relate to each other whether the issue is foreign policy or national defense. In a less extreme version, some of the units may differ from issue to issue but the overall patterning of the relations and the character of the circle is about the same from issue to issue.

Note that the definition of circle does not require that a national establishment have a clearly defined set of leaders but only that some units be more central than others. We do not expect the man from Mars to be taken to the leader of the establishment!

The second and third points on the nature of the pegs on which the establishment is draped, and the question of who is a member of the establishment, as well as another issue which is often not raised — the amount of divergence of opinion within an establishment — all raise the question of legitimacy to which we now turn.

A legitimate establishment is one in which the large majority of its members, as well as the public at large, accept its inevitability as well as acknowledge, more or less, its right to rule. At the very least, the acceptance is indicated by the fact that few people expect to take to the barricades or the mountains in the foreseeable near future to contest the establishment. Note that since the concept of the power circle with various connections is ours, not one which is always invoked by the participants or the public, this acceptance is seen as fragmented. That is, there may seem to be a separate acceptance of the government, of businessmen, of labor leaders, of intellectuals, and so on, in so far as these sectors are in fact linked together to form a national establishment. Thus we come to our first proposition which is indeed quite radical.

If there is a national establishment in the sense defined here of a single power circle, then to the extent that any institutional sector within the establishment is legitimate in the sense defined here, *all* the sectors recruited to the establishment are also legitimate. That is, if it can be shown that Communist party leaders in a Western European country are regularly linked in power brokerage relationships with businessmen, if only through a third party, and if business, labor, media, government, etc. are all represented in the national establishment, then businessmen will in general acknowledge the legitimacy of Communist party leaders, and the latter will recognize the legitimacy of businessmen.

In power circle terms there is no requirement that affects flow through the system, only power and influence on a regular basis. Thus, there is no requirement that national establishments be love feasts or that connections be established on the basis of affect. There is only the requirement that different parties be willing regularly to discuss differences and formulate policy. Though every national establishment can tolerate only a certain range of permissible opinion, this range is much larger than is often imagined, and power circles are hardly like-minded. In general, a single national power circle, if it is legitimate, tends to represent all shades of permissible opinion, more or less in proportion to their distribution in the national elite at large. Even within the central power circle of Yugoslavia, at the time we studied it, there were considerable splits of opinion on a number of important issues, including economic development and attitudes to the Soviet Union. In part, I support Field and Higley's (1973) view that such circles of power are 'unified elites', but in part I have to deny it. In their terms, unified elites are

> sufficiently cohesive and freely communicative internally so that regardless of the different political affiliations which its members may maintain and the different interest positions in the society with which they may associate themselves as spokesmen, they share a basic consensus about the nature and the desirability of the society they direct and manage (p. 9).

The requirement that power circles share a basic view of the desirability of the society in which they live seems, however, unnecessarily stringent, and contrary to the facts of some Western European power circles as I see them.

To understand my view of legitimacy, it is only necessary to imagine that there is more than one major power circle in a country. That means that there are few if any connections from one to the other. It can be shown from network theory that dense connections are built up from regular interaction (one of our few transplants from micro-network theory). Each circle can then operate without having to bargain with the other, though to be sure they must take the others into account. As Durkheim long ago pointed out, contrary to liberal contract theory, bargaining requires some common overarching willingness to abide by some rules and some minimum trust. And in general, the more frequent the bargaining and the more mutually satisfactory the results, the greater the trust that is developed. Moreover, the force in establishment power circles is towards inclusiveness, ever bringing more groups in, rather than towards fragmentation and exclusiveness.

Thus, it seems likely that power circles without regular bargaining relationships will not hold each other to be legitimate. None of this is to deny that every nation will have specialized power circles, but that this specialization will take place within the context of a larger central circle.

Before giving some examples of legitimate central power circles based on careful research, let me impressionistically observe that France and Italy, for example, probably have a central power circle that includes the Communist Party, that these circles are legitimate, and that this fact confounds some American observers. Furthermore, the main problem for Spain and Portugal is to include parties of the Left within the national central power circles without plunging the countries into the crises of legitimacy that they had previously and painfully experienced. They are going about solving their problems in different ways, but in formal terms the problems are the same.

And this brings me to the obvious major flaw in my present state of theorizing about power circles. I can tell you what they are like, that in fact they are split under some circumstances and not others, but I do not at present have a theory of change: that is, what are the conditions that make for separate power circles coming together, and what are those which make a single one split into two or more. But some insight into this crucial problem may come from a brief look at our four examples.

The four examples — Norway, Yugoslavia, Australia and the United States — are all based on careful surveys of positional elites, with the addition of some persons named often by the original sample. Each study was collected by a different team and with somewhat different methods. They probably represent not the 'ultimate' power-holders, if any, but those who run the country on a day-to-day basis. Here we shall not go into the methods of data collection or analysis but merely try to summarize the results.[2]

In each study, positional elites were asked who they talked with or had the most contact with on matters of national policy. In the United States and Australia one particular policy issue was chosen by each respondent; in Yugoslavia and Norway the referent was more general. These connections were then clustered by a computer program which essentially put those people together who had the most contact with each other and whose density of relations was statistically greater than that of the overall set of relations of the elite sample. Although each country also had a number of satellite circles, here we are focusing on the central power circle, representing almost 60 percent of the sample. Relations in this circle were the most dense of the four countries, with 7 percent of the possible relations actually existing. Australia was the largest, with 419 members which included 273 sample members. The US was the next largest, with 220 persons overall, a density of 4 percent, and included 30 percent of the sample.

Yugoslavia was a special case. When the Yugoslav data were analyzed in the same way as for other countries, no central circle emerged. Rather, a larger number of relatively small cliques emerged. No clique, group or circle was large enough or composed of enough important persons, or had members with sufficiently diverse views to function in the manner in which a central circle might function. Does this mean that the regime in Yugoslavia in 1968, when we gathered our data, was not legitimate? Perhaps. But note that when our clustering technique was relaxed to allow for interaction via one other person as the basis for forming the initial clusters (see Alba and Moore, 1978, for an explanation of the details of the technique), then a relatively diffuse (density of only 2 percent) cluster of 192 persons was found which included 25 percent of those we sampled.

Let us for the moment assume that a central circle exists in Yugoslavia, though a much more loose one that in the other countries we studied. Then, later in this paper we will entertain the notion that the circle in Yugoslavia was not only quantitatively different from the others but that its very looseness created a qualitative difference that almost led to questions about its legitimacy, questions that were resolved but at some cost.

Whatever the details, it is obvious that there is a relation between some features of the nation and the relative size and density of the central circle. In turn, the characteristics of the central circle are related to the degree of governmental legitimacy. At this point we can offer only informed speculation rather than hard proof. First, we are limited because we have, after all, only four cases. Secondly, there are limitations in the comparability of our data since each study used somewhat different sociometric questions and somewhat different methods of data gathering. These differences in method may have affected some of the characteristics of the central circles. Nonetheless, here are at least some plausible hypotheses about central circles. (1) Federal systems, as found in the United States, Australia and Yugoslavia, increase the number of persons required to run the country. (2) The existence of separate commerical, cultural, and industrial centers also increases the size of the elite and may also increase the degree to which it is differentiated. (3) Small population size, geographic propinquity, and the intimacy which often accompanies such physical arrangements, may make for a smaller and more dense central core. (4) The presence of more than one important ethnic group increases the dispersion and fragmentation of the elite central core. (5) Finally, some ideological hegemony is important in insuring cohesion.

Norway, then, is the archetypical 'tight' and small system. The elite is largely concentrated in one or two cities, it is not a federal system, the population is small and the elite are intimate with one another. Finally there is but one major ethnic group. While the United States is large and federal, with many different commercial centers and with the government center separate from the commercial center, its ethnic diversions are not as great as Yugoslavia's, at least not as represented in the elite. Thus, the US has a large but not as dense a central circle as the Australian one, which represents an equally large and federal country but one with a much smaller population and with greater ethnic homogeneity. All countries exhibit an ideology which has hegemony over competing ideas.

Other things equal, the smaller the central power circle, the greater the legitimacy of the establishment. The reasons for this are fairly obvious. The larger the number of independent sources of power, the larger the power circle, because more units (people or organizations) have to be checked with or taken into account. A large number of independent units raises the possibility of power circle splits, yet on the other hand insures greater flexibility. So federal systems such as in Australia, Yugolsavia or the United States serve to incorporate various centers of local power and so increase the size of the central circle but still maintain legitimacy. Note that the size and density of the central circle is not entirely dependent upon the size of the population of the country but rather also on the number of sources of power, the structure of the state, and ease of communications within the elite.

At the heart of the legitimacy issue is what kind of people and institutions are represented by the central circles. In all four countries the government, including political leaders out of power but in the legislature and political party leaders, are an important segment of the central circle but these political institutions are more important in Norway (57 percent) and in the looser cluster in Yugoslavia (61 percent) than in the United States (47 percent) or Australia (37 percent). The different is caused by the weak representation of political parties in the United States, as might be expected, and the importance of business and labor in Australia. The legislature is more important in the central circle than some might have predicted, given the predominance of the executive in modern nations. In legitimate establishments in modern countries, the legislature may not have power, but it is an important switching point.

Business is very important in Norway and Australia, as is labor, but both are slightly less represented in the United States than their numbers in the positional elite sample. The apparent equivalent of business in Yugoslavia, the economic managers, hardly count at all. Intellectuals are under-represented in all countries but less so in Yugoslavia, though in that country there is a sharp different between intellectual establishment technocrats and Marxist-Humanist intellectuals. The former are in, the latter are out. This capsule review which omits some important details gives a conventional view of the four countries. But that is the whole point. A legitimate central circle in fact captures the major institutions of control in the country. If it does not, then the establishment is not legitimate.

But the obvious can be overdone. Of course the Party (actually the League of Communists) is important in Yugoslavia. Our analysis shows it to be a key linking device. And surely labor unions and top business leaders are important in Australia and Norway (but the Norwegian shipowners hold themselves out a bit). And business is important in the US, while political parties count for almost nothing. On the other hand, other groups are also represented. A review of some of Gwen Moore's (1977) work with the American elite data in instructive.

Moore set out to discover if the Domhoff – C. Wright Mills thesis of the importance of social class, class-linking mechanisms such as the Social Register, the right schools, the right clubs, etc., together with class political committees such as the Council on Foreign Relations, were in fact important in making a member of the positional elite also a member of the inner central circle. Essentially what she discovered was the Mills' and Domhoff's views were indeed correct but only if one paid attention to the business elite. Elites in other sectors came to be members of the central circle in other ways, with media visibility and output not at all important. And in Yugoslavia, mere participation in the War of Independence or having been a delegate to a key congress was not enough; members of circles and cliques had more particularistic ties than those.

The point is that given the fact of a central circle in legitimate governments, and given the fact that these circles actually include a fairly wide representation, there is no one obvious way that all types of persons enter. Rather, it does depend on the dynamics of each sector represented and on the particular ways in which persons rise in given sectors at given points of time in different countries.

Some of the changes in Yugoslavia since we collected our data in 1968 give some additional perspective to our theory of legitimacy. We presented two pictures of the Yugoslav elite. By the criteria of other countries they were a fragmented elite which did not exhibit the central circle structure we found in other countries. On the other hand, with slightly relaxed criteria, they showed considerable structure and unity. The Yugoslav elite was interviewed in 1968 during a period in which the major direction of Yugoslavia had changed from a social and political system dominated by a centralist statist model to one which attempted to decentralize and liberalize (Denitch, 1977). These attempts tended to increase the diversity of Yugoslavia's cultural mosaic; economic decentralization tended to increase the gap between the developed and underdeveloped sectors of the economy as well as between developed and less developed regions. The League of Communists attempted to divest itself of formal decision-making posts in the governmental structure and hoped to involve other institutions in the decision-making process. The result was the creation of a large number of intimate circles each quite prepared to go their own way. If our arguments have been correct, this situation could have led to a serious crisis of legitimacy, a view apparently shared by the Yugoslav top leadership, which after several years of drift engaged in various attempts to pull things back together. One need not necessarily approve of the particular steps taken by that leadership to agree that they faced a serious problem. The leadership's ability to pull the country more or less together, for the time being, rested on the fact that there were several contradictory bases for power circle formation in Yugoslavia at that time. On the one hand, there were particularistic ethnic and national similarities, common opinion, and war-time or other kinds of buddyship on which to base small, fairly tightly-knit but disparate circles. On the other hand, buddyship can be and was mobilized to produce an entourage-based, loosely-knit central circle in which some of the members were politically important while others were not. This latter base, still residual in part from the war, together with the reasserted cohesive potential of the League, allowed Yugoslavia to tighten up its latent, loose, but nonetheless real, central circle. There seems little doubt that despite some rumblings, the government retained its legitimacy while still advancing its federal tendencies. Had there been no underlying central circle, however loose, rule and power might have been retained but without legitimacy. Nonetheless, the looseness of the basic underlying structure of the central federal elite, as opposed to the possible greater coherence in the national elites, remains a problem for the legitimacy of Yugolsavia as a single entity.

To recap our thesis. There is indeed a ruling committee in the societies we looked at, and I suspect in most modern, developed societies. These committees or central circles tend to be representative of major forces and institutions in those societies, and persons are generally recruited to the central circle according to the differing rules of each sector. If there is more than one power circle, or if many circles are not at least bound loosely together, then none of them is likely to be legitimate, and the result is instability, which may be a good or bad thing, depending on how you look at it.

NOTES

1. Studies of corporate overlap and interaction are examples of network analysis of inter-organization connections. See Levine (1972), Mokken and Stokman (1974) and Sonquist and Koenig (1975) for examples of work in this field.

2. The United States study was conducted by the Bureau of Applied Social Research in 1971 under the direction of Allen Barton, Bogdan Denitch, Charles Kadushin and Carol Weiss. The data on elite networks reported here were analyzed by Gwen Moore (1977). The Yugoslav study was conducted by a team of Yugoslavs in 1968 and reported in Dzinic (1969). The network data reported here was analyzed by Kadushin, Abrams and Moore. Some of it is reported in greater detail in Kadushin and Abrams (1973) and in Kadushin, Alba and Moore (forthcoming). The Australian data was collected in 1975 by Higley et al (1976). It was analyzed by Kadushin, Moore and Higley (forthcoming) in Kadushin, Alba and Moore.

3. These figures include persons not interviewed but named by persons interviewed. The percentage of the sample is based on the number of interviewees in the central circle divided by the number of total interviewees.

REFERENCES

ALBA, R. D. and MOORE, G. (1978) 'Elite Social Circles', *Sociological Methods and Research*, 7, 167-188.

DENITCH, B. (1977) 'The Evolution of Yugoslav Federalism', *Publius* 7 (4): 107-17, and references cited there.

DZINIC, Firdus, ed. (1969) *Stvaraoci mnenja u Jugoslaviji.* Belgrade: Institut Drustvenih Nauka.

FIELD, G. Lowell and HIGLEY, John (1973) *Elites and Non-Elites: Their Possibilities and Some Side Effects.* Andover, Ma.: Warner Module 13, pp. 1-38.

HIGLEY, J., SMART, D. and DEACON, D. (1976) 'The Australian Leadership Study', *Politics* 11 (May): 96-99.

KADUSHIN, Charles, and ABRAMS, Peter (1973) 'Social Structure of Yugoslav Opinion-Makers: Part II, Formal and Informal Influences and Their Consequences for Opinion', in Barton, Denitch and Kadushin, eds, *Opinion-Making Elites in Yugoslavia.* New York: Praeger.

KADUSHIN, Charles, ALBA, Richard and MOORE, Gwen (1978) *Circles of Power,* forthcoming.

LEVINE, J. H. (1972) 'The Sphere of Influence', *American Sociological Review,* 37 (Feb.): 14-27.

MOKKEN, R. J. and STOKMAN, F. N. (1974) 'Power and Influence as Political Phenomena', University of Amsterdam: Institute for Political Science, mimeo.

MOORE, Gwen (1977) 'The Structure of Elite Influence in the United States', Ph.D. dissertation, New York University.

SONQUIST, John and KOENIG, Thomas (1975) 'Interlocking Directorates in Top US Corporations: A Graph Theory Approach', *The Insurgent Sociologist* 5 (3) (Spring): 196-229.

8

ELITES, INSIDERS, AND OUTSIDERS:
Will Western Political Regimes Prove Non-viable?

G. Lowell Field
University of Connecticut, USA
and
John Higley
Australian National University, Australia

During the modern historical period, roughly 1550 to 1950, the legitimacy of some regimes and the absence of legitimacy in others could best be explained in terms of variations in the character of national elites. Where elites shared a consensus as to ultimate political values, and where they were unified in their willingness not to pursue partisan interests beyond the point at which the stability of institutions was endangered (e.g. England after 1689, Sweden after 1809, Mexico after 1933), regimes enjoyed substantial legitimacy. That is, most elite persons, and varying proportions of non-elite persons, thought existing political institutions worth preserving, and they acknowledged that those who happened currently to operate those insitutions had a right to do so.

Conversely, where, as in the majority of societies, elites viewed power as personalized and directly dependent on the support of organized coercive forces (e.g. France, Germany, Spain, Portugal throughout their national-state histories), regimes had little legitimacy. In this more usual situation, elite persons, and most non-elite persons, saw power and rulership as flowing from the success of individuals and groups *qua individuals and groups* in gaining at least temporary control over the principal means of coercion and force.

Underlying this association of legitimacy with elite consensus and unity is the idea that the operation of all relatively stable and peaceful regimes is in fundamental respects a holding, steadying, and adjustive process. The aim is to prevent conflicts from reaching proportions that would leave discontented groupings with no alternative to violence. In this view, *management* of conflict, rather than any full and frank pursuit of the apparrent interest of one or another 'side' in a conflict, is the central nature of political activity in any stable and peaceful polity.

To be effective, management of conflict requires that influential persons cooperate in suppressing, distorting, or otherwise manipulating issues which, if expressed and acted on openly and widely, would result in disastrous conflict. Such concerted action by influential persons is possible over any long period only if they are in essential agreement about the desirability of a politically stable system, and only if they are unified in observing specified limits to partisan activity.[2]

Because the legitimacy of a regime depends on elite consensus and unity, and because consensus and unity appear to be reliably self-perpetuating once they are created, it follows that the delegitimation of a regime can only occur when a consensual and unified elite fails to contain conflicts among non-elites. This has never happened, according to our examination of the modern histories of regimes operated by consensual and unified elites.[3] Whether there is reason to think that it might happen in the foreseeable future is nevertheless an interesting and important question.

In addressing this question, we shall explore in very broad fashion the twò principal conflicts which pose increasingly ominous challenges to the political managerial capacities of consensual and unified elites in contemporary Western societies. These are (1) the growing conflict between these elites and that portion of Western populations that remains reasonably well integrated into the productive and social systems, persons we will call 'insiders', and (2) the growing conflict between these insiders and the many persons located in strictly marginal or wholly superfluous work and dependency statuses in these societies, persons we will call 'outsiders'.

Our contention is that both these conflicts threaten to impede and to render ineffective the managerial role of elites. Indeed, this threat to elite effectiveness has grown to such proportions as to raise the question of the possible non-viability of Western political regimes in their current configurations.

THE EMERGENCE OF
INSIDERS AND OUTSIDERS

Quite unforseen by nearly all observers, during the past ten to twenty years the populations of the most developed Western societies (at a minimum the United States, Great Britain, the Netherlands, the principal Scandinavian societies, and Canada) have begun to divide into two loose interest and attitude camps.[4] The boundaries of these camps are not contiguous with the boundaries of the classes and strata which derived from the agricultural, manual, and non-manual work force components familiar historically during the process of socio-economic development.

One of these camps is the very large population component we shall call 'insiders'. It consists of all those persons who are fairly securely and satisfactorily employed in the work forces of developed societies, plus the many persons who occupy fairly honorific and comfortable dependency statuses in them. Thus, the insider category contains (1) the bulk of the non-manual work force component, especially those who are reasonably secure in relatively interesting and decently paid jobs (e.g. middle- and upper-level managers, professionals and their assistants, specialists in many services); (2) reasonably prosperous members of the less organized agricultural and artisan work force components; (3) some portion of the manual work force component (e.g. skilled industrial workers in reasonably secure employment), especially where current economic prosperity makes this group comparatively well-off; as well as (4) persons located in more or less honorific and comfortable statuses of dependency upon the working population (e.g. many housewives, the better-off retired people, the more ambitious and career-oriented youth in educational pursuits).

The other population camp which has begun to emerge consists of persons whom we shall call 'outsiders'. However, this outsider category contains two population segments that are of distinctly different social origins, and this discrepancy in origins and experience prevents outsiders from acting very effectively as a single self-conscious political unit. One segment consists of persons who grow up in conditions of poverty and who are therefore outside the dominant culture of the developed societies, plus an indeterminate number of persons suffering severe personal handicaps of a physical or an emotional kind. Most of these persons tend to reach adulthood without marketable skills and/or without the attitudes necessary for regular employment in a sophisticated work force. Organizations simply find it uneconomic to pay them a living wage for any jobs they may be able and willing to undertake. This is in part because no pressing need exists for the kind of unsophisticated manual labor which they might qualify to perform.

The other population segment making up the outsider category consists of many persons who grow up in circumstances approximating enriched leisured living in the developed societies. As is readily observable, the more fortunate majority of young people in these societies experience what are essentially leisure-class upbringings. While there is probably a tendency in all urban settings to treat children as luxury items to be pampered and displayed, a steady decline of available employment for youth in highly urbanized developed societies exacerbates this tendency.[5]

Nevertheless, income levels in such societies are high enough so that idleness and boredom do not become serious problems for the better-off children and youth until at least their later teenage years. Until that time, activities of a reasonably satisfying sort are provided them by parental and community arrangements. Many affluent youth even manage to find temporary paid employment from time to time and for short periods while they are growing up. But in the typical case this employment is neither seriously time-consuming nor continuously necessary in any urgent sense. To some considerable degree it is itself a distraction from idleness and boredom. Consequently, it does not contribute to an appreciation of the fundamentally constraining character of most aspects of social reality.

Most activities in which affluent youth in developed societies engage have no serious ulterior purpose, except for possibly an educational one. Because of this, these activies cannot be related plausibly to the needs of other persons or of the society as a whole. Consequently, such youth have few opportunities in which to develop a willingness to accommodate the seriously inconvenient wishes of others or to defer their gratifications in the face of a social demand to practise self-discipline. Moreover, because this kind of upbringing is for a long time comfortable, relatively few youth who experience it develop substantial personal ambitions. Unlike most youth in developing societies, they do not wish to escape from their conditions. These several aspects of the conditions of affluent youth in developed societies effectively prevent teaching them reasonably prudent standards of adult behavior, just as in the past it was difficult to instill in the individually favored and indulged rich offspring of privileged groups a provident and responsible character.

It is ironic that the pleasant and absorbing activities of many youth in developed societies should provoke problems of adjustment in later life, but there is a good deal of evidence that this occurs. One reason is that the affluence of most youth in developed societies is in fact quite limited. It depends almost entirely on their parents' limited incomes. Although these are far above historic levels, they are nevertheless closely tied to the holding of specific occupational positions. Relatively few of these parents are additionally well off in terms of extensive property holdings. Thus, once the parents of affluent youth retire or die, the youth have no prospect of growing up to adult lives that will in any sense be as leisured as the upbringings which they have experienced. In fact, as they approach adulthood prospects inevitably seem to many affluent adolescents increasingly grim. This is why they lack the strong desire of most young persons in historical societies to escape the limitations of youth for a greater freedom and a more interesting life as an adult. In historical perspective, in fact, developed societies quite perversely reverse the course of the life prospects of many youth.

Except for individuals who are especially self-confident or exceptionally ambitious, therefore, affluent youth in developed societies tend to face adult life at most with resignation, and often with a desire positively to evade its responsibilities. Needless to say, many youth with this background and outlook are likely to be as unemployable as those who come from the most unfavorable circumstances of poverty and deprivation. Just as there is little need in the economies of developed societies for the kind of unsophisticated manual work that persons who have been deprived in youth might be able to perform, there is also little need to involve the immature, the inexperienced, and the wholly unenthusiastic in service or bureaucratic positions. In any case, many affluent youth fail to find employment that is for them interesting enough, challenging enough, and perhaps prestigious enough to entice them into doing it well.

Thus, although their backgrounds and social locations differ dramatically, persons in the two segments comprising the outsider category have in common the inability or reluctance to participate effectively in the work force, the labor market, and the occupational career structure of developed societies. This is naturally reflected in the corresponding inability or reluctance of responsible administrators to employ them. Therefore, the outsider category consists of (1) unemployed persons, (2) persons precariously employed in less desirable jobs or in 'make-work' jobs openly created to absorb them, (3) persons who manage in one way or another, because of some obvious or at least plausible incapacity, to be supported in meager and non-honorific statuses by society or by individual benefactors, and (4) the dependents and hangers-on of all these persons.

The size and visibility of the outsider category increases with the length of time societies are at the most advanced level of development. Thus, in societies that have only recently reached this level, like Australia, Norway, Switzerland, and France, the phenomenon has not as yet grown much beyond its embryonic stage, nor spread beyond the major urban areas. But it is much more visible in the older developed societies of Great Britain, the United States, and the Netherlands, in all three of which the distinctiveness of some of the outsiders is accentuated by the racial heterogeneity of the populations involved.

The emergence of these insider and outsider categories, then, is the principal consequence of prolonged experience with the highest level of socio-economic development. As was the case with differing work force components and with the classes and strata which they spawned during the process of socio-economic development, it is the relations between these categories, and between them and elites, which are the principal source of social and political conflicts in developed societies. We shall now attempt to specify the nature of these conflicts.

THE RELATION OF ELITES
AND INSIDERS

The pervasively bureaucratized structure of work in developed societies probably contributes to a much greater understanding and acceptance of the necessity for power acts by socially remote persons, and thus implicitly of elite behavior and functions, than is the case in developing societies. This is because the daily experiences of the largest group of workers in developed societies — non-manual workers — involve the more or less constant instrumental exercise of power in extended and impersonal organizational hierarchies. With one or more of them belonging to most nuclear families, these non-manual workers spread what is essentially a 'managerial' orientation toward power throughout developed societies.

The result is the creation of a more sophisticated culture as regards organizational matters. There is at least an implicit recognition that elites, like less strategically placed power wielders, are engaged in manipulating the behavior of other persons and thereby making large-scale bureaucratic endeavors possible. Moreover, there tends to be widespread acceptance, among those persons belonging to the insider category at least, of the view that large-scale bureaucracies are necessary to attained levels of productivity and affluence, whether or not they are humanly satisfying in their own right.

But this widespread, if mostly implicit, understanding of elite functions and behavior does not necessarily lead to equally widespread acceptance of the roles, statuses, and behavior of specific elite persons as such. Many non-elite persons in developed societies can generally acknowledge the necessity for organizational hierarchies and for 'elites' to head them up, and yet still suppose that the manipulation of personal conduct for organizational ends might be better (i.e. more humanely, more wisely) done by persons other than those who currently have elite status. Similarly, many non-elite persons can consider as both plausible and attractive various proposals for altering the conditions under which elite persons obtain and exercise their status — by choosing elites more democratically than at present, by insisting on shorter elite tenures, and so on. In the recrudescence of populism in all the developed societies in recent years, moreover, many non-elite persons have toyed, rhetorically at least, with devices aimed at ensuring that major organizational decisions be taken democratically by organizational participants themselves. Yet most bureaucratic structures in developed societies are so constituted with respect either to private property rights or the rights of superior political authorities as to cause this last proposal for democratic decision-making by organizational participants to be stoutly and effectively resisted as a matter of principle.

In the face of such resistance, and because the necessity for organizational hierarchies is so widely, if tacitly, recognized in developed societies, the discontent of many non-elite persons with specific elite roles and statuses in large-scale organizations has predominantly moved in a somewhat oblique direction. This is the very widespread demand for procedural safegurards designed to allow the greatest possible 'input' of interested opinion and sentiment into the decision-making processes of these organizations. In effect, non-elites are demanding a thorough-going 'judicialization' of these processes so that while persons located in elite positions will still make final, formal decisions, their

actual latitude of choice will be slight. This formalization of organizational decision-making has been most elaborately and enthusiastically
urged, and to some extent adopted, in universities.

Given that the bureaucratic structure is probably more facilitative
than indispensable for the principal institutional tasks of universities, it
is possible to argue that this demand to formalize decision processes in
them is merely time consuming. Yet even in commercial firms and
various regulatory organizations, where the bureaucratic structure is
presumably essential to the performance of nearly all tasks, widespread
encouragement of committee decision-making accompanied by
encounter-group exercises and such mass-oriented techniques as sensitivity training indicates a similar, less formalized trend to restrict the
decision-making latitudes of elite persons. Moreover, in virtually all
collective bargaining contexts, between labor and management as well
as in relation to white-collar and professional employees, rules and
regulations severely formalizing all serious personnel decisions have
been widely adopted. This is especially the case with respect to
personnel decisions affecting those who have tenure or seniority rights,
but it also extends to employees seeking those rights and to the hiring
of new personnel.

Should it continue unchecked, this trend to formalize organizational
decision-making and to make it more open and more subject to the
pressure of interested parties would, either by the nature of things or
by human will, eventually largely eliminate elite decision-making and
the status of elite persons. That is a prospect that is wholly peculiar to
developed societies. In developing societies the elimination of elites and
of elite decision-making in organizational matters is literally impossible
because most members of the work forces of such societies are insufficiently sophisticated as regards the functioning of complex organizations to be able to bring it about. In addition, the line-up of political
power in such work forces guarantees that experiments in this direction
never get much of a trial. The possible exceptions to these statements are
the rare levelling revolutions in largely agricultural societies that involve
the full or partial destruction of pre-existing elites. But these, as the
French and Russian revolutions clearly showed, are always brief, they
always involve drastic declines in productivity, and they are always
followed by a prompt return to organizational hierarchies headed up by
new or restored elites who usually have more latitude for decision-
making after the revolutionary experience than was available to elites
before it.

With respect to these considerations, however, one cannot be sure of the situation in developed societies. We have already said that the work experiences and numerical dominance of non-manual workers in these societies gives to developed populations a greater political and social sophistication as regards organizational matters. The trend toward formalizing elite decision-making that we have sketched indicates, at any rate, that developed societies have already taken significant steps in this direction, and organizational disaster has not as yet resulted. The interesting question thus becomes how far developed societies can move in the direction of eliminating elite decision-making. Are further moves in this direction 'impossible' in the less literal sense that bureaucratic organization would fairly quickly become paralyzed so that the resulting chaos and famine would rapidly lead to either retrogressive development or to a crude and dictatorial reimposition of elite decision-making?

We think that the elimination or even the gross restriction of decision-making by strategically placed elite persons in the organizations of developed societies is indeed 'impossible' in this latter sense. That is, it would render large-scale organizations very nearly inoperative and paralyzed, and it would therefore produce chaos and catastrophe. We think this would almost certainly be the result for several reasons which relate to the general theoretical analysis of elites.

Most major organizational decisions, even when they are not explicitly personnel decisions, have important implications for the careers of persons or categories of persons belonging to the organization in question. In respect to these decisions these persons are vitally interested parties, and they cannot be expected to show restraint or impartiality in the processes leading to these decisions. If anyone can be expected to judge impartially in the interests of the organization (or of the society, or of the civilization) in such matters it is those people whose own careers have already been successful enough so that further advancement for either themselves or their potential allies is no longer a pressing concern. Normally, such persons occupy the most strategic, uppermost, or 'elite' positions in large-scale organizations. In old-fashioned bureaucratic and hierarchical structures, where there was little formalized 'input' and relatively few procedural safeguards of the kind that are currently urged in all developed societies, it is likely that major decisions affecting directly or indirectly the careers of organizational members were made as prudently and as responsibly as they ever can be.

The contemporary trend toward formalization and procedural open-ness, on the other hand, makes it unlikely that generally acceptable organizational decisions can be reached in most cases. This is because the rival interests of persons vitally affected by such decisions stand in the way. The reforms that are being advocated serve to make these rivalries more public, and in so doing they exacerbate the feelings surrounding them. Measures aimed at formalizing and opening up the ways in which choices between rival interests are made are therefore likely to lead to postponements, evasions, and compromises as great efforts to placate all interested parties are made. A further complication arises when it is remembered that, while the making of choices, which decisions represent, is usually necessary because of limited resources, which choice to make is very often an arbitrary matter except from the selfish standpoint of the personal interests that happen to be affected. For an elite decision-maker to make such choices privately (even if in secret he draws lots in order to do it) is probably less harmful in the long run than to pretend publicly that a rational choice has been impartially made on the basis of a full airing of claims and arguments.

The implication is that elites in developed societies must find policies that will preserve the essence of their decision-making power and latitude as these have recently existed in societies before they reached the 'developed' level. Elites must do this not merely to defend their own interest, but because if they allow themselves to become enmeshed by procedural safeguards and requirements of openness in reaching decisions, then the essential organizational mechanisms of developed societies will be paralyzed. This would presumably gravely impede both the material productivity and the political orderliness of these societies.[6]

The next question to ask is whether elites in developed societies will be able successfully to defend their essential powers and functions. Is it possible to develop policies under which the making of most day-to-day organizational decisions will continue to be the function of strategically placed elite persons and which yet will be generally acceptable to the insider category of the developed society? Clearly, and as we said at the outset, consensual and united elites have been able to maintain such a situation over long periods in developing societies. What is peculiar about developed societies, then, that creates so much pressure for procedural safeguards and openness in decision-making processes?

We think that bureaucratic employees (or insiders) in developing societies were readily managed by elites because they were willing to

trust elite decision-making to serve their own interests. Most fundamentally, this inclination on the part of bureaucratic employees to trust
elites rested on the essential self-confidence of most of those
employees. In general, those who complained or sought to restrain the
operations of influential persons revealed their own insecurity and
weakness, a revelation that was usually inexpedient.

In earlier developing societies bureaucratic positions and statuses
were rationalized in terms of what may plausibly be called a 'merit
system', even if the formal organizational features which this term
suggests were not always present. Those who did non-manual work
were mainly persons who were convinced of their own qualifications
for the positions which they held or aspired to, even in the face of
serious competition for those positions. While they feared that
favoritism might sometimes lead to the advancement of the wrong
persons, by and large they counted on their own qualifications to
impress superiors with the need to employ them initially, to retain
them in service, and to advance them suitably in the appropriate
circumstances. In this mood, they had no serious distrust of elite
decision-making per se.

Large numbers of non-manual workers could feel this way in
developing societies because it was readily apparent to them that the
number of persons qualified and available for responsible bureaucratic
positions was small. Only a limited portion of the population had the
opportunity to acquire the sophistication, the verbal skills, and the
formal education (to the extent that this was necessary) that such
positions required. To be in non-manual employment at all (especially
if one had to work for a living) was a substantial assurance of one's
personal qualifications, and these, many easily supposed, could hardly
be overlooked by elite persons.

Obviously, the situation is very different in developed societies. For
most bureaucratic positions, especially for those in which persons are
employed initially, the qualifications needed are not specific and technical. Instead, they consist of linguistic and social skills and a broad
acquaintance with social structure. Most children and youth who grow
up in what we have called cultivated leisure in developed societies
necessarily acquire some sophistication, a good deal of social knowledge, and much social skill. Advanced education, moreover, is fairly
readily available to a much larger portion of the population than was
ever the case in the past. Indeed, in most developed societies opportunities for higher education have evidently increased more rapidly than

have the available positions for which such education is considered a necessary or sufficient qualification. As a result, most non-manual workers in developed societies are not very confident as individuals that their qualifications for the positions they hold or seek will impress and persuade some remote elite persons operating in private of the need to employ, retain, or advance them. They are uncomfortably aware that many, perhaps even most, other persons have similar qualifications.

This is a source of the pressure to judicialize the decision-making processes in the bureaucracies of developed societies. Insecure insiders are trying, quite rationally, to defend the positions to which they have attained, or to which they seek to attain, on the basis of qualifications in which they themselves have little confidence. Consequently, they are trying to impose procedural safeguards against arbitrary, and from their standpoint, uninformed decisions affecting their careers. They are demanding greater participation in the processes leading to these decisions in order partly to present their individual credentials in the best possible light, and partly to prevent those processes from going against them. Given the outsized competition for insider positions, the uniformity of most of the competitors' qualifications, and the remorseless insistence on 'merit' (in the sense of measurable credentials) for employment and advancement in bureaucracies, it is plausible to think that this pressure to formalize and restrict the decision-making latitudes of elites will increase indefinitely in developed societies. Yet we have already reasoned that beyond some (probably early) point it can only result in organizational paralysis and, with that, a catastrophic developmental retrogression.

This, then, is the first of the two major tensions and conflicts which elites in developed societies must solve if their own statuses and the more general political legitimacy of the regimes they operate are to be sustained. We do not think there is any simple solution, however. Fairly obviously, if pressure from insiders for procedural safeguards and openness of organizational administration is to be held to manageable levels, a great deal of respect for acquired rights and statuses will have to be afforded. Specifically, the price of continued privacy and latitude for elite decision-making will be an acceptance of the acquired rights of all employees located in the more responsible and visible bureaucratic positions. These include their right to a say in an organization once they have gotten there, and their right to count on being considered with substantial preference as against candidates from outside the organization for their positions and for advancement to higher positions that open up.

Only by emphasizing such 'rights of possession' at the expense of more meritocratic and ostensibly egalitarian principles can the insecurities of insiders be abated and their discontents thereby placated. In the longer run, more problematic policies might be devised. Conceivably, for example, the currently widespread opportunities for higher education could be reduced, or specialized prestige schools could be superimposed on the universities (as in France) so that the number of persons formally qualified for various bureaucratic positions would be more nearly limited to the number of available jobs. Conceivably, the whole question of how children grow up could be profitably dealt with. In any case, a successful policy in this area will almost certainly be a compromise. Elite persons will lose some of their freedom of decision, but they may be able to hold on to enough of it to avoid the paralysis of complex organizations and the political chaos that that would entail.

THE RELATION BETWEEN INSIDERS AND OUTSIDERS

As we indicated when we defined this second problem earlier, the populations of developed societies show signs of dividing into two loose interest and attitude camps. In the insider camp are persons who either are regularly and fairly satisfactorily employed or who occupy accepted and honorific dependency statuses. In the outsider camp are persons who do not belong to the accepted and honorific categories of dependency and who are more or less unemployable for objective or subjective reasons.

Naturally, in societies as humane and affluent as developed societies at least initially are, most of the outsiders, rather than being relegated to beggary or starvation, are reluctantly and grudgingly accorded some public support. This is the more possible during the initial state of full development because there appears to be no serious need for additional persons in the work force. High economic productivity, in which vast quantities of goods are produced on the basis of very small direct applications of human labor, is characteristic of developed societies. Great quantities of food are produced on farms by 5-15 percent of the work force at most. An unprecedented quantity of material goods is turned out by 30-40 percent of the work force, employed mainly in factories at what by historic standards are short hours and easy working conditions. In general, the material productivity flowing from the direct efforts of about half the work force is more than sufficient to absorb all the monies which consumers can be induced to spend on material goods. While this creates some work for specialists in advertising techniques, there is hardly a need for many more farmers and factory workers.

The other half of the work force — plus or minus 10 percent depending on how long a society has been at the 'developed' level — is employed at tasks whose products, although very important, are essentially intangible and not convincingly measurable. Thus, no one really knows with any certainty whether more of these kinds of workers are needed. No one knows for certain in any given situation, for example, whether more teachers or more policemen or more accountants would actually produce more of whatever it is that teachers or policemen or accountants produce. Possibly more would produce less, but no one can really say. In any given situation much would depend upon the inclination of additional children to be taught, the disinclination of additional persons to be forced to respect the law, and the willingness of those who spend organizational or public funds to report carefully the necessary data which more accountants could then analyze. Obviously, bureaucratic or white-collar personnel interact with each other in complicated ways. In many situations it is not clear whether more of them are needed to do necessary work, the definition of which is itself unclear, or whether a new plan of operation could be devised to make the work easier. What is clear is that, as with farmers and factory workers, there is normally no pressing need for many more bureaucratic personnel in developed societies.

All these considerations mean that there is no strong inclination in these societies to find work for those who are either unable or reluctant to do whatever work is currently available. This led many persons within the student movements of the 1960s to conclude that developed societies are affluent enough to make work strictly optional. The students observed that there were enough persons working at necessary tasks to support all the population at a high standard of living. They inferred from this that if persons (like themselves) are not sufficiently attracted to any available work to want to pay the costs of qualifying themselves to do it, then let them paint pictures, sing songs, or raise babies at public expense.

Unfortunately for this easy way out of the situation, however, affluence in developed societies is not the objective fact that it sometimes appears to be when the attention of affluent young people is first drawn to it. Probably few working adults feel really affluent. Many who are located in less fortunate employment or dependency statuses are seriously deprived according to the prevailing standard of living. Yet there is no way in which support for them can be generally increased without a serious sacrifice on the part of many who by no means regard themselves as affluent. This is why the impending taxpayers' revolts in all the developed societies do not arise among the wealthy. Rather, they are located in the far more numerous middle strata of the populations.

Moreover, the possibility of improving the lot of outsiders in developed societies through a redistribution of income is impeded by a lack of necessary empathy between those who work regularly or are presumed by the society to be entitled to fairly generous support, the insiders, and those who do not work regularly and have no strong claim for support, the outsiders. The inevitable difference of outlook between these two groups leads to the insider's question, 'Why should I sacrifice to help them?'

We interpret these considerations to mean that the outsider category in developed societies probably cannot be made to disappear, short of some draconian measures aimed at drastically reducing the populations of these societies. Indeed, in the absence of such measures, and assuming that some decline in the size of work forces relative to populations will occur as a result of further technological innovations and various constraints on employment as a consequence of energy and other resource shortages, the outsider category will probably grow. What will be the likely consequences of this? We think that it will threaten in a very fundamental way the already fragile and tenuous social control mechanisms of developed societies.

A far greater proportion of the populations of developed societies escape the more convincing forms of social control than in any past societies. Let us suppose, although it is no longer strictly true, that agricultural and manual factory workers are still engaged in work activities the material productivity of which is sufficiently obvious so that any one of them is readily aware from direct observation whether he or some fellow worker is working or is loafing. By contrast, it is impossible for the very numerous non-manual workers in developed societies to be in any similar way aware of whether they are producing much or little. The policeman, for example, is present as much to discourage the commission of offenses as he is to arrest those who nonethless commit them. Similarly, the accountant or auditor exists as much to discourage persons from misusing or stealing funds as to detect and report the embezzlements and deceptions which nonetheless occur. A managerial official with line authority doubtless has the function of dismissing the employee who draws his pay and *openly* does not work, if there ever should be such a person. But perhaps this empty theoretical function is the manager's major reason for being. In other words, bureaucratic or non-manual work often has as its major purpose a forestalling of what *might* otherwise happen.

In this sense the productivity of most non-manual work is essentially unmeasurable. Its productivity can only be imagined in terms of some postulation of what would happen in the absence of what non-manual workers do. How many children would learn arithmetic if there were no teachers regularly employed to teach them? Some certainly. How many emotionally distraught patients would eventually work out their problem if there were no psychiatrists to help them? Some certainly. In other words, the questions that have to be asked in order to try to measure the productivity of much non-manual work are inherently without a definite answer. Whatever answer may be given depends upon too many unspecified and unspecifiable matters.

In developed societies, therefore, a very large part of the work force cannot be held to any convincing standard of work accomplishment. This is even more true, of course, of the large body of dependents which the affluent developed condition justifies and makes more or less routine. Almost the whole body of non-adults, a large but somewhat declining proportion of married women, and a large and increasing number of retired persons are in dependency statuses involving very little measurable work. If, in the extreme, we take all dependents together with all non-manual workers, it can be argued that upwards of two-thirds of the populations of developed societies escape the historically normal requirement to satisfy themselves and other persons that they are doing their part of the necessary work of society.

This is why the social structure of developed societies is distinctly soft and tenuous. It takes a great deal of political consensus, empathy, and lack of seriously divisive grievances and discontents to keep the bulk of the population reasonably responsive to social needs. Moreover, as the troubled industrial relations of just about all the developed societies clearly indicate, it is difficult indeed to keep those relatively few who still perform regular, measurable, difficult and burdensome work sufficiently diligent to prevent a lapse from the high level of material productivity without which the population in its present numbers could not continue to exist.

It is this minimal and precarious social structure that any considerable further growth of the outsider category threatens to disrupt. For there is nothing in the circumstances of outsiders that inclines them to respect even minimal definitions of responsible and moderate behavior. Having no stake in the social system, and small chance of ever obtaining one, they can eke out acceptable standards of living only by tactics that amount to beggary or brigandage. Their demands are essentially non-negotiable because they have little or nothing to lose in pressing them as far as the traffic will bear. In making these demands their single lever is the threat to disrupt in fairly horrendous ways the already precarious social structure of the society which has relegated them to the outside. Thus, if the numbers of outsiders should increase significantly it is hard to see how the performance of those doing necessary tasks could be continued, unless, of course, the outsider category as a whole was seriously stigmatized, deprived, and repressed by force. In this respect, the continued growth of the outsider category is a basic threat to the maintenance of liberal and humane values in developed societies, and to the legitimacy of their political regimes.

Elites will therefore have to devise policies aimed at terminating the trend toward the division of developed populations into insider and outsider categories. But the room for compromise that is probably available with respect to the relation between elites and insiders does not appear to be present in this second problem area of the relation between insiders and outsiders.

Obviously, there is no simple solution. Conceivably, although it has little practical possibility, limiting procreation among the more prosperous families would reduce the number of affluent youth who are ambiguously oriented toward the pursuit of adult careers and at the same time leave more positions available for more deprived youth. This would help restore the ambitious, upwardly mobile person, familiar in the Western experience of industrialization, to numerical prominence in developed societies. Short of such an unlikely expedient, however, it is necessary to make the experiences of affluent youth more relevant to the needs of adult life. Possibly this can be done to some extent by involving them in meaningful civic activities. Perhaps the growth of ecological problems will open up possibilities in this direction.

It may also be possible to redefine a body of adult statuses in special areas like community recreation, entertainment, and adult education so as to create publicly acceptable work roles for persons who lack strong career ambitions. In addition, wherever outsiders have been assigned their statuses on the basis of identifiable group characteristics like race or religion, and wherever they may therefore plausibly claim to have systematically suffered neglect and discrimination, deliberate placement of some of their number in prestigious occupational positions may be helpful. This kind of 'affirmative action', which is now practised with respect to blacks and some other minority groups in the United States, will increasingly be appropriate in several European societies, Australia, and New Zealand as regards foreign workers and various other minority groups that these societies have admitted from the developing societies. Finally, the problem of job security can be reduced somewhat by defining honorific dependency statuses more broadly than at present. Earlier retirement ages and more direct legitimation of fairly lengthy and recurring periods of student status are the changes that come to mind most readily in this last respect.

While most of these modifications are probably to some degree feasible, it nevertheless seems likely that several of them at least will be viewed as undesirable politically and ideologically. To a considerable degree, therefore, their adoption depends upon political and intellectual innovation by elites. Not only must the problem of the relation between insiders and outsiders be recognized much more clearly than at present, but a distinctly less sentimental version of liberal social doctrine than that which is currently widespread in developed societies must also be elaborated and disseminated. We may fairly ask whether the hard-pressed elites of developed societies are in a position to undertake this. But even if an affirmative answer to this question can be given, doctrinal revision and consequent reform of the sort we have sketched may not suffice to eliminate the problem we have been discussing. In the last analysis, substantial net population *decline* in developed societies may prove to be necessary.

NOTES

1. In a fuller treatment of the connection between elites and legitimacy, a third type of elite which is unified around a single defined ideology and which

reliably represses all challenges to existing institutions, would have to be discussed.

2. See J. Higley, G. L. Field and K. Groholt, *Elite Structure and Ideology: A General Theory with Applications to Norway,* New York: Columbia University Press, 1976, esp. ch. 1.

3. We exclude as outside the universe of discourse the outcomes of subnational conflicts that have a distinct geographic base (e.g. the American Civil War, the Irish Rebellion, 1916-18). Obviously, these much more intractable territorial conflicts have not always been managed successfully by consensual and unified elites, or by any other kind of elite.

4. We have elsewhere tried to provide a theoretical conceptualization and an empirical measure for levels of socio-economic development. See Higley, Field and Groholt, op. cit., pp. 41-52. By this measure, a society is 'developed' when 40 percent or more of its work force is performing non-manual labor. Roughly fifteen societies currently meet this criterion.

5. Gilbert Bloch and Michel Praderie, *La population active dans les pays développés,* Paris: Cujas, 1966.

6. It should be clear from the context that in no sense is this an argument for curtailing the functions of major representative bodies, political parties, or electoral systems as they now operate in developed societies. As utopian critics frequently maintain, this generalized institutionalization of representation does not seriously restrict the influence of elites. It does, however, ensure that major questions will be referred to general forums which symbolize the public interest. In addition, it operates to make major choices of leading personnel when necessary, and to provide peaceful means by which incompetent and unworthy leaders may be removed when necessary.

9

LEGITIMACY IN A DIVIDED NATION:
The Case of the German Democratic Republic

Peter C. Ludz
University of Munich, FRG

The major problem in any social science analysis of legitimacy can be summed up in the question: How does one develop a concept of legitimacy that is both historically meaningful and (empirically) applicable? In order to answer this question it is useful to distinguish between the general and the specific problems involved.

The general problems will be clarified by introducing some terminological and conceptual distinctions which can be gathered from the growing literature on the subject. The specific problems will be discussed with respect to a specific case – the German Democratic Republic (GDR).

Before we turn to the details of terminological and conceptual problems, a question should be broached: Is legitimacy a moral concept? Perhaps in the last analysis it is a moral or normative concept. As such it more or less resists empirical research, but occupies a firm place in political theory and political philosophy. The moral implications of the concept of legitimacy have always been tied up with the idea of sovereignty and its various historical manifestations. Despite this fact, political theory so far has not succeeded in operationalizing this linkage, and the analytical rank of the moral or normative elements has hardly been determined.[1] Thus, concerning legitimacy there exist severe deficiencies in political theory which, however, barely affect empirical social science analyses on legitimacy.

When applying the concept of legitimacy to a specific area, to a special political and social system, two problems come to the fore. First, what time-span should be included? Since legitimation is a process, it is rather difficult to make statements about legitimacy for an exact date or only one period of time. Secondly, legitimacy as a concept needs points of reference. The analyst has to decide on such questions as 'for whom' and 'for what'. Such an understanding indicates that legitimacy can only develop if competing interests and demands of specific social and/or political groups are met. In this context it is necessary to consider if highly industrialized Communist systems can exist without legitimacy or legitimation.

SOME GENERAL PROBLEMS

Terminological distinctions

Legitimacy and legitimation. Legitimacy and legitimation are often used as synonyms. They do, however, express two different meanings (cf. Max Weber and Hermann Heller) and thus should not be confused. *Legitimacy* denotes a quality of political power (a quality attached to authority relationships). *Legitimation* denotes the process that leads to legitimacy. So we should speak of legitimation if we are dealing with a historical process. Furthermore, Max Weber utilized the concept of legitimacy in different ways. Joseph Bensman has made out seven definitions of legitimacy in Max Weber's works.[2]

Legitimacy and illegitimacy. To determine what legitimacy means, we also have to refer to its antonym: *illegitimacy.* Illegitimacy covers a wide range of meanings in political life as well as in political science: moral doubts; civil disobedience; political apathy; dissatisfaction of the masses (despite features of obedience and of certain loyalty to the political system).

Conceptual distinctions

In order to test the applicability of a meaningful concept of legitimacy in the case of the GDR, it seems necessary to review some of those concepts of legitimacy that are widely used in social science literature, i.e. the concepts of Max Weber, Seymour Martin Lipset, and Jürgen Habermas.[3] How can these concepts be applied to Communist systems of rule, to Communist elites?

Concerning Communist systems of rule, Max Weber's distinction between legitimate and illegitimate rule seems inappropriate. Weber concerns himself with the temporary legitimacy of power created in genuine revolutions, and he terms this legitimacy 'charismatic'. The revolutions in Eastern Europe after World War II on the whole were not genuine, because the eventual distribution of power was profoundly affected by the presence of the Soviet armed forces. This is especially true for East Germany where approximately 250,000 Soviet troops have been stationed since 1945.

Max Weber's concept of legal rule is also not applicable to East Europe. The concept of legal rule refers not only to the people's adherence to a political system and the authority of the rulers, but also stresses the factual, i.e. objective validity, of legal rule. Thus, a reference to truth is inherent in the concept of legal rule. This has serious consequences for the concept as such. Rule in Weber can be legitimate rule only when the existing normative order is positively acknowledged by the public at large and when the citizens believe in its legality. Legality means the formally correct procedures of law-making and law-enforcing. Jürgen Habermas has rightly criticized this Weberian view by emphasizing that in Weber faith in legitimacy becomes reduced to faith in legality.[4]

Seymour Martin Lipset places his concept of legitimacy into the broad context of 'social conflict and democracy'. At first glance his understanding seems to be quite useful. He acknowledges that the term 'legitimacy' contains value elements, namely values carried and applied by specific political-social groups.

This group approach to legitimacy, at least in an abstract perspective, makes it possible that legitimacy be used as a concept not only in research on differing social groups, but that it can also be applied to various forms of political organizations, including Communist and Fascist organizations. In addition, Lipset's group approach provides a kind of tool to 'measure' degrees of legitimacy.

Lipset focuses his attention on crises of legitimacy. Crises of legitimacy are, for example, defined to exist when a newly established system cannot fulfil the expectations of those groups that are crucial to the political-social process. In addition to legitimacy crises, loss of legitimacy can – according to Lipset – be rather easily identified. Loss of legitimacy usually occurs when a political system no longer has the capacity to provide adequate access to the political process for new social groups rising from below. For both, the crises and the loss of legitimacy, Lipset provides a number of historical examples. Finally, Lipset stresses a third aspect: a decrease in the capacity of a political system to govern may endanger its legitimacy.

Thus, legitimacy is viewed against the background of democracy. Lipset is mainly concerned with an analysis of Western industrialized societies of the nineteenth and twentieth centuries and with their changing conditions.

Although for the purpose at hand some of Lipset's suggestions can be taken over, his approach as such (including such contextual terms as 'tolerance', 'democracy', and 'group conflict' cannot be applied to an analysis of legitimacy in the GDR.

Jürgen Habermas's concept of legitimacy also lacks applicability. His view that a community of individuals, who participate in a 'practical discourse', decide on the validity of norms and take a vote on which norms are 'right', i.e. legitimate, cannot be employed when investigating Communist systems or subsystems in Communist societies. Rather it applies to small groups in the late eighteenth and early nineteenth centuries.

In other words, neither Max Weber, Seymour Lipset nor Jürgen Habermas provide a concept of legitimacy that is suitable to investigate or 'measure' legitimacy or legitimation in the GDR. Even more so, as far as I can seen, there exists no such concept at all. Research on legitimacy in the GDR (or, as a matter of fact, in other East European societies) has to be carried out on a more modest methodological level.

LEGITIMACY, LEGITIMATION AND ILLEGITIMACY APPLIED TO THE GDR SYSTEM OF RULE

Systematic observation and description for a given time period constitute the point of departure of all research on legitimacy in the GDR. Such systematic observations and descriptions concentrate on processes of legitimation as well as on indicators of illegitimacy (e.g. riots, mass rebellion, disobedience, and emigration). In any case, a two-sided perspective is mandatory: legitimacy, legitimation and illegitimacy must be approached from the side of the rulers as well as from the side of the ruled.

The first point in question is the legitimacy of the ruling party in the GDR, i.e. the Socialist Unity Party of Germany or *Sozialistische*

Einheitspartei Deutschlands (SED). To acquire legitimacy the SED has used different instruments, namely coercion, socialization (education), organization, rewards, and a nationalist ideology ('socialist nation').[5]

The application of these instruments has varied throughout the short history of the GDR. For analytical purposes it seems useful to distinguish between four stages of acquiring legitimacy:

1946-1952: the attainment of power by the SED (coercion, socialization);
1952-1961: the stabilization of power (coercion, socialization, organization);
1961-1967: the structuring of power (socialization, organization, rewards — mainly during the period of the 'New Economic System', 1963-1967);
1967-1977: the attempt to gain legitimacy (organization, rewards, nationalist ideology).

Each of these periods reveals different aspects of the legitimacy problem.

Furthermore, the SED's open attempts to gain legitimacy occurred at a rather late date of GDR history — at the end of a long socio-political process. Such observation raises the question whether or not legitimacy is in fact a major objective of a ruling Communist party. Or are there other more important objectives?

In the history of the GDR at least four major objectives of the SED can be discovered: (a) the establishment of strict party hegemony; (b) the 'integration' of different political and social forces (i.e. the former Social Democrats and Communists, the Liberals and Conservatives as well as the various organizations and institutions of the former German Reich); (c) the maintenance of self-identity (as proclaimed by Ulbricht in April 1946, when in East Germany the Communist and Social Democratic Parties merged to the SED, and confirmed in 1959, when the 'construction of socialism in the GDR' was proclaimed) and (d) the restructuring of the society in accordance with the party's actual ideological goals (i.e. for the time being the 'developed socialist society').

The SED has always had difficulties in combining these four objectives. The difficulties are increasing, since the costs of control become higher and higher. Totalitarian controls or party hegemony cannot fully be implemented in a highly industrialized social setting. For example, the SED has to listen to the materialistic wishes of the people if it wants to raise the productivity of work. Higher work productivity, on the other hand, is a major prerequisite for the attainment of the developed stage of socialism.

In other words, for a Communist party like the SED to gain legitimacy is at best one goal among others. Recent events again testify to this fact. What happened in the GDR in the winter of 1976/77 and in spring 1977 clearly demonstrates that party security and hegemony occupy a higher rank.

Legitimacy as a goal may only then become a prime issue in SED politics after the GDR will have lived through a longer period of domestic social and in particular political stabilization and consolidation.

So far this stage has not been reached, and there are many reasons for this. Eurocommunism, West German television and millions of tourists from the West as well as consumer aspirations of the GDR population have been severe obstacles to domestic consolidation. Now, as before, the political system in the GDR lacks stability, the SED maintaining only a pseudo-authority.[6]

At this point it may be helpful to introduce the distinction between 'indigenous' and 'derivative' legitimacy, which is sometimes used in Communist studies. 'Indigenous' is the kind of legitimacy which a Communist party gets from its own national heritage and which belongs to the very party 'naturally'; it must not be borrowed from other countries. 'Derivative' denotes the type of legitimacy that a Communist party 'has accumulated by virtue of its association with the Communist Party of the Soviet Union (CPSU)'.[7]

In the case of the SED there exists a two-fold deficiency in indigenous legitimacy. The division of Germany (cf. below) is as pertinent as the SED's own historical origin. The political forces that shaped the SED were German Communists who had been trained in the Soviet Union for many years. They returned to the Eastern part of Germany after World War II as a Soviet-oriented and Soviet-supported group, and they managed to occupy all politically and socially important posts. Those German Communists and left-wingers (e.g. the Social Democrats) who had been in Hitler's prisons and concentration camps had no chance against the Moscow group.[8]

Only in later years — in the late fifties and early sixties — did the SED develop some kind of independence from the Soviet Union. Economic and social achievements were as important in this process as the revival of nationalist ideology. Paradoxically, the late Walter

Ulbricht became the protagonist of a nationalist ideology — and this was one of the reasons for his removal. Less pretentious than Ulbricht, his successor as party chief, Erich Honecker, tries to establish indigenous legitimacy through social policies; but so far he has hardly been successful.

On the other hand, there is no doubt that the derivative legitimacy has been declining in the GDR over the years. Even more so, at present, this legitimacy may exist rather as a belief than as a real phenomenon. Many SED functionaries may still believe that the SED as the ruling party in the GDR is legitimized through its ideological and political ties with the CPSU. Thus, they may not realize the necessity of indigenous legitimacy. Be that as it may, such an attitude enables them to assign first priority to the stabilization of power, including socialization and coercion, as well as to the continuous creation of new forms of organization and rewards.

LEGITIMACY IN THE DIVIDED NATION

Legitimacy in the GDR can hardly be discussed without taking the political and social system of the Federal Republic of Germany (FRG) into consideration. At all times, and particularly since the conclusion of the Basic Treaty, the FRG has been a challenge to the GDR — and this has been so regarding all aspects of social, intellectual and political life. This challenge has intensified since 1972, i.e. since millions of people from the FRG and West Berlin have visited the GDR.

Three areas of contest between the two Germanys are pertinent here, and all are crucial to the legitimacy problem. They represent substantial FRG challenges to the SED.

The constitutions

Legitimacy in the FRG — in terms of political science, not necessarily in legal terms — is based on the principles of representative democracy and people's sovereignty. This implies that in a democratic process legitimacy can only result from alternatives that allow a consensus to build up. This also means that there exists the permanent possibility of new initiatives to create a new consensus and to meet competing interests.[9]

Now, as before, one of the main instruments of the democratic political process is free, secret, and general elections. Although often ridiculed, the general elections in the FRG, which take place every four years, perform important psychological and political functions. Elections still make the people (or at least a vast majority of the people) feel that they have a chance to influence the political process, that they can change the composition of the ruling bodies.

In the GDR Constitution, on the other side, the state is defined as 'the political organization of the working people . . . who, guided by the working class and its Marxist-Leninist party, implement socialism'. The main instrument to achieve this goal has been the so-called 'democratic centralism', i.e. a principle of organization invented by Lenin. The SED has ordered democratic centralism to become the guiding principle of all party and state organization in the GDR. Democratic centralism is meant to combine centralized authority with democratic participation. The individual organs within each apparatus are arranged hierarchically. Each higher organ is elected by the lower one. But the flow of decisions runs from the opposite direction — from top to bottom. Decisions taken at the top are not subjected to discussion or control at the lower ranks; they have to be carried out. Democratic centralism also includes the postulates of strict submission to the majority and of party discipline; it prohibits the formation of (party) fractions.

Thus, the GDR system of rule represses all political alternatives. Furthermore, elections — as is generally known — have no real democratic political function in the GDR. They are used by the ruling SED to mobilize the people.

Since legitimation and legitimacy can only occur in a political climate of exchanges between the rulers and the ruled, lack of legitimacy in the GDR becomes strikingly apparent when the two German constitutions are compared.

The idea of human rights

The human rights question became more important for the people in the GDR after the SED had signed the Final Act of Helsinki (1975) and published it fully in *Neues Deutschland*. It has gained additional relevance through President Carter's initiatives since January 1977, and through the broad coverage by the mass media in the FRG.[10]

The issue within the human rights complex with which average GDR citizens are mainly concerned is the so-called *Ausreiseverbot*, i.e. the fact that they are prohibited to visit Western countries and to emigrate from the GDR. Only a few thousand privileged individuals may travel to the West, and so far a small group of applicants has been allowed for humanitarian reasons to leave permanently. The circumstance that he is not granted the fundamental right to choose the country in which he wants to live has shaped the average GDR citizen's political attitude significantly. It has become a much stronger factor bearing on legitimacy than social and political aspirations in Lipset's terms.

The political process

In the FRG the parliamentary majority forms the government while the parliamentary minority functions as the opposition to the government. Political decisions that affect the FRG as a whole arise from bargaining between the government and the opposition. However, political decision-making is not an affair of the parliamentary and administrative bodies alone. It also involves the political parties, the various pressure groups, the mass media, the legal and business communities and the intellectuals.

In contradistinction, political decision-making in the GDR is more or less restricted to the top ranks of the SED. Like other socialist countries, the GDR has established a system of rule that intrinsically links the state to the party. According to the official doctrine as well as to political reality, the party will is transferred to the state. Furthermore, the SED has no competitor at the party level, and it controls the mass media and the four other parties in the GDR as well.

However, at the top of the social system there existed a certain plurality during one specific period of GDR history. Besides the leading functionaries in the party and state apparatuses, new technological, administrative, economic and cultural elites more or less were formed groups. As an 'institutionalized counter elite' they constituted a functional alternative within the system.[11] But again it is difficult to assess the role of this elite within the overall context of legitimacy or legitimation. Also, as stressed before, we have to be aware of the time factor. Between 1963 and 1967 these elites played a certain role in political decision-making. However, since 1971 – since Honecker came to power and since the new *Ostpolitik* began to have some effects – the members of the former counter elite have been either integrated or shelved. In any case, the number of experts who can participate in top level political and social decision-making has been reduced to a considerable extent.

In addition, the political process in the GDR is affected by orthodox Marxist-Leninist ideology. The GDR Constitution decrees that 'the social system of socialism be improved continuously'. Such programmatic statements affect political reality in the GDR, if one takes into consideration that the semantics of Marxism-Leninism — directly or indirectly — shape the individual's everyday life.

Finally, the political process in the GDR is characterized by attempts of the ruling authorities to get everybody involved in the political process ('mass participation'). In political everyday life this induces a clearly hierarchical system of 'participation'. On each level of party and state organizations, groups, commissions, etc. are set up by various mass organizations, and each citizen is called upon to participate in those groups to which he is commanded to belong. Participation, as outlined above, follows the principle of democratic centralism. Rhetoric cannot disguise the lack of real participation in the political process by the people or by social and political groups outside the SED.

THE PEOPLE'S APPROVAL/NON-APPROVAL OF THE SOCIO-POLITICAL ORDER

In the preceding section the problem of legitimacy has in part been approached from the point of view of those affected — of those subjected to SED rule, i.e. of the populace at large. This aspect of our overall theme will dominate our further discussion.

The 'people' in the GDR Constitution are identical with 'working men and women'. The 'working class' and its party guide the working men and women. According to its self-image, the SED is the true representative of the people in the GDR; it is the agent of legitimacy and sovereignty. Thus, from this official ideological aspect legitimacy is not questioned at all. As a policy goal, legitimation has definitively been pursued by the SED relatively late in GDR history, namely since the beginning of 1963. Since 1969/70 SED policy has been strongly influenced by reactions to the FRG *Ostpolitik*. A nationalist ideology and an emphasis on social policy improvements gradually emerged as the major instruments of attaining legitimacy.

However, both nationalist ideology and emphasis on social policy have not been very effective in bringing about legitimacy. The 'national question' is not a really pressing issue for the people in the GDR; much more important to them are improvements in their daily lives, such as higher pensions, more freedom of movement, and a better supply of consumer goods. Also, social policy improvements within the margin conceded by the party no longer contribute to increase legitimacy; people rather take them for granted. The expectations of the people rose much faster than the possibilities of the SED to fulfil them. Therefore it is not mere speculation to state that if the SED were more active and effective in complying with the materialistic and psychological expectations of the people, then an *Ersatz* legitimacy would be likely to develop. It might replace the people's latent hopes of reaching a state of (democratic) legitimacy. But for the time being the SED is not in such a position – owing to the ponderousness of the planning bureaucracies as well as to the lack of funds and resources.

Under present conditions the people in the GDR are not satisfied. Discontent, as we just stated, rises from the SED's social and cultural policies which remain below the level of the people's expectations. This may be the major reason why people in the GDR do not acknowledge the SED as the legitimate ruler. Even though many by now take the political organization of the GDR more or less for granted, they may not accept the SED as the sole political force – not now and not in the future. A wide range of attitudes opposing the SED regime exists, including illegal and legal emigrations, disobedience, political apathy, adherence to Western standards of living and Western life styles, seeds of an inner opposition (certainly in ideological terms).

The SED's claim to legitimacy is further undermined by the fact that the GDR is one state, one society in a divided nation. A variety of nebulous influences which affect the people's attitude flow from the FRG to the GDR; but there are also what may be called official influences, the idea of self-determination held by the FRG government among them. The FRG claims that there still exists one legitimate German nation – mainly on the grounds of identity of ethnic groups, homogeneity of cultural tradition, language and history, similarities in the stage of economic-technological advancement. The FRG links these claims with the German people's right to self-determination.

In addition, ideological influences from the FRG to the GDR can be traced at the party level. The ideas of left-wing West European parties (Eurocommunism) spread more and more within the GDR and have recently (1976/77) brought about some cases of open ideological rebellion.[1][2]

On the other hand, when discussing the perspective of the ruled, we must mention that since 1945 attitudes, the reference system and the cultural values of broad masses in the GDR have been changing. The proletarianization of life, which the German Communists returning from Russia had exemplified and during the history of the GDR forced through, is the most obvious sign of this change. Furthermore, those who might have been in a position to represent democratic norms and values have been repressed by the Soviets or the SED. Sooner or later they left the GDR for the West, submitted to their fate or were silenced and put in labor camps.

In other words, what we are discussing here is a very complex subject. The investigation of legitimacy in the GDR, in terms of the ruled, has to take a number of differing factors into account. For the evaluation of the present situation, however, the most decisive factor is that the people in the GDR, owing to their everyday experiences over years, no longer expect from the SED regime something that could be termed democratic legitimation or legitimacy.[13]

Besides the hard core of SED functionaries, only relatively small groups of privileged elites, among them parts of the younger generation, are really committed to 'their' state. On the other side of the spectrum, there exists a small number of dissenters who fight the SED ideologically.

Thus, concerning legitimacy at least four groups within the GDR population can be distinguished: the believers, the satisfied, the dissatisfied and the dissenters. To a certain extent these groups may be identified more exactly by applying Lipset's approach.

Finally, the picture would be incomplete unless we mentioned that since the events of 17 June, 1953, there has been no open crisis of legitimacy in the GDR. This, of course, has mainly been achieved by the almost perfect system of spying and surveillance and by the fact that most dissenters no longer live in the GDR. They may have been allowed to leave the country or − after imprisonment − may have been redeemed by the Federal government. However, the SED's general policy line has become equally important in maintaining stability. In the GDR as in other East European states, we find a sort of dialectic between coercion and rewards. The coercive nature of these regimes is beyond doubt. Rewards have also long been used by the ruling parties as power instruments. Both instruments, however, have been refined during the history of SED rule. In the GDR the 'dialectical' policy of coercion and rewards has been successful in so far as hundreds of thousands of functionaries and employees have not resisted SED efforts to adapt themselves to everchanging forms of organization and control. This policy has helped the SED in its efforts to achieve legitimacy.

CONCLUSIONS

The SED's proclamations of nationalism and patriotism as well as its domestic policy measures may not have failed completely in establishing legitimacy. But ideological influences from the FRG as well as from Eurocommunism and the effects of the CSCE in Helsinki and Belgrade seem to have had an impact on the situation in the GDR. And above all, it is impossible to establish full legitimacy in one part of a divided nation (and this holds for both Germanys). Thus, if at all, only an *Ersatz* legitimacy can be observed in the GDR.

With regard to legitimacy in the GDR, we have to concentrate our attention on four factors: the time dimension, the major objectives of the party, the instruments it uses to achieve legitimacy, and the people's attitudes towards party policies. For each situation these factors have to be investigated individually. Only then will we be able to make meaningful statements on the legitimacy of the SED.

Principally speaking, legitimacy is not a primary goal of ruling Communist parties. It may rise to the forefront in situations when the party is so isolated from society that its functionaries feel relatively 'secure'; or when the level of anti-party sentiments has sunk to a point at which the party can strive for legitimacy without taking risks.

From the methodological point of view, the concept of legitimacy as formulated by Western social scientists can hardly be used in empirical analyses of Communist-ruled societies; it provides only a few aspects that may be utilized.

Legitimacy should always be investigated from the perspective of both parties involved: the rulers and the ruled. In other words, the questions 'for whom' and 'for what' must be materialized in the research design. Furthermore, research on legitimacy has to acknowledge differences by time and by country. Research on legitimacy in the GDR will necessarily be occupied with other foci than legitimacy studies concentrating on Poland, Hungary, Rumania — or the Federal

Republic of Germany. For the GDR, scholars cannot neglect the issues of the divided German nation. They also have to take into account the quite common feeling of superiority among the citizens of the GDR vis-à-vis the Russians and other East European neighbours, and/or their still rising aspirations.

NOTES

1. Peter von Kielmansegg, *Volkssouveränität: Eine Untersuchung der Bedingungen demokratischer Legitimität*, Stuttgart: Klett, 1977.
2. Joseph Bensman (CUNY) told the author about his discovery, on which he has not published yet.
3. Cf. Max Weber, in J. Winckelmann (ed.), *Wirtschaft und Gesellschaft: Grundriss der verstehenden Soziologie*, Vol. I, 4th new ed., Tübingen: J. C. B. Mohr and Paul Siebeck, 1956, pp. 122 ff.; Seymour Martin Lipset, *Political Man: The Social Bases of Politics*, New York: Doubleday, 1960; Jürgen Habermas, *Legitimätsprobleme im Spätkapitalismus,* Frankfurt/M.: Suhrkamp, 1973.
4. Cf. Habermas op. cit., pp. 133 ff.
5. Some of these instruments were also used by other East European Communist parties of the post-World War II period, cf. Alfred G. Meyer, 'Legitimacy of Power in East Central Europe', in S. Sinanian, I. Deak and P. C. Ludz (eds.), *Eastern Europe in the 1970s,* New York: Praeger, 1972, p. 56.
6. Cf. Peter C. Ludz, 'Two Germanys in One World', in P. C. Ludz et al., *Dilemmas of the Atlantic Alliance*, New York: Praeger, 1975, pp. 28 ff.; also P. C. Ludz, *Die DDR zwischen Ost und West: Politische Analysen 1961-1976*, Muenchen: C. H. Beck, 1977, pp. 260 f.
7. Rudolf Toekes in his 'analysis' of A. G. Meyer's article, cf. *Eastern Europe in the 1970s*, op. cit., p. 81.
8. For details cf. Henry Krisch, *German Politics under Soviet Occupation*, New York and London: Columbia University Press, 1974.
9. The word 'interests' includes a variety of types here, for example rational interests or interests to be perceived as well as the actual interests of differing social, economic, and political groupings or organizations.
10. Television and radio broadcasting in the FRG reaches approximately 85 percent of the populace of the GDR.
11. For a detailed discussion of the 'institutionalized counter elite' in the GDR in the early sixties, cf. Peter C. Ludz, *The Changing Party Elite in East Germany*, Cambridge, Mass.: The MIT Press, 1972.

12. For example, Rudolf Bahro. His book, *Die Alternative: Zur Kritik des real existierenden Sozialismus*, Frankfurt/M.: Europäische Verlagsanstalt, 1977, was published in the FRG.

13. Jean-François Revel treats this loss of (democratic) perspective as a general phenomenon of 'totalitarian' systems. Cf. Revel, *Die totalitaere Versuchung*, Berlin and Wien: Ullstein, 1976, p. 23, translated from the French *La tentation totalitaire*.

10

SOVIET INDUSTRIAL WORKERS:
The Lack of a Legitimation Crisis?

David Lane
University of Cambridge, UK

The approach of Richard Rose to the problem of legitimation is useful in at least one respect: it builds a temporal element into social and political analysis (Rose, 1968-69). For Rose, time itself helps to establish legitimacy. As he puts it: 'The longer a regime can remain in power, the more the turnover of generation works to its advantage for its presence becomes normal in a cognitive sense and one may hypothesize in a normative sense as well' (Rose, 1969: 619). But the passage of time in my view does not necessarily lead to the legitimation of a regime. Whether this is so or not depends on the nature of the inter-changes between various parts of the societal system: the extent of social and system integration, the adaptability of the new incumbents to traditional values and beliefs, and the administrative ability of the new elites to process outputs to meet certain thresholds of public demands. Though the passage of time is some evidence that one might expect all or most of these problems to have been solved. By focusing on society as a behavioural unit, the relevance of a legitimacy crisis may be appraised, for a society may not collapse even if a crisis of legitimacy may be apparent. Such a crisis may be a necessary but it is not a sufficient condition of social instability leading to social change. Institutional control (physical oppression, massification) may prevent the articulation and organization of alternatives to the existing order. The ruled may become resigned, apathetic or anomic.

This essay draws substantially on my book, co-authored with Felicity O'Dell, *The Socialist Industrial Worker* (London: Martin Robertson & Co. Ltd., 1978).

By considering, in the manner of Parsons and Habermas, the inter-relations of the social system, rather than focusing narrowly on the 'regime', or the political order, we may define three distinct types of crisis: problems of political output (the incapacity of the government to fulfil existing demands); problems of system integration (inability to secure compliance); and legitimation crises proper (the lack of diffuse supports). Here we are concerned principally with the last two of these types of crisis in so far as they affect the Soviet working class. I suggest three hypotheses: first, that the supply of motivational commitments of the Soviet industrial working class is congruent with the demands of the elites. Secondly, that forms of system integration are more power-ful in the Soviet Union than under Western capitalism and ensure that crises of outputs in the political system will not result in system disequilibrium. Thirdly, that the extent to which there is a crisis, it should be located in the supply of output from the political system. That is, aspirations conditioned in the system of motivation may not be fulfilled through the day-to-day allocation of resources, defined in the broadest terms.

Following Rose's plea to consider a regime across time, in this paper I shall describe first the major features of the development of the Soviet industrial working class since the Revolution and how they relate to the problem of legitimacy. In the following two sections I distinguish between *social integration*, which centres on the 'orderly or conflictual relationships between actors' and *system integration* which has as a frame of reference the parts of a social system (Lockwood, 1975: 371). System integration is to do with forms of managing and control and is an important means of achieving 'compliance' in the sense used by Rose. I shall consider the ways the administrative structure of the Soviet enterprise promotes the control and participation of the worker and the forms alienation may take. Social integration is concerned with patterns of orientation, and under this heading I shall discuss the Soviet worker in terms of three ideal types of the industrial worker's world which have been devised in relation to the British working class. Finally, I shall suggest an ideal type of the 'incorporated' worker which, I believe, is more appropriate to describe the modern Soviet industrial worker (see also Lane and O'Dell, 1978).

The industrial manual worker is an important social category for two reasons. First, in the USSR, manual workers from the largest single social group: officially in 1976 they accounted for 61.2 percent of the occupied population (*Narkhoz 1975*: 9). Secondly, and of greater importance, for Marxists industrial workers play a key role in the economic and political order of industrial society. I would define industrial workers as a component part of the working class: they constitute that group of wage labourers employed in manual or semi-manual tasks in direct production in large-scale technologically advanced and capital-intensive industry, they form a substantial part of the working class which might be defined as all manual and non-manual labour occupied in publicly-owned institutions concerned with production, distribution and exchange.

The events of October 1917 have affected the Soviet industrial worker in many ways which place him in a quite different context to the industrial worker under capitalism. In the Marxist sense the class structure and political culture of the USSR differentiate the Soviet worker from his Western counterpart. For more than fifty years he has been employed in nationalized industry. A class of private capitalists owning the means of production is unknown. The absence of a process of an economic market does not, to quote Habermas, 'secure for the owners of the means of production the power, sanctioned in civil law, to appropriate surplus value and to use it privately and autonomously' (Habermas, 1976: 26). Even before the Revolution, industrial workers formed a large part of the RSDLP and by 1976, 41.6 percent of CPSU members were by social position manual workers. Compared to the West, there is less internal competitiveness between various strata such as trades and industries. The lack of competitiveness is furthered by the absence of structural unemployment. The homogeneity of the industrial worker is conditioned by the non-existence of wage-bargaining unions with 'trade' interests: this was the case in Tsarist Russia and has been so for the past fifty years of Soviet power. Also, the high rates of industrial growth and social mobility have led to the recruitment of managers, executives and technicians from within the working class. Compared to his counterpart in Western Europe, the Soviet worker is surrounded by the appearances of a workers' state: these are symbolized by the October Revolution and myths about it, participation (albeit often symbolic) in the ruling Party, a high level of social and economic security, and possibilities for individual social mobility through educational competition and an endless path of 'alternative routes'. While the internal stratification of the working class by educational achievement, occupational position and even Party membership becomes more important, the class structure in a Marxist sense has become over time more homogeneous. Now let me turn to consider, in terms of system integration and social integration, the hypotheses I mentioned above.

In the modern system of Western capitalism the market in politics and economics serves to regulate various relatively autonomous groups and interests. In the Soviet Union, society is formally arranged to further the integration and participation of various groups in it. Exchanges are limited and control is secured through the mediation of administrative institutions. As far as the industrial worker is concerned these arrangements, I believe, do effectively further his incorporation into the industrial enterprise and into society.

Consideration of the organizational structure of the Soviety factory points to some important differences in comparison with the West. The notion of a bureaucratic form of organization derived from the work of Max Weber would not appear to be a very useful description of the way that the factory is organized in the USSR. It is true that many of the processes are 'bureaucratic' in character. The form of organization is hierarchical, promotion is (or should be) on merit, there are stipulated areas of competence for various officials, and organizations are achievement oriented. But organizational structures in the Soviet industrial enterprise appear to me to differ in three major ways from the model drawn up by Weber. First, there is a plurality of institutional structures within any one enterprise: Party, State, trade union, and various associations and societies are organized for innovation, improvement of production and leisure-time activities. Secondly, strenuous attempts are made to involve or mobilize participants in the activities of the enterprise. Thirdly, 'moral pressure' is exerted on its members.

The plurality of structures is a unique characteristic of the Soviet pattern of organization. I would suggest that the tendency for bureaucratic structures to be uncontrollable and to develop along the lines of instrumental or formal rationality leading to system instability, may be countered by these arrangements – if they worked properly. Arguing along Weberian lines, one might say that the ministerial executive (the factory director) might concentrate on maximizing production capabilities: he is likely to be instrumental in orientation. The Party, however, and – to a lesser extent – the trade union, have a responsiblility to counter such tendencies. In a Weberian sense the objective of the Party is to assert or to re-establish substantive rationality. That is, its task is to see that the industrialist's or the professional's goals are congruent with the 'general goals' of society. In practice, however, I doubt whether the Party does have this superior role and its seems more likely that it has become much more a tool of management, closely identified with the fulfilment of the factory's economic plans. There is then an ongoing tension between theory and reality.

The other major way in which Soviet organizational structures differ from those in the West is that they require a greater degree of formal commitment or participation, and in this respect they are much more successful. Such participation is within the formal hierarchical structure and it does not diminish the responsibility of the management. Rather, the large number of formal groups seek to involve the worker in various forms of activity. This is an attempt to solve the problem resulting from large scale organization which gives workers few means of expression.

While I am unable to prove this scientifically because no systematic comparative research has been done, general levels of participation and involvement in the USSR appear to be higher than in the West. While calling for caution in interpreting the data collected by Soviet sociologists about the quality of commitment and the extent of participation, the trend is clear. White, in reviewing numerous Soviet empirical studies concludes: 'The average amount of time devoted to sociopolitical activity is estimated to have increased almost seven times over the period of Soviet rule, while the proportion of working people involved is estimated to have increased eighteen times over the same period' (White, 1975: 31). This is supported by the findings of numerous Soviet social surveys (see Lane and O'Dell, 1978; Mukhachev and Borovik, 1975; Kuznetsov, 1974). The results of such surveys are sometimes rejected in the West, and are seen as reflecting the ideological preferences of their sponsors. This is a charge which has also been made against Western social research by its critics. While there is obviously a component of 'received ideology' in any piece of empirical research, this by itself does not invalidate its use. Soviet research shows important variation in results over time and between different populations. It is by concentrating on trends and variations in responses that we may build up a reliable picture. It is also important to bear in mind that many users of Soviet research, who object to it on ideological grounds, are quite happy to rely on it when it confirms their own views. Many *émigrés* adopt the practice of their former masters' interpretation of capitalism: they eagerly cite sources which show it in a negative light and suppress data about its positive features.

A second characteristic of this participation is the differential activity of various groups of workers. Of the participant respondents of Mukhachev and Borovik (1975), 38 percent were Party members, and

58 percent were manual workers (pp. 33-34). This shows important stratification of activity within the enterprise where 14.6 percent and 75 percent of the work force were Party members and manual workers, respectively. White has summarized ten different Soviet research studies of socio-political activism and has shown that for technical staff the average level of participation was 67.7 percent (range 57.3 to 84.1 percent) and for manual workers the average was 35.37 percent (20.5 to 55 percent) (p. 48).

It should be borne in mind that these data all show that many employees, especially among the manual workers, do not participate and many do not think it necessary to do so. Also, the effectiveness of much of the activity is open to question. In the Urals worker participants in the Permanent Production Conference were questioned about their effectiveness; 47 percent thought that they had improved the organization of production, 31 percent thought that they had improved the organization of work, 30 percent – a strengthening of production discipline, 23 percent – a raising of the productivity of labour, 20 percent – an improvement in the quality of production, and 15 percent thought that they influenced a reduction in the cost of production (Mukhachev and Borovik, 1975: 198). But many workers in the factory, including those who were not members, did not have a very high opinion of the effectiveness of many of the voluntary participatory institutions: only just over a third of workers surveyed thought that organs of People's Control had sufficient influence over production. Complaints were made about the 'formal character' of meetings, and that the factory administration, Party organs and unions often did not give sufficient attention to the units of popular control and to proposals put to them (Iovchuk and Kogan, 1972: 204). Even so, we should not lose sight of the fact that the institutional arrangements and levels of social, political and economic participation in the enterprise are much higher than in industrial enterprises in the West.

How these forms of industrial organization and means of participation influence the level and kinds of alienation of the industrial worker is again difficult to ascertain with accuracy. The Soviet industrial worker creates a world of objects. For Marxists such 'objectification' does not necessarily lead to 'alienation' which only takes place under certain social conditions. Objectification leads to alienation when man's product assumes an existence not only external to him but also alien to him. The division of labour and the existence of capital are not in themselves alienative. In Marx's theory, especially in the *Economic and*

Philosophical Manuscripts, the source of alienation is found in capitalist property relations and not in technological factors.

Many contemporary Western studies of alienation analyse components of workers' attitudes independently of ownership relations. For instance, Blauner (1964) in his work on American workers identifies four components of alienation: powerlessness, meaninglessness, social isolation, and self-estrangement. This is, to be charitable, a reinterpretation of Marx, for Blauner considers the essence of alienation, or rather of attitudes towards and happiness in work, to be derived from technological factors, not property relations. This is not the same as the essentially structural conditioning of alienation meant by Marx. It is important not to confuse these two kinds of relationships. Alienation in a Marxist structural sense is not directly applicable to the Soviet workers' situation and hence is not a latent source of systemic conflict. But 'alienation', in a sense of dissatisfaction with work, with instrumental attitudes, with forms of 'powerlessness' over the work situation is still a feature of the Soviet worker and in some ways is comparable to workers' attitudes revealed by Western non-Marxist studies. Alienation then may be said to have a multidimensional character: psychological, social, economic, and political, which derive from non-property factors.

Data collected by Zdravomyslov et al. (1966) help to show the extent of dissatisfaction by workers with their work, and this may be used as an index of motivational commitment. Again, caution is necessary in interpreting the published results and one should focus on the different responses of various groups and the rankings rather than on absolute levels. The authors found that satisfaction with occupation varied from a negative attitude among unskilled manual labour to a strongly positive one among the highly skilled. The 'social significance of work' is another measure of worker attitude, and here we again find that the more highly qualified workers (especially panel setters) had positive attitudes, whilst the unskilled manual workers did not; machine operators also had a low score. The factors in the work situation which gave rise to satisfaction were the following: content of work (index score 0.72), pay (0.61), possibility of improving skill (0.58), variety in work (0.48), organization of labour (0.38), management's concern for workers (0.35), and finally physical effort (0.32) (Zdravomyslov et al., 1966: 114). Other studies have come to similar conclusions (for more details see Lane and O'Dell, 1978). Aitov's interviews with 10,707 workers in Ufa in 1972 showed that attitudes towards work were most positive among the more qualified and better educated workers (Aitov, 1974). Mukhachev and Borovik found variations in the attitudes of different groups of workers when they studied their conceptions of 'ownership relations' towards the factory. They asked the question (in sixteen lathe-building factories): 'Do you consider yourself to be one of the proprietors (*khozyaev*) of socialist production?' 47.2 percent said yes; 22.5 percent, no; 22.1 percent did not know, and 8.2 percent did not answer (Mukhachev and Borovik, 1975: 53-54). Workers with a good education and skilled occupations would appear to have higher levels of 'consciousness' in terms of participation and a feeling of working in 'their' factory.

These results are not dissimilar to those revealed by studies of workers conducted in the West. Greater dissatisfaction exists among unskilled workers doing repetitive jobs than among more skilled workers; manual workers have no control over the rhythm of their work. The perception of the social significance of work is lowest among the unskilled manual groups. Political activity is greater among skilled than unskilled, and non-manuals rather than manuals. Such dissatisfaction, in my view, is determined partly by the technology of modern industry which — in both the USSR and the West — requires some workers to be involved in routine production. Many of these workers see factory labour as instrumental. A secondary factor giving rise to job dissatisfaction is the incapability of the system to provide a suffcient number of jobs which require the levels of education and attainment achieved by many of those in factory work. Thirdly, there are imperfect and contradictory forms of socialization: these in practice tend to emphasize achievement through qualifications at the expense of minimizing the desirability of manual unskilled work. These are forms of inadequate and inappropriate political output.

There is, then, among Soviet industrial workers a certain lack of unity between man and his work, between subject and object. Whether this amounts to 'alienation' in a *Marxist*, i.e. a structural sense, is debatable, and I would say that these attitudes rather are evidence of work dissatisfaction. The Soviet worker is still subject to various forms of estrangement from his work, his fellow men and his environment; and some groups of workers may even form an alienative sub-culture. It is particularly important to note that the worker does not directly control the means of production. The state rules on behalf of the working class rather than there being direct working class decision-making. To this extent I would disagree with Soviet sociologists such as Shkaratan who say that the Soviet working class is a class 'for itself'. Control of the means of production is essentially centralized, but mediated by various forms of checking (*kontrol'*) by groups of workers at the industrial enterprise.

I would also call in to question Ticktin's analysis that 'the [political?] elite have only limited control over the surplus [of labour] – more limited than under capitalism' (Ticktin, 1976: 43). Rather, I see a more effectively socialized and incorporated working class: workers may influence and even seek to alter the pattern of exhange between them and the political elite, but they have little independent class power to resist the rulers. But I would disagree with writers such as Blumberg whose emphasis on control excludes property relations and puts the Soviet worker in essentially the same relationship to the means of production as the worker in a capitalist society. 'State management of the economy perpetuates the alienation of the worker from the means of production, for he has no more control over them than he ever did' (Blumberg, 1968: 177). 'Control' is only one element of alienation and I would suggest that the relationship to the means of production has undergone a structural change; this places all employees, management and workers in a factory in essentially the same class as regards their relationship, in a property sense, to the means of production, which is not the case under capitalism. This makes for a greater homogeneity of *class* interest, in the Marxist sense, of managers and workers, and of the various interests making up the Soviet factory.

What is true, however, is that there is a stratification among the work force and this may involve forms of 'unequal exchange' between various groups and an imbalance of power and rewards in favour of managerial/executive strata within the enterprise. Although there are exceptions, the more highly skilled and educated workers and employees have greater positive commitment to the work process and to 'control' within the framework of Soviet management, and their participation in the dominant Party is greater. What is absent, as many critics of Soviet society have noted, is direct management by the working class, and this gives rise, even in a Marxist sense, to partial forms of alienation. I also do not wish to imply that there is a unity of interest between the various groups working in the Soviet enterprise; there are important distinctions which stem from the social and cultural division of labour, occupation being the most salient.

I feel justified in concluding that the evidence suggests that the Soviet industrial workers' identification with the production enterprise is strengthened by the structural arrangements of the factory. I would argue that there is no legitimation crisis in the USSR in the sense of an inability of the political elites to secure compliance at the place of work. This high level of system integration might be compared with the polar case of low compliance in Eastern Europe — that of Poland. In that country the political elites have had less time to inculcate a belief system. The population is more politically heterogeneous with stronger alternative foci of values in the Catholic Church and on intensely nationalistic cultural intelligentsia. The Communist Party (PUWP) is, and always has been, much weaker as a social and political force in Poland, and it has been unable to provide an effective integrating role at the work place.

In the next part of this paper I shall examine the kind of social integration which characterizes the world view of the Soviet industrial worker, and the levels of diffuse loyalty to 'the system'.

On the admittedly inadequate and somewhat fragmentary data at out disposal, it is impossible to make a definitive statement about the work orientations and socio-political attitudes of the Soviet working class in general. Indeed, research findings show that the working class is socially and politically stratified. Lockwood (1975) and others have attempted to categorize in British society three main types of working class milieu: the traditional, the deferential and the privatized. I shall discuss the Soviet working class in terms of these types and then define a fourth ideal type, the incorporated, which I believe is more apposite to the Soviet worker.

The traditional 'proletarian' worker under conditions of modern capitalism is part of a highly homogeneous social group with respect to life styles. Also he sees society in essentially dichotomous power terms: of 'them' and 'us'. (Lockwood, 1975: 18). Alec Nove to some extent has attempted a similar power type of analysis of Soviet society, he makes a 'qualitative distinction between . . . 'we' and 'they', between rulers and ruled . . .'. Nove asserts that this imagery of society 'impregnates people's consciousness in the Soviet Union' (Nove, 1975: 624). No evidence is marshalled to support this contention, and I feel that the centre of gravity is misplaced in this model. I would agree that there appear to be closely-knit social networks among factory workers which 'emphasise mutual aid in everyday life and the obligation to join in the gregarious pattern of leisure which may express itself in a public and present-oriented conviviality . . .' (Lockwood, 1975: 17). Also, Party organizations are located in the enterprise — unlike under capitalism.

But I have found no evidence to suggest that the Soviet working class as such has developed an alternative counter-culture to the dominant one of Marxism-Leninism. Rather, these traditional life styles which in this model are thought to support social and political opposition to the ruling class in Britain, are in the USSR fostered by the factory through the *kollektiv*.

One radical critic of Soviet society sees 'working class opposition [being] expressed principally through so-called "deviance" and "social problems" ' (Holubenko, 1975: 8). Holubenko points out that drunkenness is the 'most prevalent outlet for frustration' (p. 8). But drunkenness, however important, is not solely an expression of the Soviet working class and is as much a Russian cultural and peasant artefact as a working class one (Connor, 1972: 39). Some studies suggest that the incidence of drunkenness among the working class is greatest among the least educated and most unskilled strata (Tundykov, 1967: 47). In my view the phenomenon is more likely to be explained in terms of traditional Russian culture, the strains of industrialization, and maladjustment to urban life, rather than as an expression of political discontent. Such 'traditional' attitudes do not appear to be linked to protest in the form of strikes. Our knowledge about strikes is extremely fragmentary and unreliable. Holubenko points out that they take place in 'areas removed from the Moscow-Leningrad region', in the 'periphery' of the country (Holubenko, 1975: 8). This again would suggest (as far as our interest here is concerned) that such activity is linked to the newly mobilized working class, rather than being an expression of traditional solidarity. Unlike Habermas, who has analysed traditions in terms of supports and buttresses to the dominant culture of capitalism, I see traditionalism at the place of work in the USSR as undermining the system of industrial production. This is because in Russian culture before the Revolution there had hardly developed a work ethic comparable to the Western 'Protestant ethic', which underpinned capitalist development (see Habermas, 1976: 77).

The 'deferential' worker views his bosses with respect, he perceives of himself in a legitimately inferior position, he provides his labour power in return for the traditional expertise and paternalism of the management. I would suggest again that this stratified yet complementary world of management and worker is untrue of the Soviet Union. The worker does not regard his leaders as having 'the intrinsic qualities of an ascriptive elite' (Lockwood, 1975: 18), though they may be regarded as pursuing the 'national interest'. The levels of participa-

tion in management and politics by the Soviet worker and his higher
levels of aspirations and social mobility lead me to conclude that
deferentiality is not a major trait of Soviet workers. What does seem to
be a feature of the world of Soviet industrial workers is that they are, in
Lockwood's terms, brought 'into direct association with [their]
employers or other middle classs influentials and hinder[ed] from
forming strong attachments to workers in a similar market situation to
[their] own' (p. 19). This would suggest that there is an integration of
worker and management — but not of the traditionalist deferential
type.

The 'privatized' worker is one who is isolated at work and in the
community: social divisions are seen in terms of 'differences in income
and material possessions' (p. 21). His work is instrumental, the money
nexus predominates: ' . . . the single, overwhelmingly important, and
most spontaneously conceived criterion of class division is money, and
the possession, both material and immaterial, that money can buy' (p.
24). Such workers may be in trade unions but union membership is not
the 'symbolic expresssion of an affective attachment to a working class
community but a utilitarian association for achieving [the member's]
private goal of a rising standard of living' (p. 23). The latter could not
be said of union membership in the USSR. The privatized worker is
apathetic, he does not question the political, economic and social
arrangements which confront him.

In the USSR, some of the orientations of a privatized worker, in my
view, may be shared by a member of a sub-culture, i.e. a group which
does not subscribe to all the major values of a society and which has
different priorities from the governing elites. Podorov's investigation of
violators of labour discipline not only found that this group of men
(only 8 percent were women) was mainly interested in work for
instrumental pecuniary reasons but that also their interests were mainly
passive, revolving around drinking, meeting friends and playing
dominoes; they rarely participated (only 1 percent) in social activity, or
read educative literature (Podorov, 1976: 73-74). But such pecuniary
interests are not part of a 'privatized' worker's world as stipulated by
Lockwood. As Lockwood points out, a pecuniary model of society can
only be internalised by a worker in so far as 'his social environment
supports such an interpretation' (Lockwood, 1975: 26)' Despite a
movement towards a consumer revolution in the USSR, no Soviet
theory (or counter ideology) supports such an interpretation.

A comparison with Poland is again instructive. Here there are much weaker boundaries around the society. The image of the West is stronger and is continually reinforced by an inflow of expatriots and foreigners. Motivational commitments to work involve greater instrumentalism. The 'money nexus' is stronger: the market for consumer goods is more important in reconciling demand for goods than in the USSR. The system has been less able to inculcate the value of postponement of gratification and the abstemious aspects of Marxism-Leninism (Lane, 1974) have not been internalized by Polish workers. 'Consumerism' provides a much more potent motivational commitment than it does in Soviet Russia.

Workers who are privatized are apolitical, but it would be incorrect to view such men as in principle being not prone to strike activity. On the contrary, workers' expectations for a higher standard of living may be so strongly internalized that if they are not met − through increases in wages − then intense industrial conflict may occur. Such conflict is essentially economistic and does not entail any criticism of the political order in the USSR. The strikes which occurred in Novocherkassk in 1962 (Boiter, 1964) were in protest against price rises and increased work norms, as were other cases of trouble in 1963 (Brown, 1966: 235). Much of Holubenko's analysis may be interpreted in this vein. He emphasizes the fact that industrial unrest has occurred 'in response to three basic issues: (a) low wages − in particular a sudden drop in bonuses or in wages due to revised work norms announced by the factory management; (b) food and consumer goods shortages; (c) inadequate housing' (Holubenko, 1975: 14). I would emphasize along with Brown (1966) and McAuley (1969: 251), that strikes in the Soviet Union are exceptional events: not only are they mediated by labour disputes procedures and other methods of control, such as the police, but the Soviet worker 'lacks any tradition of pressing for improvements' (McAuley, 1969: 251). While Holubenko concedes that strikes in the Soviet Union are 'localised events' which raise 'limited demands' (Holubenko, 1975: 16) due to the fragmented character of the working class. He sees the development of a hereditary proletariat as leading to class consciousness. I see no evidence of this tendency in the sense of a political counter-culture or, as writers such as Westergaard would define it, a 'radical class consciousness' involving a 'recognition of common interests of wage workers in other occupations' and a 'tentative vision of an "alternative society" ' (Westergaard, 1975: 251-52)'

Worker unrest has been manifested in strikes and demonstrations to a much greater extent in Poland. This is to some extent a resurgence of traditional forms of worker-management relations which have continued from pre-war Poland. They should not be considered as systemic types of conflict. They are, like strikes in the West, overwhelmingly economistic in aim. Workers' demands for the strengthening and democratizing of unions are indications, in my view, of workers perceiving the union as an effective bargaining counter against the State to improve their own working conditions and standards of living. As under capitalism, strong trade unions help make workers bargain within the context of the system and are not system destructive. Strengthening the unions in Poland might be an appropriate way of incorporating the working class into a more politically stratified society than is the case in the USSR.

Whatever its limitations, the typology of the 'privatized worker' does provide an explanation of the basis of social solidarity for the modern industrial worker. If a man does not work for the monetary return he gets from his labour, then why should he toil under the conditions of modern capitalistic industry? Many critics of the Soviet Union, ranging from Robert Conquest to Holubenko, have emphasized the role of coercion and repression. I would change the emphasis considerably to take into account socialization and incorporation of the working class.

The 'incorporated worker' shares many of the traits we have seen in the above ideal types. He has certain forms of solidarity with the factory. He accepts the authority structure on the basis of its performance capacity. He participates actively in improving production, and he is closer to the administration both socially and politically than the worker in a capitalist society. But he does not actively shape the overriding values of his society which are largely determined by the ruling political elite. While there are tendencies towards 'privatization' of life in the sense that family orientation (not discussed here) and economistic attitudes are strengthening, the dominant ideology of Marxism-Leninism and the institutional forms of polity and economy place these attitudes in a quite different context to that of the privatized worker in the West. Also, I see such privatization as leading to an *apolitical* status rather than, as suggested by Habermas, to a growing politicization of private life: this is because following the October Revolution the family, at least in urban areas, was weakened in its traditional 'solidaristic' functions. These indeed are currently being strengthened in the Soviet Union and the family is becoming a more important form of integration.

Westergaard (1975: 255-56) has called for attention to be directed to the 'macro-structural' features of societies which promote or hinder class identity and opposition. The structural features of Soviet society undoubtedly inhibit opposition. The incorporation of the worker is ensured by the pervading but not perfect forms of socialization and by the complex institutional arrangements of Soviet society and factory. What the Soviet political and administrative system has succeeded in doing is to provide mechanisms to integrate a relatively unsophisticated labour force into the industrial system. Its dynamics lead to the incorporation of the natural leaders among the workers: not only by occupational promotion, but also through the Party and other organizations the worker becomes increasingly identified with the factory. The Soviet working class is non-revolutionary for similar reasons to the British: it is inculcated with pragmatic aspirations, and has a general conception of serving the 'national interest' (see McKenzie and Silver, 1968). But the Soviet worker is part of a contest educational system (rather than a sponsored one as in Britain): he has high levels of occupational aspirations. These are 'cooled out' through an endless process of educational selection. As Brown has emphasized, in an earlier study, there are many channels open to a worker to resolve disputes (Brown, 1966: 236-38). The worker finds his immediate demands fulfilled at least to some extent by his employers and by the ruling elites (Ticktin overplays, to my mind, the accommodating nature of the authorities, as Conquest exaggerates the role of coercion). Here stability of employment and a rising living standard are important. In my view inputs of mass loyalty are not absent in the Soviet Union and there is no crisis of legitimacy in terms of system inputs.

A major difference in other states in Eastern Europe stems from system boundary maintenance. The legitimacy of East European governments is compromised by the subservience of their governments to that of the USSR and the sovereignty of the nation is sometimes questioned. Hence, internal discord between various elite interests may involve intervention in the internal affairs of such states by the USSR. Support of the national interest by the working class therefore may take a different form than in Britain or the USSR and may involve workers demonstrating in favour of a particular elite group; in such cases their demands are in effect focused on external factors. The greater relative independence of their governments in recent years has increased their legitimacy: but the possibility of invasion, such as in

Czechoslovakia in 1968, raises legitimacy problems of a completely different kind to that of the USSR.

Much more important in the USSR than crises of legitimacy proper are what Habermas has called crises of rationality, that is to say, problems of political output. This calls into question the ability of the system to fulfil at various levels the expectations of the population. There are two particular problems which are of concern: first, the satisfaction of pragmatic economistic expectations of the working class by the provision of a constantly rising standard of living; secondly, an increasing provision of specialist and higher education and the jobs that are thought appropriate for their graduates. In both of these instances the government is faced with intractable 'supply' problems. On the one hand, consumer demands, particularly in Eastern Europe but also in the USSR, are becoming more sophisticated and the economy needs to adapt to meet them. Aspirational deprivation, where consumer demands rise and supply does not increase to meet it, seems to be a likely development in the USSR. On the other hand, people have higher expectations about the type of work and education which they think appropriate to themselves and their children. The decline in the rate of growth of the economy has led to a fall in the rate at which non-manual occupations can be created and in the educational provision which is necessary to train people for these statuses. But even here the contest educational system is one which (both in the US and the USSR) successfully 'cools out' ambition through competition, it postpones a final realization of ambition until late in life and deflects failure in the competitive process away from the societal system to the individual. Social tension, then, is likely to rise as a response to inadequate economic performance and to the frustration of education and work aspirations of youth (and their parents).

Problems of political output have even greater saliency in the other Eastern European states. In Poland, not only is there aspirational deprivation but also decremental deprivation and relative deprivation. Examples of the former precipitated unrest in 1970/71 and 1976 when the government appeared to be unable to meet the existing levels of expectation by raising food prices. In Poland, comparison with the East Germans, visitors from the Baltic and ex-patriot Poles raises levels of expectation and gives rise to an external standard. Hence, the range and types of demands on the political system are greater in Poland than in the USSR and structural integration is weaker which gives rise to greater system instability. It is much more difficult to implement what is known in Britain as a social contract between workers and government.

To conclude, while my analysis is one which has maximized a crisis of legitimacy in the USSR, in the sense of support inputs, it is true that inadequate political output may through time have unstabilizing effects on levels of commitment. In the short run, however, a crisis of legitimacy is unlikely. As in Britain, which is also undergoing a political crisis, my prognosis is that discontent can be contained within the parameters of the system. As far as the Soviet industrial working class is concerned, I would anticipate demands involving the priorities of government, rather than any systemic cleavage as suggested by writers such as Parkin and Giddens. This is because values and beliefs of the working class are generally congruent with those of the political elites. This is much more the case in the Soviet Union than in Poland. The Soviet elites have developed effective means of system integration which not only hinder the aggregation of a radical alternative, but provide, to a far greater extent than in the West, postive ways for the incorporation of the working class into Soviet society.

REFERENCES

AITOV, N. A. (1974) 'Izuchenie struktury rabochego klassa promyshlennogo tsentra', *Sotsiologicheskie issledovaniya*, no. 1.
BLAUNER, R. (1964) *Alienation and Freedom.* Chicago: Chicago University Press.
BLUMBERG, Paul (1968) *Industrial Democracy: The Sociology of Participation.* London: Constable.
BOITER, A. (1964) 'When the Kettle Boils over . . .', *Problems of Communism* (Jan/Feb.).
BROWN, E. C. (1966) *Soviet Trade Unions and Labor Relations.* Cambridge, Mass.: Harvard U.P.
CONNOR, W. D. (1972) *Deviance in Soviet Society: Crime, Delinquency and Alcoholism.* New York: Columbia U.P.
HABERMAS, J. (1976) *Legitimation Crisis.* London: Heinemann.
HOLUBENKO, M. (1975) 'The Soviet Working Class', *Critique* 4.
IOVCHUK, M. T. and L. N. KOGAN (eds.) (1972) *Dukhovny mir sovetskogo rabochego.*

KUZNETSOV, E. M. (1974) *Politicheskaya agitatsiya.* Moscow.

LANE, D. (1974) 'Leninism as an Ideology of Soviet Development', in E. DeKadt and G. Williams, *Sociology and Development.* London: Tavistock.

LANE, D. and F. O'DELL (1978) *The Soviet Industrial Worker: Social Class, Education and Control.* London: Martin Robertson.

LOCKWOOD, D. (1975) 'Sources in Variation in Working-Class Images of Society', in M. BULMER (ed.), *Working Class Images of Society.* London: Routledge.

McKENZIE, R. T. and A. SILVER (1968) *Angels in Marble: Working-Class Conservatives in Urban England.* London: Heinemann.

McAULEY, M. (1969) *Labour Disputes in Soviet Russia 1957-65.* Oxford: Clarendon Press.

MUKHACHEV, V. I. and V. S. BOROVIK (1975) *Rabochi klass i upravlenie proizvodstvom.* Moscow.

NARKHOZ 1975 (1976) *Narodnoe khozyaystvo SSSR v 1975g.* Moscow.

NOVE, A. (1975) 'Is there a Ruling Class in the USSR?', *Soviet Studies* 27 (4).

PODOROV, G. M. (1976) 'Opyt sotsiologicheskikh issledovaniy trudovoy distsipliny na predpriyatiyakh Gor'kovskoy oblasti', *Sotsiologicheskie issledovaniya* 4.

ROSE, R. (1968-69) 'Dynamic Tendency in the Legitimation of Regimes', *World Politics* 21.

TICKTIN, H. (1976) 'The Contradictions of Soviet Society and Professor Bettelheim', *Critique* 6 (Spring).

TUNDYKOV, Yu. N. (1967) 'Znanie kak predposylka formirovaniya nravstvennoy lichnosti', *Dukhovnoe razvitie lichnosti.* Sverdlovsk: Filosofskie nauki no 3. 1967.

WESTERGAARD, J. H. (1975) 'Radical Class Consciousness: A Comment', in M. BULMER (ed.) *Working Class Images of Society.* London: Routledge.

WHITE, Stephen (1975) *The USSR: Patterns of Autocracy and Industrialism.* Glasgow: Dept. of Politics (Cyclostyled paper).

ZDRAVOMYSLOV, A. G., V. P. ROZHIN and V. A. YADOV (eds.) (1967) *Chelovek i ego rabota.* Moscow: Translated by S. P. DUNN (1972) *Man and His work.* New York: International Arts and Sciences Press.

11

THE MEN WITH GUNS:
The Legitimacy of Violent Dissent

J. Bowyer Bell
Columbia University, USA

Europe, East and West, has not seen a boundary change in thirty years and, unlike the generation of stability after the unification of Germany and Italy, there are no serious irredentist claims.[1] Not only have the boundaries been static but also to a very large extent so have the state institutions. Efforts to modify by various means the Eastern Marxist regimes failed in Poland and Germany without recourse to the direct Soviet military intervention that proved necessary in Hungary and Czechoslovakia. In Greece there has been the interregnum of the colonels while Portugal and Spain have moved from authoritarianism toward democracy. Elsewhere, except for the emergency of the De Gaulle Republic, European institutions have been unchallenged and, quite often, even in the West, a single party has dominated the political processes.

As a general rule the opportunity fr men with guns to murder for the cause does not exist in efficient, brutal, authoritarian states. The swift and adamant repression by the threatened center – and the absolute acceptance that maximum coercion will be used – dissuade even the most frustrated and the most ambitious. In Eastern Europe the challenges to authority – essentially Soviet control – have arisen spontaneously. Budapest in 1956 was not the end result of a conspiracy or an urban guerilla campaign, there were no gunmen involved in Polish demonstrations or in the government offices of Prague. Only in Yugoslavia, where a relatively open internal society on top of old ethnic flaw lines, might there now be room for the gunmen. Certainly the Croatian diaspora has sought to bring the struggle into the homeland but have been more visible and more effective elsewhere in employing the techniques of spectacular terror in hijackings, assassinations, and escapes. For Eastern Europe, then, the operative word has been effective; for ineffectual repression, the end product of incompetence or the restraints of a democratic society or failing of will or talent, permits armed dissent and brutal, ineffectual repression encourages it. At the present time, then, all that exists in the East is a distant potential, perhaps not so distant in Yugoslavia but as yet invisible to most observers.[2] Some of the pressures of bloc conformity have been eased and with them the tensions that endanger the existing regimes. In very slight diversity there is strength and hence stability.

Rather, the reverse seems to have been the direction of events in Western Europe. There the three decades have been a tide toward interdependency. The outward symbols have been the creation of various regional political, military, and economic institutions – the EEC, the European Parliament, Euratom, NATO. These formal structures largely reflect the gradual and as yet imperfect creation of Europeans – those who with French nationality work in London for Royal-Dutch Shell, wear Italian shoes, drive German automobiles, and holiday in Sweden. There remain, of course, vast national-bound differences, not the least being language; but the trend, definitely and irreversibly, has been the erosion of splendid isolation, the fashioning of Western European institutions, and the rise of a single, post-industrial, style of life. Europe is, of course, still pocked with regional habits, parochical concerns, and those by-passed by the new consumer society. The assumption of most, however, has been that national differences will continue to decay, that Western Europe will incremently move toward a unity retaining ample diversity to satisfy local values and the American tourist. Tomorrow will be like yesterday.

Continuity does not necessarily mean stability and, for Europeans with unsatisfied national aspirations, does not even bestow legitimacy. There are those who see the present European state system – especially its economic success and stability – as institutionalized tyranny that denies just national aspirations or the appropriate form of government or even the inevitable triumph of a liberated proletariat. Simply *because* the system is effective, has been stable, and appears beyond serious challenge, those who dissent have become desperate. Few believe, as did those with unsatisfied desires in 1875 or 1895, that sooner or later a European war will shatter the old molds. After 1870 the French anticipated, sooner or later, conditions that would permit the return of Alsace and Lorraine, and the revolutionary anarchists a capitalist war that would sap the system. The Greeks awaited the collapse of Turkey, the Serbs the fall of the Austrian-Hungarian Empire, the Poles some transformation that would free Warsaw. Violent change was not only desirable but also probably. In 1977 a war in Europe in an era of uneasy detente, under the nuclear shadow with the inevitable confrontation of the two great powers, while hardly unthinkable appears first unlikely and secondly a certain disaster for all but the most frantic. If an interstate war as a *deus ex machina* of change cannot seriously be envisaged, then those who dispute the present order must seek other means. Because the tides of interdependency run swiftly, they must do so *now* rather than at some future moment when the appropriate objective revolutionary conditions exist. Thus, at the very time that most observers and nearly all participants in the new Europe recognized the direction of history, the nature of the future, as the end not of ideology but of parochial nationalism and violent politics based on universalism or particularism − then, now, a new generation of revolutionaries have appeared. Under various strange devices they deny the legitimacy of the new order, speak in the names of peoples, classes, and nations either long ignored or thought long satisfied.

ETHNIC SEPARATISM

With few exceptions those who seek to liberate nations unnoticed except by specialists and antiquarians accept that the tides are against them. In ten years or twenty the language will be lost, the young will have migrated to the Saar, the old farmers and old ways will die out and the houses be bought up by Dutch businessmen for vacation villas or torn down. One need only go to the West of Ireland to see the ruined stone hovels of a peasant population now living in a Celtic diaspora − Boston or Liverpool or Sydney. They now speak English, now are lost to a nation that is but a pale copy of English fashions, a park for tourists, a site for branch offices. It is not romantic Ireland that is dead and gone but a vital, living people with their own language, their own ways, but no control over their future. And everywhere on the periphery of Europe the process continues to the anguish of the Basques or Corsicans or Welsh. Consequently, the submerged nations have been breeding grounds for separatist movements, some little more than folklore societies, others engaged in national liberation struggles by recourse to guerrilla war. To a greater or lesser extent all the separatists deny the legitimacy, if recognizing the capacity, of the center, no matter that at the center is a democratic government, no matter that at the periphery is a 'nation' that has been submerged for centuries. All want a devolution of authority, if no more significant than support for regional differences, even the 'right' to name children in Bretton rather than choose a 'French' name from an authorized list. Some, however, want to fashion an independent nation – a Basque Republic.

The separatists, in nearly every case, form a triangle. At the bottom nearly everyone wants to emphasize the speical differences – in dress or habits or tongue – if it is to local advantage: i.e. helps the tourist trade or neighborhood pride. Often submerged nations on the periphery have been scorned – their dress or habits or tongue decried from the capital as crude, obscure, the outward symbols of those left behind by events who in time would give up Gaelic for English, Catalan for Spanish, put away 'peasant' clothes, live like the others. Thus, a first step in separatism is the creation of pride, a new national commitment to counteract the lures of the center – and the center offers tangible societal advancement, incorporation into the universalist future, prizes of the pocket and place in preferment. Thus, a national literature must be discovered or created and distributed, national sports and games must be introduced and imposed, the national language lauded and used, the old symbols imbued with new meaning. The pragmatist, however, must be convinced that Basque or Irish has a value that Spanish or English does not, that speaking Welsh will not assure an economic penalty in an English world. Obviously, all of this is a slow process. This old nationalism, eroded by the charms of the modern world, often resides in the most pragmatic or rural populations who have retained the old ways and tongue by necessity not choice. Even with all the resources of the state and the use of coercion, the Irish government has not been able to revive the Irish language as a living tongue. The Catalans or the Basques therefore have ample evidence that devolution can come too late, that the central language has incalculable drawing power, that the time to act is now. Thus, further up the triangle are those who want simply to be different and to encourage that difference but also to possess the power to protect that difference. They advocate regional authority, control over the existing assets, the devolution of real power from the center as a right. Thus, the Scottish Nationalists include both those who simply want to be different and those who have formed a particular separatist political party to seek devolution of political and economic power by democratic means. In this they followed part of the Irish pattern of agitating for Home Rule within the parliamentary system – and as yet unlike the Irish have not produced those who advocate recourse to violence, civil disobedience, mass protests, boycotts and assassination, or any mix of such tactics. In fact, as one moves toward the peak of the separatist pyramid those fewer and fewer want more and more – a Welsh Republic, not some squalid little regional council conceded grudgingly from Westminster. And they are willing, as their aspirations become more extreme, to seek more extreme means than the system will tolerate – symbolic Breton bombs in Paris, a shot fired at the French Foreign Legion in Corsica, and ultimately an armed struggle waged with limited resources and irregular tactics. These, the nationalist rebels, have always been few, certainly in the beginning when someone, someplace must strike the first blow. They speak, however, for the nation – a nation that need not be polled for they need look only into their own hearts to know the desires of the people.

These separatists claim for themselves the authority of an inchoate nation, repressed through the years by alien conquerors. Once the submerged nation is liberated many of the inherent problems, e.g. a decaying economy, emigration, a decay in the cultural and linguistic heritage, and the importation of foreign foibles, will be solved, usually by the introduction of some form of socialist equalitarianism, and the redistribution of the national assets, the end of manipulation from the center, and the appropriate exploitation of national resources. In some cases, e.g. Scotland, such a program, now advocated by a minority, has a basis in reality in others – Brittany or Corsica – less so; but in any case the problem facing the militant separatists is to convert the skeptical – or at least secure their toleration – and to fashion a counter-state, a shadow institution draped in historical legitimacy.

IRELAND

In Ireland in 1969-70 the Provisional Irish Republican Army (IRA) evolved out of a split over tactics within the Irish Republican movement in response to the sectarian troubles in Northern Ireland. The Provisionals seek to establish in all thirty-two counties of Ireland a small farmers' and workers' government – an aspiration that would remove the six counties of the North from the United Kingdom and replace the Republican government in Dublin with an all-Ireland successor. The Provisionals are thus opposed by Westminster, by Dublin, and by whatever regional government might exist in the North. This is particularly so for the prime means the Provisional IRA has used in attempting to 'break the connection with England' has been physical force — guerrilla warfare: rural ambushes, letter bombs, assassinations, extortion, theft, sabotage, arson. The whole spectrum of the tactics of irregular warfare has been employed not only in the North but also in English cities. In Dublin, as well as London, the Provisionals are scorned as terrorists, unsavory murderers whose claim to represent anyone but themselves is ridiculous. The Provisionals speak for no one. No one respectable in Britain or Ireland recognizes their claims and postures. They receive at best few votes when they go before the electorate. Their 'military' campaign is brutal, murderous, and counter-productive. Their talent is minimal, their future lies in prison or in conversion to reason and the claims of legitimacy authority. The position was made quite clear over fifty years ago by the then Irish Minister of Justice, Kevin O'Higgins:

> We will not have two governments in this country, and we will not have two armies in this country. If people have a creed to preach, a message to expound, they can go before their fellow-citizens and preach and expound it. But let the appeal be to the mind, to reason rather than to physical fear. They cannot have it both ways. They cannot have the platform and the bomb. (*Dail Debates*, Vol. X, col. 280).

In 1923 O'Higgins was speaking to those who belonged to a movement — the IRA — that could trace its organizational roots back to 1849 and the Irish Republican Brotherhood and beyond that to the example of Wolfe Tone who in 1798 merged th ideals of the French revolution with those of Irish nationalism:

> To subvert the tyranny of our execrable government, to break the connection with England, the never-failing source of all our political evils, and to assert the independence of my country — these were my objects. To unite the whole people of Ireland, to abolish the memory of all past dissensions, and to substitute the common name of Irishmen in place of the denomination of Protestant, Catholic, and Dissenter — these were my means.

The men of physical force, disdaining electoral means or even riotous protest, sought again and again from 1798 to 1916 to break the connection. And in the Easter Rising of 1916, the rebels shattered the

British assumption that Ireland was at peace, at last destroyed the center of Dublin, and fashioned a blood sacrifice which inspired the new men, who struck again at Britain during the Tan War of 1918-21. They, the leaders of 1916, all dead or executed except Eamon De Valera, spoke in the name of an Irish people — the same people that jeered them as British troops marched them off to captivity. Dead, the 1916 leaders were transmuted into martyrs and the Irish people into militancy sufficient to sustain the guerrillas of the IRA. The Tan War was brought to an end by an Anglo-Irish treaty that permitted the establishment of an Irish Free State but not the Republic. Six counties of Ulster had opted out and in the South there was still an oath of loyalty to the Crown and British bases — and for the dedicated within the IRA such an agreement was treachery. The representatives in the Dublin parliament, the Dáil, voted for the treaty; but according to De Valera the people do not have the right to be ,wrong. Civil War followed, the IRA was smashed and went underground. The Irish Republican leadership, even when elected, refused to take their seats in the illegitimate Dáil. The *real* government was represented by the old Dáil members who had voted against the treaty.

Those less pure broke away from the IRA and the Sinn Féin party and under De Valera founded Fianna Fail, a 'slightly constitutional party' that in time went into the Dáil and in 1932 came peacefully to power. The IRA in time discovered that they had traded the devil they did know — the old Free Staters — for one they did not — De Valera. De Valera did away with many of the treaty symbols, rewarded old Republicans, wrote a new constitution, and eventually negotiated the return of the British bases. In 1936 he outlawed the IRA and arrested the Chief of Staff. He, no more than the Free State government, had a need for a second army or a second government. The IRA, however, persisted. The remaining members of the Second Dáil ceded their powers — as a government-in-exile — to the IRA Army Council. The IRA embarked on a British bombing campaign. The outbreak of war made the IRA a danger to Irish neutrality and their continued resort to the gun forced an even harder Dublin policy of internment and repression. The police of Northern Ireland had always pursued a hard policy. In Britain police outraged at the bombing attacks crushed the IRA by the end of 1940. By the end of the war the IRA was in shambles. The pretentions to be the 'government' attracted very few. The Sinn Féin party was a tiny group of devout — without power or prospects. In the IRA, however, the faithful rebuilt a small underground army, raided into Northern Ireland and England for arms, and in 1956 launched a guerrilla campaign that finally dwindled away in 1962. Again the IRA was in disarray. After each adventure there seemed fewer of the faithful and fewer remaining chances to use physical force.

When the civil rights campaigns of 1968-69 in Northern Ireland sparked sectarian violence so extensive that the British Army was sent into the province in August 1969, the IRA was too weak to play any significant role as a defender of the Nationalist population. The result was the split that produced the Provisionals – the classic descendents of the men of physical force who had found a new role and a new popularity in the North, new toleration by some in the Fianna Fail government in the South, and a new source of aid and comfort in the Irish diaspora. By 1971 their new campaign was underway, tolerated by the Nationalist population, angered by the British army's apparent bias against them. The introduction of internment in August 1971 – a measure to punish the minority rather than to round up known IRA people – permitted escalated IRA violence. By the end of the year the British Home Minister, Reginald Maulding, could only hope at some future date that security forces would achieve a tolerable level of violence. The next year saw Bloody Sunday in Derry, the end of the Northern Ireland Parliament, talks between the Provisionals and British cabinet officers, a truce, renewed violence, and the beginning of a five-year campaign of attrition.

During this time the Provisionals' position remained that they represented the ideals of the Irish nation, that Britain was an alien occupying power, that the Dublin parliament was a pawn of the British, that any Northern assembly was equally illegitimate, and that only all the Irish people – North and South – had the right to decide the institutions of the nation. Ireland was occupied by an imperialist British army in the six counties in the North and their Irish allies in the South. Outside the Republican movement few took these pretensions very seriously; most, however, took the Provisionals very seriously. They had a veto power over any political initiative in the North and the capacity to cause untold harm in the South. And no matter how unsavory their military campaign might become they could not quite be disowned by the Northern minority who feared that someday the Protestant majority might turn on them using the security institutions of the Province. If such an attack were tolerated by London and unhindered by the Dublin government, doomsday would come. Thus, there had to be some Provisional defenders on the ground. So the IRA was tolerated by many, North and South, whose fear of doomsday was greater than their loathing of IRA violence. And, the Provisional IRA did in fact have real assets as well.

Traditional legitimacy

The foundation that permits the operation of the Irish Republican movement has quite literally been centuries in the making and cannot readily be eroded by right reason or by the grating of a new reality. The Republicans have been strengthened by nearly two centuries of uncompromising efforts to break the British connection. They have claimed, and their claims until recently have seldom been denied by those seeking office, that the Republican revolutionary tradition has been largely responsible for what freedom Ireland has gained — that violence works. This legacy of patriots has been accepted in Ireland as real history, not myths or legend. Those who would deny the benefits accrued through an armed struggle, balance politics, agitation, and concession against physical force, have until recently been in a minority. Even today a great many of the Irish read their past as a long confrontation with British power and accept the present IRA as, deserving or no, heirs to a heritage of struggle. Almost all the effective symbols of the state, almost all the most gripping patriotic myths, almost all of the stuff of history so authorizes this legitimacy.

When at the funeral of a fallen volunteer, the Provisional IRA march slowly to the wail of pipes, impassive under black berets, hidden behind dark glasses, awaiting the final volley over the grave of another patriot and martyr, there is a moment of deep emotion that no rite of the Dublin state can equal. No one believes for a moment that Fianna Fail is truly a 'Republican' party and all that this means in Ireland, no one much feels deeply about an Irish army parade or the opening of the Dáil. For over fifty years the elected politicians have employed the Republican rhetoric — praised the old heroes, advocated their goals, accepted their means. After all, De Valera's new 1937 Constitution insisted that Dublin's writ should run over all thirty-two counties. No one seeking office wanted to draw the bounds to the nation. Most of all, no one wanted to point out the distressing impact of incorporating a million Protestants into a system that worked quite nicely for the Church, the men of some property, the existing parties and institutions. So, for almost all the history of the state there was no dissent on the 'national issue'. The various efforts of the major Irish parties to defuse the Republican bomb in no way tampered with Republican ideals and in no sense created a parallel rhetoric. In fact, the strongest single attraction of the Republican movement increasingly became the obvious hypocracy of the legitimate insitutions. Men who cried havoc on the platform were all to content to concentrate on getting a penny more on milk. Politicians who served in the 'official' Republican party were all too willing to jail and intern those who sought to turn oratory into action. Thus, a Republican commemoration is real — a real young man is dead, the flag on his coffin is not just a banner, the volley over his grave is not a sordid ritual but a reward and a promise. The state has been left without the rites of legitimacy — five decades of overt hypocracy has allowed these assets to slip into militant hands. And emotive ritual dramas cannot be easily re-possessed or new ones easily created.

The old ideals

What the IRA ritual summons forth in public is an attitude toward history and toward existing insitutions. For a great many of the Irish, all with long and exacting memories, there has seldom been an intimate connection between justice and law, law and order. The agencies of order were often considered, justly, as imposed; the laws constructed to preserve others' privileges, and the Crown's justice no more than mean self-interest. Forbidden their religion, paupers in a green land, denied education, advancement or common decency, few could see a communality of interest with the Ascendency landlords, with the agencies of the Crown, with *them*. Laws were to be evaded or changed, not obeyed. Opposition, silent or violent, was the only legitimate means of change. Concession, compromise, changing times, prosperity or prospects did indeed erode this posture. But in the South basically an abiding suspicion remains. No one, of course, really considers the Irish uniformed police as agents of the Crown or plots to evade democratically elected laws. In the North, injustice was, and many feel still is, institutionalized. 'Political crime' truly exists in Ireland; and the IRA, whether engaged in train robbery in the South or random bombing in the North, can continue to feed on a considerable pool not so much of sympathy — certainly not lately — but rather toleration. The informer, no matter how highly motivated by democratic ideals, by loyalty to the state, remains hateful. Thus Ireland, a really most law abiding state, still is populated by those whose dedication to democracy, to the proposition that now law and justice are truly linked, still somehow, cannot easily betray those Dublin calls 'men of violence'. And most especially so, when over the past decade at times the only defender of the embattled Northern minority has been the volunteers of the IRA. No matter how brutal or unsavory the IRA may appear they at least are *there*. This by no means indicates that all the Irish tolerate the IRA, only that the habits of the past coupled with the situation in the North create an ambivalence.

A new role

It is in fact the events in the North that give the present IRA a legitimacy related neither to the old rituals nor the old attitudes. Once the civil rights movement had engendered a Protestant backlash, very few in the South trusted the policy or the British army to defend — effectively, or in time, or perhaps at all — the Northern minority. The 'Republican' Fianna Fail had opted to stand back. The victory of the opponents in 1973 did bring to the fore those who at last, if haltingly, in public denied the historical aspirations of the nationalists. There was no longer an inalienable right to unity and increasingy there was no longer any interest in a unity that would cause chaos and undesired change North and South. If civil war came to the North — and surely the victims would be the outnumbered minority — then Dublin would, could, do nothing. That very few people *really* wanted a united Ireland, that very few in the South would benefit by a united country and many might suffer, that without harsh sacrifices no Dublin government would be capable of acting on Northern events, all might be true. But the desertion of the Northern Catholic population whether logical or inevitable, caused grave concern and some guilt. Thus, *at least* the IRA was there, doing something, holding a thin line. If the IRA were hounded and crushed, what then?

So the IRA has three factors to exploit: possession of living historical rituals that grant legitimacy of a long tradition, the reluctance of the population to betray those who advocate the old ideals of the people, and a position as Catholic defenders in the North. It would appear that certainly the first two and perhaps the last are wasting assets. Yet old

ways and old dreams change – but slowly. There is a charm about
myths that the new realities of the democratic state cannot quickly or
easily erode. Fifty years of political cant are not suddenly discarded –
there are years of debts still to fall due. New rituals and myths cannot
be fashioned at will, new attitudes summoned up by emergency legislation, and old responsibilities not discarded in the name of practicality.
Ireland has not always been a very practical country, has often preferred the old myths to the new realities, and still can be touched by
the old dreams made manifest in the old ways.

The Irish case is special, most cases are; but the ideological pretensions are similar to those found elsewhere. The movement speaks for
the nation, no matter how often the nation denies them at the ballot
box, and for a higher and more compelling authority – the people' And
the movement, being pure and unwavering, beyond cant or compromise, holds true to the national ideals without the need to mess in
the day-to-day political process of compromise and manouever and the
corruption of high purpose. Possessed of the truth, the movement also
demands the moral right to resort to physical force – more important
in Ireland than elsewhere – to oppose the oppressor who can 'only
thus' be defeated. Politics, like prostitution, is alluring but corrupting.
Only an armed struggle will win the nation. Presently in Europe small
groups of patriots in submerged nations have accepted many of these
assumptions, speak for old nations, if in recent revolutionary rhetoric,
and call for violence in the people's name. Far larger groups in these
submerged nations deny the gunmen's presumptions but in turn share
some, occasionally all, of their aspirations. And toleration for the
guerrilla is sufficient in the Basque country now, perhaps in Wales or
Scotland tomorrow.

The greatest risk of disorder arising from ethnic separatism exists
where a real rather than an imaginary community exists with a different
religion or a different language and always a different heritage. If there
can be a Maldive Island Republic why not a Basque Republic or a Free
Scotland? Elsewhere on the European periphery the advocates of a Free
Sardinia or a Bavarian Republic seem unlikely to appear or manage to
fashion an alternative nation. Sicilians want more from the Italian
system rather than separation. There are, as well, in Europe little noted
pools of ethnic isolation quite without historical legitimacy or present
national aspirations: Turks in Germany, Algerians in France, South
Moluccans in the Netherands. As time passes they come to live in two
worlds, part of neither, increasingly alien to the Turkish village or the

Spice Islands, yet not German not Dutch. Again it seems more likely that their aspirations will be toward absorption — as yet an alien option in much of Western Europe. The Portuguese colonialists or the French Algerians are easy to manage, coming back to a 'home' they never knew, disgruntled and often violent: in time they can be melded in the homeland. The 'foreign' workers and their families are another and more difficult matter — as a new generation of South Moluccans demonstrated. In any case so far their aspirations do not reflect on inchoate ethnic legitimacy bur rather interest in a better deal. The real alternative legitimacies remain those of the Catalans or Brettons or Scots. There, without the greatest of care, the inevitable process of devolution may lead to the violence of the Basque country or Ulster when the old myths clash with new realities.

IDEOLOGICAL REVOLUTIONARIES

Although the Basques may be Marxist-Leninists and the Provisional IRA have a social-and-economic program, the rock on which they stand is nationality, ethnic separatism. There are in Western Europe, however, those who seek to either liberate nations or peoples enchained by an oppressive system. Those on the far Left may envision, in fact, a nation-free world at some distant point in the future; but those on the far Right are deeply nation-bound highly suspicious of almost all universalist trends, especially those bedded in Marx-Lenin-and-Mao. Yet both share a conviction that the existing system, however defined, is corrupt, oppressive, a facade for injustice and betrayal. Both claim historical roots that legitimize their present posture. And both accept that only recourse to force will be effective. In these matters Colonel George Papadopoulos and Andreas Baader, however abhorent the thought might be to each, share much; for someone, someplace must strike the first blow, time is running out, evil men hold power and bemuse the masses with guile and heresy. Papadopoulos had more assets than Baader but both sought through force to shape the future to their luminous vision.

The Right

After World War II the European Right appeared in terminal disarray.

Monarchy was an anachronistic institution, Fascists discredited
absolutely, authoritarian regimes in Spain and Porugal isolated and
irrelevant. In thirty years, apparently Spain and certainly Portugal are
again within the Western mainstream, and except for the Colonels'
interregnum in Greece between 1967 and 1974, parliamentary democracy everywhere is triumphant, even the Communists – now Euro-
communists – apparently co-opted. From time to time the more
sensational newspapers report a secret meeting of a neo-Nazi or neo-
Fascist underground but in most countries Fascism at best is a vestigial
remnant, often a lure for the disturbed. The Greek colonels, however
unsavory some of their actions, were not neo-Fascists and very Greek,
narrowly parochial, devout, political simpletons with village suspicions
and an abiding fear of 'Communism' – a label for much of the world
they did not understand nor accept, a world beyond the hill towns.
Communism corrupted the young, betrayed the national ideals, and led
sooner rather than later downhill to disaster. Certainly in Portugal and
Spain the loyal supporters of the old ways have not simply disappeared
or been totally converted, they may reappear in alarming guises when
the new systems run into difficulties. In both there has been evidence
that secret organizations do exist, certainly the basis for them exists.
There are in Spain Guerrillas for Christ the King and bombers from the
Right in Portugal. In France, during the post-Algerian period, the
Organisation Armée Secrète the ultras, brought the colonial war back
to the homeland – as the Portuguese colonials may yet do. Mostly the
forces of the Right, denied power, have been advocates of conventional
ideologies and usually capable in time of adjusting to the system,
organizing a monarchist party rather than a coup d'état. Only in Spain
and Portugal would it seem likely that Ibernian Colonels might emerge
at some future date speaking in the name of the people to save the
nation from democratic corruption and the Communists. Even there
the avowed Fascists seem few on the ground and faint of will. Elsewhere the Fascist wave of the future that broke in 1945 is hardly to be
found – except in Italy.

Italy

Elsewhere Fascism is an attitude of mind or a coterie of cranks; in Italy
it must be taken seriously. Within, if barely, the parliamentary system is
the *Movimento Social Italiano* (MSI), those who in public claim to be

merely a nationalist party but who in private are suspected of loyalty to Fascists ideals and aspirations. It was hardly surprising that the Mussolini era in time attracted the nostalgic, those who gloried in the old days, some ultra-nationalists, and the young eager to serve under stirring slogans. While the monarchists faded away, maintained only briefly by charisma and habit, MSI managed to enlist new recruits and attract the old faithful, not enough to make any real difference in the Chamber of Deputies or the Senate, but sufficient to maintain a real presence, to be a catchment for the disgruntled Right. The MSI leadership insists that the movement is not Fascist, which would have been against the law, but repeatedly slipped into Black Shirt rhetoric, and remained critical of the democratic system in terms that implied a loyalty to the old anti-democratic ways. MSI over the years wavered on the edge of respectability but was increasingly isolated, abhored by nearly all. From time to time either in speech or action, MSI appeared to condone or encourage violence — particularly after regional differences in Reggio-Calabria led to violent demonstrations, soon manipulated in part by MSI cadres. Mostly, however, they were not men with guns.

Beyond the MSI there were strange fringe groups with romantic names dreaming of a Fascist revival, fondling in secret meetings the beads of the Old Order. Some, like Prince Junio Valerio Borghese, the Black Prince, were silly anachronistic 'aristocrats', others were ultra-nationalist officers, and a few were strange idealists of violence known, if at all, only to the police. The core movement was founded in 1954 as the New Order by those dissatisfied with MSI's political approach. In 1973, the New Order produced a journal, *Year Zero*, the initials of which were often used in proclamations. In April 1974 *New Order-Year Zero* was transmuted into the Political Movement of the New Order and at later times into the Black Order. There may have been no more than a few hundred members. There were other tiny groups, even a weird Nazi-Maoist cell, and a variety of Right conspirators with or without romantic cover names. The Italian Left was deeply suspicious of this murky fringe of the MSI. Some of the new Fascists were obscure, some quite prominent like retired Lieutenant-General Giovanni De Lorenzo, who the Left accused of organizing his own *coup* in 1964 and who marched in MSI processions. Until 1968, however, there had been no visible recourse to violence, conspirators might plot and neo-Fascists meet — but out of sight.

Between April 1968 and April 1969, seventeen 'symbolic' bombs

exploded in Italy. No one seemed to know who was responsible —
perhaps anarchists — and no one seemed greatly to care. In August
1969 bombs were detonated on seven trains in northern and central
Italy injuring twelve people. Matters were more serious. Then, on
Friday 12 December in Milan, a bomb exploded in Piazza Fontana in
front of the Banca Nazionale dell Agricolture. Bombs went off simultaneously in Rome. The 16 dead and 140 wounded could not be
ignored. The country was shocked. Italian politics have never been
quite the same. The Milan bomb incident and the subsequent investigation revealed much about the nature of the farther fringe of Italian
politics. First, the police began by arresting dozens of suspects —
although they were only suspected on faint grounds. Within days 244
persons were questioned and 55 held. From the first, anomalies dogged
the investigation. The police first charged Pietro Valpreda, a known
anarchist, with complicity. Valpreda insisted he was being framed and
when jailed continued to shout his innocence from his cell. Eleven more
anarchists, or members of extreme Left-wing political groups, were
'believed to be involved'. Three more arrests were made, but several of
the wanted slipped through the net. Then the police announced that
one of the suspects, Giuseppe Pinelli, had jumped to his death from the
fourth floor office of Dr Luigi Calabresi, the department head of
Milan's police political bureau. Pinelli's suicide, according to the police,
'. . . . bore all the signs of self-accusation'. Although an anarchist 'plot'
had at first seemed a satisfactory explanation, the rush to close the case
after Pinelli's death seemed strange to some.

The formalities dragged on month after month. Other oddities
occurred. Witnesses began to die. At the very first, Armando Calzolari,
a member of the Right-wing group associated with Prince Borghese,
disappeared on Christmas morning 1969. He had been making accusations of murder against his colleagues. His body was found early in
January. Another Right-wing lawyer, Vittorio Ambrosini, died — a
suicide. He had voiced suspicions about the Milan bomb. There were
already doubts about the prosecution's chief witness, a taxi driver who
claimed to have taken Valpreda to the bank. In July 1971, the driver
died in his bath, apparently naturally. Three anarchists, two of whom
were character witnesses for Valpreda, died in an automobile crash. The
Anarchist-Bomb-Plot began to come apart. It was gradually becoming
clear that the Milan bomb was not a singular incident, not the responsibility of 'anarchists', but a component part of a neo-Fascist *strategia
della tensione*, the orchestration of violent incidents in order to create

conditions appropriate for the establishment of an authoritarian government. Some of the Right were even more impatient and in December 1970 Prince Borghese bungled an inane *coup* attempt and fled to Spain. On the Left the appearance of the underground *Brigate Rosse*, dedicated to an armed struggle, added further din to the continuing disorders.

Over the next seven years a variety of neo-Fascist organizations, other than the New Order, appeared: the Mussolini Action Squads, the Steel Helmet, the National Vanguard. The New Order, banned in November 1973, apparently remained the core group. During this time the Milan Bomb case continued to reflect the shifting tactics of the neo-Fascists. Ultimately it was clear that not only had the Fascists been responsible for the incident, several suspects were arrested and Valpreda released on a form of bail, but also that security officials had been responsible for the cover up and the penetration of Leftist organizations as provocateurs. Dr. Luigi Calabresi, who was blamed by the Left for Pinelli's death, was shot and killed in the seemingly irreversible round of assassinations, kidnappings, street fights, bomb attacks, and bombings. There were more conspiracies revealed – a Compass Rose plot in 1973 – rumors of *coups*, and disclosures that high military officials had become involved in Fascist plots. An all too typical exercise occurred on 10 July 1976, when the Roman public prosecutor Vittorio Occorsio was machine-gunned by the New Order while sitting in his car. A month before the *Brigate Rosse* had murdered the Genoan public prosecutor, Francesco Coco. The Fascists claimed in pamphlets scattered over Occorsio's body that he had been 'guilty' of serving the democratic dictatorship and persecuting their militants.

The Fascists of the New Order contend tht the democratic system is corrupt, does not produce those who represent the nation – only traitors. They, the New Order, represent the real nation. They defend the future that the present state has mortgaged to the Communists – the ultimate devil in their pantheon of anti-Christs. Their New Order will reflect the traditional Italian ideals. Their armed struggle is justified by both the need to redeem the nation through strength and to prevent the Marxist-Leninists from foreclosing the future. Their allies – the conspirators and sympathizers – all agree that only a disciplined, authoritarian regime can salvage a nation all but destroyed by the greed and incapacity of the orthodox politicians. And so the militants of the New Order murder in the name of the nation, to protect the future, to salvage a long heritage threatened by the godless and feckless. The only real difference in the justification of the New Order and the *Brigate Rosse* when they murder for the case is that one speaks for the nation and the other for the masses.

The Left

The extra-parliamentary Left in Western Europe in most cases arose, like the *Brigate Rosse* , from student protests in 1967 and 1968. The epitome was the wild May Days in Paris in 1968: the elegant graffiti, the endless seminars in revolutionary tactics and strategy, the prospect that the real proletariat would come out in the streets, the grandeur of De Gaulle revealed as a facade for incompetence. And then nothing changed really. The workers went back to work, the professors to teaching. Injustice remained. The war in Indo-China went on and on. In most Western European countries those who could not or would not tolerate life as usual, who could see no point in continuing futile student protests, began to contemplate moving beyond revolutionary rhetoric: the *Brigate Rosse* in Italy, the Angry Brigade in Great Britain, and the Baader-Meinhof *Rote Armee Fraktion* (RAF) in Germany.

Germany

The Baader-Meinhof Group revealed most of the characteristics of those small bands of European 'urban guerrillas'. Despite differences in style and basic ideology, they all grew out of frustration and desperation in some cases personal and in others political and turned to urban guerrilla warfare. They felt that the Fascist-Imperialist-Capitalist system had institutionalized injustice, was exploiting the people – the workers – while simultaneously tranquilizing them with the benefits of a mindless consumer culture. Color television was the opiate of the masses. They admired the efforts of the Third World to resist the repression of imperialism – in Indo-China, in Africa, and in Latin America. Their heroes were Che Guevera, Ho and Giap. Their tactics were modeled on the guerrillas in the bush or on the slopes of the Andes. In the face of the frozen power of the state, they wanted to act – as did the Palestinians against Israel when in 1967 all the conventional Arab armies lay shattered, burned out hulks along the desert roads. Their enemy – Fascism – was everywhere, although the arch enemy was the

United States, and the targets consequently elsewhere. If the system was to be disrupted, the masses, bemused by consumerism, had to be awakened to their *real* needs and their potential power by the few already so liberated – and the only means was violence. 'It is better to burn a store than to run one'. And so a store was burnt to protest the war in Vietnam, to rouse the masses, to begin the struggle.

By 1970

The Baader-Meinhof group, Andreas Baader and Ulrike Meinhof, had become a press and television sensation. Baader had been arrested and convicted of arson in 1968, fled while on bail and was re-arrested in Berlin, then freed in May 1970 by Ulrike Meinhof and others in a prison raid. There were bank raids, bombings, street gun battles and dramatic escapes. In May 1972 United States military facilities were twice bombed and four Americans killed and fourteen wounded. There were rumors and then evidence that members had contact with the Palestinian *fedayeen* – a new terror international in the making. On 1 June 1972, Baader, Holger Meins and Jan-Carl Raspe were arrested in Frankfurt. Baader's lover, Gudrun Ensslin, was arrested in Hamburg a week later and Ulrike Meinhof soon picked up in Hanover. Holger Meins went on a hunger strike and died on 11 November 1974. On the following day Judge Günter von Drenkmann of the West Berlin Supreme Court was killed on his doorstep. The other four were finally brought to trial in May 1975, for various crimes, including murder, in a special courthouse, constructed at a cost of some 12,000,000 Deutschmarks. During their three years of imprisonment, outside the RAF survivors were involved in one spectacular event after another, often in association with the *fedayeen*. When Palestinians seized three diplomats in the Saudi Arabian embassy in Khartoum, one of their demands was the release of the Baader-Meinhof prisoners. When their demands were not met, the three were murdered.

In Germany the RAF proved more effective. In March 1975, in West Berlin, the mayoral candidate Peter Lorenz was kidnapped and exchanged for several prisoners. In January 1976, two RAF members participated in the transnational team of Ilich Ramirez Sanchez – Carlos – in the kidnapping of the ambassadors of the Organization of Petroleum Exporting Countries in Vienna. One was Gabriele Kröcher-Tiedmann who had been freed in the Lorenz kidnapping. Another,

Wilfried Böse, later took part in the hijacking of the the Air France airbus on 27 June 1976, and died in Entebbe. The Israelis picked up two more in Nairobi. They had planned a rocket attack on an El Al plane. By then most of the original group were in prison, dead – Ulrike Meinhof committed suicide in her cell on 9 May 1976 – or scattered, leaving fifty to sixty still wanted by the German authorities. But some at least were still operative. On Monday 4 April the Chief Public Prosecutor, Siegried Buback, held a news conference to announce that warrants had been issued against two alleged terrorists, extradited from Sweden to West Germany, who had planned to kidnap a former Swedish immigration minister and trade her for the jailed RAF prisoners. On Thursday 7 April, just after 9.15 a.m. a couple on a rented Suzuki motorcycle pulled alongside Buback's limousine in the middle of the city of Karlsruhe. One produced a sub-machine gun and sprayed the car. Buback and his driver were killed and a bodyguard critically wounded. The pair abandoned the motorcycle near the Karlsruhe-Frankfurt autobahn and disappeared. The West German news agency DPA received a call from the Ulrike Meinhof Special Action Group taking responsibility: 'you'll hear from us again'.

During the long period before the trial the government found that the prisoners had a considerable number of sympathizers and supporters, and no difficulty in remaining in contact – one of the reasons for the construction of the special courthouse. For some on the German Left, the *Rote Armee Fraktion* was a legitimate revolutionary organization participating in an armed struggle against the common capitalist-imperialist enemy – but not for very many. Those who had become apologists for the Munich massacre, could be hired to hijack and kidnap with a slogan, who though that burning a department was an effective protest against the Vietnam war might be the *enfants terrible* of German violence but for the orthodox Left they remained pretentious and dreadful children. They were a self-destructive elite easier to explain by recourse to psychology than parsing political postures.

The new European gunmen could not care less abou the self-serving analysis of the comfortable. They *know* that the masses have been bemused by consumer bribes – color television as the opiate of the masses. Some one person, someplace must set the first bomb, ignite the power of the people, strike at the heart of the state, kill. They abhor the institutions of democracy – Dublin Dáil or the Italian Chamber or the German constitution – such institutions are pawns that manipulate the people through a parliamentary process. At times, often those struggling for a free nation may, indeed, be supported by vast majorities of the submerged. Yet most of the people will not sacrifice themselves and may, given the opportunity, even vote against those who act in their names. In *theory* the minority in Northern Ireland – and the majority in the Irish Republic – want a united nation, but in practice and during polling they display little evidence to this effect. Those whose banners carry only ideological slogans can muster even less evidence that their claims are founded on the unarticulated aspirations of the nation or the masses. Some support does, indeed, exist: fifty thousand students rampaging through the streets of Rome in protest at the death of a Left leader; the eulogies of respectable Leftists on the death of Meinhof; the rabid election rallies of the MSI; and the conspiracies of high Italian officers – enough anyway that the forces of order in as diverse corners of Europe as Ireland, Germany and Italy remain challenged. And challenged they are by those who claim for themselves what the people will not give them openly – the right to look into their own heart, articulate the people's desire, and then to shoot down those who would put bounds to the nation, betray the old ideals, and repress the masses.

NOTES

1. In April 1977 Italy and Yugoslavia formally ratified a treaty signed in 1975 that ended the long dispute over the port of Trieste – the last official European territorial problem.

2. The Soviets take a very dim view of 'nationalist agitation': for example, in April 1977 the Georgian nationalist Zviad Gamsakhurdia and two colleagues were arrested in Tbilsi – even though he once said only twenty or thirty Georgians wanted independence.

12

ETHNICITY, INEQUALITY AND LEGITIMACY

Andreas Svrakov
Columbia University, USA

Ethnic nationalism challenges the legitimacy of both old and new states. It might be expected that the newly independent states of the less developed world would need time to achieve full national integration and legitimacy among peoples still susceptible to the political claims of tribal, linguistic or religious community. It is more surprising that long-established states of the Western world should today face significant challenges to their territorial integrity from ethnic minorities such as the Scots and Basques, 'ethnographic monuments' as Engels termed them,[1] peoples whose distinctive political nationalisms were believed irrevocably extinguished centuries ago.

The emergence of nationalism is often linked with processes of social and economic change, usually referred to as 'modernization'.[2] We assume here that political movements express popular demands rooted in the socio-economic environment. New political developments such as the politicization of ethnicity must, therefore, be linked to changing socio-economic conditions. Modernization is typically characterized by increased economic specialization and hence growing contact and interdependence among various groups within a society and, at a global level, between different societies. These socio-economic developments are also associated with the expansion of the functions of the state into previously private or communal spheres of activity (e.g. education, capital and labor markets, and social welfare) in order to ensure the necessary coordination and control over an increasingly complex system. Moreover, as the state expands its competence into more functional areas, it also tends to rationalize its administrative structure by centralizing power. The economic integration of a system fosters the integration of its political structures as well; one has, in effect, fewer political centers doing more. These political developments feedback to and further reinforce trends toward socio-economic integration.

Such a descriptive outline of modernization suggests an inexorable process of integration. Greater economic interdependence and increased social contact in conjunction with the development of common political institutions would seem to lead to broad common values and interests among different groups. In multi-ethnic states, the logic of the market place and the rationalization of administration would seem to lead to the weakening of out-dated, ascriptive criteria of identity (e.g. color, birth, religion and language) and to their replacement by achievement norms which apply to all individuals regardless of their group affiliation. This is what Milton Gordon has termed the 'liberal expectancy'.[3]

It is no longer original to observe that modernization has stimulated at least as much social conflict and ethnic separatism as integration and assimilation. It is indeed true that the establishment of the modern nation-state entails 'a process that often involves the transcendence of traditional and narrower bonds to one's local place, kinship group, or caste and the growth of wider loyalties', as Paul Brass and others have pointed out.[4] It is also true that careful case studies such as Melson's and Wolpe's of Nigeria[5] as well as more general theoretical analyses[6] have established that as modernization progresses communal categories 'become more rather than less politically salient'.[7] For whereas modernization fosters the integration of regional identities *within* a nation, the modernizing process may serve to heighten exclusivism among *different* nations.

In a modernizing state in which the political consciousness of several ethnic groups is developing, the increasing centralization of power will tend to stimulate national rivalries within the state. For in a multi-ethnic state, the center will often be occupied by and identified with one ethnic group, relegating other groups to peripheral positions. Such peripheral positions with regard to political power often coincide with and reinforce peripheral economic, social and geographical positions. 'Peripheral' can be defined as 'deprived' relative to the group occupying the center. As Joseph Rothschild argues in this volume, legitimacy is in large part a function of effectiveness.[8] Obviously, a system which is perceived to lead to the relative deprivation of various ethnic groups is less likely to be granted legitimacy by these groups. At a time when social changes are encouraging the politicization of ethnicity, it is not so surprising that peripheral separatism shuld increasingly challenge the legitimacy of the state. 'In short', as Brass so succinctly puts it, 'ethnic conflict like any other kind of conflict is usually based upon the existence of scarcities or threats to the well-being of people'.[9]

We have characterized peripheral separatism and international conflict in multi-national states as a concomitant of the centralization of power and the development of center-periphery ('privileged-deprived') relations along ethnic lines. It is useful to note here that this course of events does not simply constitute 'a phenomenon of transitional societies', in the words of Hah and Martin,[10] or rather that all societies are 'transitional'. The resurgence of ethnic nationalism in the 'post-industrial' societies of Western Europe draws attention to the fact that the politicization of ethnicity and the peripheralization of ethnic groups is an on-going phenomenon which affects both more and less developed states. As Brass observes, 'Ethnic communities are created and transformed by particular elites in modernizing societies and in postindustrial societies undergoing dramatic social changes.'[11] Another was of expressing it would be to say that modernization is a dynamic, open-ended process which continues in societies at all levels of development and that the development of the Welfare State in advanced societies may activate forces of integration and conflict similar to those triggered by the introduction of a division of labor and the rationalization of administration in less developed societies.

This indicates that the disruptive consequences of ethnic nationalism are not merely a 'phase' to be outgrown but rather present a serious and continuing challenge to those political elites and social scientists who desire to regulate conflict and mitigate its destructive impact. In order to understand the basis of ethnic conflict and the threat it poses to state legitimacy we must examine how relative deprivation develops and is exacerbated in the modernization process. Is the peripheralization of certain ethnic groups a 'mechanical' matter, a result of accidents of resource allocation or similar factors, or is it due to the nature of ethnicity itself, a condition less amenable to mechanical correction? Our conclusions regarding the nature of group inequality will, of course, influence prescriptions for the regulation of ethnic conflict and the desirable shape of multinational states.

Two broad approaches can be distinguished in the study of ethnic conflict. Briefly, the first holds that ethnicity is politicized by exploited social groups which rally to ethnic symbols in what is essentially an economic conflict. Ethnic conflict may thus be seen as a form of class conflict. The second approach agrees that socio-economic inequality between ethnic groups plays an important role in defining ethnic nationalism, but insists that culture must also be seen as an independent variable at least in so far as the nature of ethnicity itself may lead to inequality and hence to conflict in multi-ethnic states. These two approaches differ primarily in the importance which each attaches to the role of cultural factors. Let us turn first to the simpler ethnic-class model.

Even a cursory examination of world conditions will confirm the observation that modernization exacerbates disparities in regional development independent of ethnic distinctions. Regional inequality seems to exist in almost all countries, including those as ethnically homogeneous as China or England. Wealthier areas with trade centers and agricultural surpluses and poorer regions of subsistence agriculture are not unusual in pre-industrial systems. Modernization often promotes greater differentiation, making the wealthy wealthier and the poor poorer. Industry concentrates in certain areas while others not only stagnate but eventually become depopulated. This process continues in post-industrial societies, e.g. Brittany and the Midi in France. The economic bases for regional inequality are, of course, obvious; they consist of differential resource allocation, soil fertility, climate, topography, location, etc. Hah and Martin note other factors which tend to increase social inequality in the early stages of modernization and which also have an impact on regional inequality. 'Wage rigidity, capital-intensive (labor-saving) technology, and the absence of institutions for income redistribution are three such factors.'[12] Since the class of employers often consists of locals of the developed region and that of employees of migrants from the poorer areas, disparities in wealth between regional groups will be intensified. And since profits are usually reinvested in the more profitable areas, the spiral of increasing inequality gains further momentum.

It would, moreover, be misleading to simply acknowledge that regional inequality pre-dates industrialization and is often increased by the uneven advance of modernization. Michael Hechter's convincing study of British national development has shown that even when peripheral regions are eventually integrated into the larger economy, this can occur in such a way as to institutionalize and perpetuate regional disadvantage.[13] He challenges the 'diffusion model' of center-periphery relations, which holds that economic development is diffused outward from the core in such a way as to foster economic and cultural homogenization. This paradigm is, in large part, applicable to the

English experience, where a common ethnic unity has developed (although regional economic disparities and cultural particularisms do persist to some extent). Hechter shows, however, that this model does not explain relations between England and her Celtic fringe. Here, the expansion of the English system assumed the form of 'internal colonialism'.

> Whereas the core is characterized by a diversified industrial structure, the pattern of development in the periphery is dependent, and complementary to that in the core. Peripheral industrialization, if it occurs at all, is highly specialized and geared for export.[14]

Economic development in the United Kingdom has produced dominance relationships based on a regional division of labor which coincides, as so often throughout the world, with ethnic divisions. Economic diffusion did not take place and hence cultural distinctiveness was not overcome by the requirements of a common system of social stratification. Indeed, the institutionalization of a regional division of labor in Britain served to reinforce the structural basis of ethnic diversity; the regional division of labor is also a cultural division of labor. And London then proceeded to politicize cultural differences through history by the adoption of discriminatory measures regarding minority languages and religions, e.g. legal disabilities directed against Welsh-speakers and Irish Catholics. Growing popular consciousness of economic inequity and its congruence with cultural identity has stimulated the emergence of ethnic nationalism in the Celtic fringe. A similar historical pattern of center-periphery relations may be observed in other established states, France, for example. Modernizing elites in Africa and Asia sometimes seem to be following the same route in suppressing and thus helping to politicize minority languages and traditions.

The above analysis indicates how ethnic nationalism can emerge as a derivative of economic exploitation. In this sense, ethnicity becomes politically salient not for its own sake but for the regional economic deprivation represented by the very existence of peripheral ethnic distinctiveness. This approach suggests certain practical steps which may be taken to end ethnic conflict, namely a redistribution of wealth and opportunity through reform or revolution. The first option is embodied in the regional development policies of many states. The second has become especially popular among Leftist intellectuals on the Continent, who welcome the resurgence of ethnic nationalism as a means to oppose the capitalist Establishment and the existing political order. Much use has been made of the decolonization precedent in the overseas empire and the 'internal colonialism' of metropolitan France. The people of the peripheral regions are said to be doubly exploited, as proletarians and as Bretons, Corsicans, etc. Contrasts between the wealth and industry of the Parisian core and the ethnic peripheries give rise to the concept of 'proletarian regions'. It is charged, for example, that Brittany, as a region, is exploited by Paris as a source of labor, natural resources and capital. In this way, the Breton nation (minus a few *compradors*) becomes part of the proletariat and Breton nationalism becomes part of the international proletarian cause.[15]

The analysis of ethnic nationalism as a particular form of class conflict penetrates beyond purely descriptive explanations of 'cultural conflict' and offers useful insight into the role of economic inequality in the politicization of ethnicity. The picture is, however, incomplete. Ethnicity may be rather more than a 'transparent variable', a simple difference in form but not substance. Can the economic situation of minorities and minority regions always be correlated with factors of resource allocation and the development of center-periphery dominance? The Basques, for example, although dominated politically by the Spanish core, enjoy an economic position superior to that of the rest of Spain. The Chinese in Malaysia, an example of a minority spatially integrated with the majority, excel in business and finance even though they are subject to discriminatory restrictions. Work in several of the social sciences indicates how ethnic identity may *in itself* contribute to differential economic development and political conflict.

If ethnicity is to have independent explanatory power with regard to the political and economic position of one group in relation to others, then culture must entail more than purely symbolic distinctions which serve merely to distinguish one group from another. Peculiar folk dances, foods and customs are only formal 'cultural markers'[16] and do not in themselves possess any greater significance than color of eyes or skin. Cultural distinctions become significant influences in determining the situation of an ethnic group to the extent that they reflect value differences. For different cultural groups with different value hierarchies will achieve differential success by a common social standard and will evince differing degrees of adaptability to the common requirements of the modernization process. The cultural factor in the differential achievement of various ethnic groups is particularly noticeable in periods of drastic social change. In Nigeria, for instance, Melson and Wolpe have observed that 'some cultural groups appear to be more predisposed than others to compete successfully for the rewards of modernization ... [and] it has been suggested that relatively rapid rates of mobilization and development in Eastern Nigeria are traceable, in part, to the receptivity to change on the part of the Ibos'.[17] The authors also caution that 'The precise role and significance of such cultural predispositions in the development process is as yet uncertain.'[18]

How, exactly, would cultural differences contribute to relative deprivation? Glazer and Moynihan have usefully adapted Ralf Dahrendorf's thesis on the origin of inequality to ethnic relations.[19] If inequality among individuals is essentially due to unequal success in conforming to societal norms, then inequality among ethnic groups, in Glazer's and Moynihan's extrapolation, is likewise due to differential success in adherence to the prevailing norms and hence in the attainment of social rewards. In a multi-ethnic system dominated, as so many are, by the myth of the integrated nation-state, it is the standards of the dominant or core group which prevail and so often condemn other cultural groups with different cultural values and achievement criteria to inferior status. Moreover, since modernization is accompanied by the expansion of the state into more and more spheres of social activity, politics becomes more important and the political inferiority of subordinate groups has ever greater consequences in terms of increasing relative deprivation. Eventually, the subordinates must either abandon their culture and its 'unmodern' values or assert themselves politically vis-à-vis the dominant group through the development of a politicized ethnic nationalism.

This theoretical sequence, however, remains essentially descriptive. To fully appreciate the cultural basis of ethnic inequality and conflict one must ask why different cultures hold different values and how and why do groups differ in terms of societal norms and achievement criteria. Some possible answers are suggested by developments in the field of linguistics. In contrast to simple regional rivalries in culturally homogeneous systems, ethnic conflict of high intensity is often manifested as linguistic conflict, e.g. in Sri Lanka or Canada . A distinguished anthropologist, George De Vos, confirms that 'Language is often cited as a major component in the maintenance of a separate ethnic identity, and it is undoubtedly true that language constitutes the single most characteristic feature of a separate ethnic identity.'[20] What are the normative consequences of language and how can language affect the political stability of multi-ethnic societies?

According to one school, which Einar Haugen has labelled 'instrumentalism',[21] there can be no deeper basis for attachment to a specific language than sentimental fancy. Valter Tauli expresses this attitude in its most extreme form when he defines language as

> a system of signs, the main purpose of which is communication. . . . It must be borne in mind that language is an instrument, a means, never an end. . . . Since language is an instrument, it follows that a language can be evaluated, altered, corrected, regulated, and improved, and new languages can be created at will.[22]

And since language is only an instrument, it follows that among rational men, not swayed by emotional appeals to unreasoned chauvinism, language could not prove a focus of serious dispute. It is in this spirit that a *francophone* official of nineteenth-century Belgium wrote to the Flemish activist and Dutch language scholar, J. F. Willems:

> Fleming or Walloon, all civilized Belgians speak French: let us take advantage of this good fortune, let us press for the complete union . . . let us move forward to the union and the greater happiness of our adored fatherland.[23]

Flemish, like the colloquial Walloon dialect of French, was to be seen as 'a simple literary curiosity, a small literature of local color, an amusement with which to pass the time, the evening by the fire'.[24] Needless to say, Willems did not abandon his linguistic nationalism.

Another, more fruitful, approach to language as a source of societal norms, communal inequality and conflict is that which accords to language the role of defining as well as expressing experience. This alternative to instrumentalism maintains that language cannot be regarded only as a system of symbols, a collection of value-neutral tools, but that words may carry meanings of their own, independent of the reality to which they refer, and that grammatical systems impose their own scheme of meaning on reality. In the words of Edward Sapir:

> Human beings do not live in the objective world alone, nor alone in the world of social activity as ordinarily understood, but are very much at the mercy of the particular language which has become the medium of expression for their society. It is quite an illusion to imagine that one adjusts to reality essentially without the use of language and that language is merely an incidental means of solving specific problems of communication or reflection. The fact of the matter is that the 'real world' is to a large extent unconsciously built up on the language habits of the group. . . . We see and hear and otherwise experience largely as we do because the language habits of our community predispose certain choices of interpretation.[25]

This linguistic tradition may be traced at least as far back as Humboldt, but has been reinvigorated and developed in more recent times by Sapir and Benjamin Lee Whorf. Those linguists concerned with the practical impact of this theoretical approach are generally found in the school called 'General Semantics'.

The theoretical statement of Sapir's and Whorf's work is the hypothesis of linguistic relativity. It can be briefly summarized as follows:

> If . . . language determines how the members of the speech community view the world and think about it, the differences among various languages lead necessarily to the conclusion that members of different language communities see and think of the world in different ways or, in other words, that each language implies a particular world view.[26]

The statement remains hypothetical but field work comparing the linguistic structures and behavioral norms of widely varying cultures has revealed some striking correlations. Harry Hoijer, for example, finds an interesting parallel between the language and culture of the Navaho Indians.

> He finds that the actor-action pattern of sentence so common in [English] is foreign to Navaho. A person is associated with an action, rather than being the author or cause of it. Motion and position are treated as being inherent in an object, rather than as being induced by some agent. Hoijer notices how consonant this is with the general Navaho attitude toward nature as reported by Kluckhohn and Leighton. They say that the Navaho does not seek to control nature or believe in doing so; rather, he attempts to influence it, often through songs and ritual. This lack of agency toward nature, as shown in practice, is mirrored in the grammatical construction which does not speak in terms of acting upon an object.[27]

Whorf reported some equally fascinating observations from his research in the language and culture of the Hopi.[28] Recent experiments in color coding and color recognition, at a more micro level, have also tended to support the conclusion that a particular language system does exert its own influence on the speaker's perception of reality.[29]

This theory has clear implications for ethnic relations in multi-national states. Cultural characteristics are reflected in linguistic structure which reinforces and conditions certain cultural characteristics. Language influences that perception of reality which forms the basis of cultural value structures. Different languages lead to different cultures which adopt different values. This in turn can lead to differential development and inequality, which gives rise to political conflict, especially in an integrating system in which political relationships assume ever greater importance with the expansion of the state.

Of course, the concept of linguistic relativity has been criticized on both linguistic and political grounds. It is charged, for example, that proponents of the hypothesis have paid insufficient attention to the universal elements of human language and of human experience, from which language is ultimately derived.[30] Soviet scholars especially have denounced the theory of linguistic relativity as a 'distorted exaggeration of the influence of language on thought and human behavior' which largely ignores the importance of socio-economic factors in determining world outlook and so contributes to 'reactionary political deductions'.[31]

We would certainly wish to avoid a facile identification of group inequality and ethnic nationalism with grammatical structure, a sort of 'linguistic reductionism', in Anthony Smith's phrase.[32] Nevertheless, in so far as the relative deprivation of ethnic groups is related to diverse cultural values rooted in language, then it is clear that increased competition and integration in multi-ethnic states can only intensify those states' political difficulties.[33] In any competition there are necessarily both winners and losers, and losers are likely to challenge the legitimacy of a system in which the rules of the game, i.e. the norms of the center, dictate either perpetual loss or the abandonment of cultural identity.

The key to the prevention and control of ethnic conflict lies in the development of political structures which maximize the political autonomy of ethnic communities while permitting that functional specialization and interdependence which is essential to socio-economic modernization. The required balance may never be completely satisfactory. The greater the degree of communal autonomy, the less efficient the system, the more costly duplication required, the greater the degree of *immobilisme* and the less capacity to respond quickly and decisively to developing crises in an accelerated world. But the more centralized the system, the greater the scope for communal domination and the greater the liklihood of ethnic conflict. Only by divorcing modernization from centralization and permitting each ethnic group to develop to the greatest possible extent within its own value framework will the multi-ethnic state retain and enhance its popular legitimacy among all ethnic communities.

NOTES

1. F. Engels, *Po und Rhein* Werke, XIII, 267, cited in A. D. Smith, *Theories of Nationalism,* New York: Harper & Row, 1972, p. 73.
2. This discussion of modernization enlarges on that of C.-D. Hah and J. Martin, 'Toward a Synthesis of Conflict and Integration Theories of Nationalism', *World Politics* 27 (3) (April 1975): 365.
3. M. M. Gordon, 'Toward a General Theory of Racial and Ethnic Group Relations', in N. Glazer and D. P. Moynihan (eds.), *Ethnicity: Theory and Experience,* Cambridge: Harvard University Press, 1975, p. 88. Cited in N. Glazer and D. P. Moynihan, 'Introduction', in the above volume, pp. 6-7.
4. P. R. Brass, 'Ethnicity and Nationality Formation', *Ethnicity* 3 (Sept. 1976): 229. In this connection, Brass cites Hah and Martin, op. cit., pp. 374-79 and R. Melson and H. Wolpe, 'Modernization and the Politics of Communalism: A Theoretical Perspective', *American Political Science Review* 64 (4) (Dec. 1970): 1126.
5. Melson and Wolpe, op. cit.
6. See especially Glazer and Moynihan, 'Introduction', op. cit.
7. Melson and Wolpe, op. cit., p. 1130.
8. J. Rothschild, 'Political Legitimacy in Contemporary Europe', this volume, ch. 3.
9. Brass, op. cit., p. 234.
10. Hah and Martin, op. cit., p. 385.
11. Brass, op. cit., p. 229.
12. Hah and Martin, op. cit., p. 378.
13. M. Hechter, *Internal Colonialism: The Celtic Fringe in British National Development, 1536-1966,* Berkeley: University of California Press, 1975.
14. Ibid., p. 9.
15. See E. Terray, 'L'Idée de nation et les transformations du capitalisme', *Les Temps Modernes* 29, (324-6) (August-September 1973): 507-8 and the article by P. Fougeyrollas, 'Question nationale et lutte des classes dans la France de demain' in the same issue of *Les Temps Modernes.* Also H. Giordan, 'Occitanie: Langue, Culture, Lutte des Classes', *L'Homme et la Societé* 28 (April-June 1973): 136.
These views are not shared by the spiritual descendants of Rosa Luxemburg, who warn that 'Toute idéologie nationale est la répétition d'un acte fondateur mythique, l'instauration de l'Etat capitaliste' (*La Taupe Bretonne,* cited in Terray, op. cit., p. 497).
16. Brass's term, op. cit., p. 226.
17. Melson and Wolpe, op. cit., p. 1116. The authors supply a small bibliography for this subject.
18. Ibid.
19. R. Dahrendorf, 'On the Origin of Inequality among Men', *Essays in the Theory of Society,* London: Routledge & Kegan Paul, 1968. Glazer and Moynihan develop their adaptation in their 'Introduction', op. cit., pp. 12ff.
20. G. De Vos, 'Ethnic Pluralism: Conflict and Accommodation', in G. De Vos and L. Romanucci-Ross (eds.), *Ethnic Identity: Cultural Continuities and Change,* Palo Alto, CA: Mayfield, 1975, p. 15.

De Vos goes on to emphasize the symbolic aspect of language as a distinctive rallying point even among groups, such as the Irish, of which the majority do not speak the national tongue. In our study, however, we will focus rather on the normative consequences of different languages commonly used by different ethnic groups.

21. E. Haugen, 'Instrumentalism in Language Planning', in J. Rubin and B. H. Jernudd (eds.), *Can Language Be Planned? Sociolinguistic Theory and Practice for Developing Nations*, Honolulu: University of Hawaii Press, 1971, p. 282.

22. V. Tauli, *Introduction to a Theory of Language Planning* Uppsala: University of Uppsala Press, 1968, p. 9. Cited in Haugen, op. cit. p. 282.

23. Cited in C.-F. Becquet, *Le Différand Wallo-Flamand* Nalinnes, Belgium: Institut Jules Destrée, 1972, vol. I, p. 28. My translation.

24. Ibid., p. 27. My translation.

25. E. Sapir, cited in B. L. Whorf, 'The Relation of Habitual Thought and Behavior to Language', in J. B. Carroll (ed.), *Language, Thought, and Reality: Selected Writings of Benjamin Lee Whorf*, Cambridge: MIT Press, 1956, p. 134.

26. H. Hörmann, *Psycholinguistics: An Introduction to Research and Theory*, trans. H. H. Stern, Berlin: Springer-Verlag, 1971, p. 310.

27. H. Hoijer, 'Cultural Implications of Some Navaho Linguistic Categories', *Language* 27 (1951): 111-20. This discussion is taken from P. Henle, 'Language, Thought, and Culture', in P. Henle (ed.), *Language, Thought, and Culture*, Ann Arbor: University of Michigan Press, 1958, pp. 22-23.

28. Whorf, op. cit.

29. A discussion of these experiments can be found in Hörmann, op. cit., pp. 316-19.

30. See Hörmann, op. cit., pp. 321-22.

31. G. A. Brutyan, 'A Marxist Evaluation of the Whorf Hypothesis', *ETC.: A Review of General Semantics* 19 (2) (July 1962): 220, 212.

32. Smith, op. cit., p. 143.

33. One might add here that religion can play a role similar to that of language in predisposing a believer to certain perceptions of reality, hence values, etc.

13

ITALY IN 1978:

'Where Everybody Governs, Does Anybody Govern?'

Sidney Tarrow
Cornell University, USA

In **September 1973**, Italian Communist leader Enrico Berlinguer launched what has come to be called the strategy of 'historic compromise'. By July 1977, the PCI had joined in a six-party accord that was accepted by the caretaker Christian Democratic government of Giulio Andreotti as the basis of a program with which to confront Italy's mounting crisis. Between these two events, Communist strength had steadily grown until the party held a virtual veto over all major legislation and controlled vitually every large city in the country. Italy, from struggling centrism in the early 1970s, had evolved in the space of four years to a situation in which the Communist party was the linchpin of future political change. The PCI is very suddenly in the system. To some, it *is* the system, or, at least, the system can survive only with its political sufferance. Italy, in the words of one pundit, has moved from the First to the Second Republic without benefit of constitutional convention, coup, revolution or changing of the palace guard.

But a number of questions can be posed of this apparently inexorable development of Italian politics in a leftward direction over the past five years. First, regarding the Berlinguer strategy: was it as new as some observers proclaimed, and how responsible would it be for the dramatic rise in PCI political fortunes between 1974 and 1976? Second, on the nature of PCI participation in the Italian state: is the system legitimizing the party, the party legitimizing the system, or is there a risk of de-legitimation for both in the current crisis? Finally, is Italy entering a profoundly new stage of social and political development combining mass mobilization with political consent, or is the current

This paper was submitted in June 1978 and discusses the situation in Italian politics up to that time.

arrangement no more than a picturesque Italian form of the 'waning of opposition' of parliamentary regimes that characterized some other European systems during earlier periods?

I. HISTORIC COMPROMISE, POLITICAL EVENTS AND PCI ADAPTATION

To begin with the PCI, Berlinguer's strategy in 1973 had three main themes: popular unity, defence against reaction, and the Catholic-Communist entente. 'Our essential task,' he wrote in September 1973, 'is to gather the great majority of people around a program of struggle for the reform and democratic renewal of the entire society and the state, and to develop around this program and this majority a spectrum of political forces capable of realizing it.' And, he continued, writing on the heels of the Chilean military coup: 'The unity of the parties of the workers and of the forces of the left is not a sufficient condition to guarantee the defense and progress of democracy where there exists a bloc of parties from the center to the extreme right of the political spectrum.' 'This is why', he concluded, 'we speak of the political need for collaboration and understanding between the popular forces of communist and socialist inspiration with those of catholic inspiration, as well as with those of other formations with a democratic orientation.'[1]

Hailed by the PCI, vilified by the extreme left and greeted with the utmost reserve by conservatives in the US and in Italy, the 'historic compromise', it was agreed by all, represented something profoundly new in the history of Western European Communism: the prospect of an alliance of popular forces that would extend from the proletarian left through the 'democratic' middle class to elements of the very core of capitalism, excluding only the forces of economic and political reaction. Coming as it did on the heels of the Chilean disaster and presaging the onset of 'Eurocommunism' in 1975 and 1976, the historic compromise seemed to augur a profound change for European politics as a whole, with a possible bloc of socialist and communist governments linked together from Portugal to Yugoslavia. 'Sellout', cried the extreme left! 'Trojan horse', warned the Italian right and Kissingerian foreign policy establishment! 'Neither', responded the PCI's powerful cultural and political machine, backing up its position in a spirited, but serious polemic with the non-Communist left, especially after the stunning Communist electoral successes of 1975 and 1976.[2]

On looking back at Berlinguer's article of 1973, one is forced to conclude that neither the right nor the left were justified in their accusations, although this hardly meant that the PCI's self-confident apology could be accepted at face value. The strategy set out in 1973 was neither entirely new, nor was it – on the face of it – responsible for the fundamental changes that have shaken Italian politics since 1973. But it was favored by these changes, and it contained within it the seeds either for a PCI strategy of mobilization with consent or for a more traditional one of consent replacing mobilization. It was the first alternative that PCI apologists would stress in selling the new strategy to their members. But it is the second, I shall argue, that has been favored by events since 1973.

1. How new was the *compromesso storico?* The events surrounding Berlinguer's announcement of his party's new strategy are too complex to recite here in detail.[3] But two in particular have often been mentioned. First, in economic trouble since 1969, Italy's plight was worsened by the Arab oil embargo and by the threefold increase in the price of energy that followed. Second, always politically sensitive to international currents, Berlinguer and the PCI were profoundly shaken by the failure of the Chilean revolution. The economic crisis, it could be argued, gave Berlinguer the opportunity to appeal to new sectors of the middle class and peasantry, while the Chilean coup demonstrated the inevitable isolation of popular front governments that were not, in some sense, 'covered' by conservative participation in their governments.

I do not think that so tactical an interpretation fits the facts of Berlinguer's initiative. Although both sets of conditioning factors were relevant, the Italian economy was *reviving* in September 1973 – a month, it will be recalled, before the Yom Kippur war – while the early lines of the new PCI strategy had already been sketched in Berlinguer's report to the Central Committee in July, fully two months before the Chilean coup.[4] The inflationary effect of the Arab oil embargo would hit Italy as hard as it did because Italian planners were *reflating* their economy from the 1971 recession in the fall of 1973, while the Chilean coup – like Khrushchev's secret speech at the 20th party congress[5] – was an unexpected international bombshell that helped PCI leaders to justify a policy decided upon earlier for domestic reasons.

In fact, as Berlinguer has never ceased to remind his countrymen, the *compromesso storico* followed in a direct line from the strategy set out by Togliatti in Salerno on his returning from Moscow in 1943, and from its renewal, after the worst years of the Cold War, at the PCI's eighth congress in 1956. In the same now-famous article in which he launched the new slogan, Berlinguer recalled that earlier 'turning point', and the need that the PCI had then felt to come to terms 'with all the historic forces — of socialist, catholic and other democratic inspiration — that were present on the scene of the country and struggled at our side for democracy, independence and unity.'[6]

The fulcrum of both Berlinguer's strategy in 1973, as in Togliatti's thirty years earlier, was the concept of alliances. Calling for a 'new party' in 1944, Togliatti had stressed the need for 'a national party'. 'When we speak of the nation', he observed, 'we mean the working class, the peasant class, the mass of the intellectuals, the mass of laborers of thought and action, white collar workers and professionals.'[7] How similar to Berlinguer's call, in 1973, for broad alliances, which he called 'the decisive problem of any revolution and of any revolutionary policy, and therefore decisive also for the affirmation of a democratic road.'[8]

But underlying the emphasis on alliances, Berlinguer continued to assume the need for a mobilization of the masses. Quoting the words of his predecessor, Luigi Longo, he wrote, 'To whoever asks himself . . . how will it be possible to gather enough forces to ward off reactionary attacks, we answer "by pushing to its utmost the organization, the mobilization and the combativeness of the people," and by "consolidating and extending every day the alliances of combat of the working class with the popular masses".'[9]

'Alliances of combat': to anyone familiar with the history of Communist alliance strategies, Berlinguer's term obviously referred to *social* alliances, and his goal of increasing the 'mobilization and combativeness of the people' was recognizable as a version of the earlier concept of the popular front from below. Thus the strategy in 1973 combined mobilization with alliances, popular pressure with elite accommodation, a hand outstretched to Catholics with more traditional reliance on leftwing unity.

2. But if the main lines of the new strategy were inherited from Togliatti and Longo, there was a greater emphasis on alliances, both social and political, as a direct outcome of the social and political

situation in 1973. Italy had just gone through an explosive period of labor unrest and a round of large wage and fringe benefit increases that had strained industry's competitive position and given the workers a taste for greater social gains. This took the form of a 'strategy of reforms' put forward independently of the PCI by the now-closely cooperating national trade union confederations.[10] The reaction from the right was both inevitable and sharp: with a revolt of the subaltern classes in the South which could degenerate, as in Reggio Calabria in 1970, in a reactionary direction; a middle class backlash against the large wage increases granted to organized labor; and a dramatic increase in the neo-fascist vote in the elections of 1972.

It was to these events that Berlinguer was reacting in September 1973. For example, his emphasis on alliances was directed clearly against the pretensions of the trade unions to set out a strategy of reforms independent of the PCI. He observes: 'The [unions] strategy of reforms can . . . only be affirmed and advanced if it is supported by a strategy of alliances.'[11] His appeal to the middle class was similarly affected by fear of the growing polarization of Italian society. Thus Berlinguer downplayed class altogether. 'We must', he maintained, 'include in a well-defined spectrum of alliances not only social figures and well-defined economic categories, but entire groups of the population, social forces *not classifiable as classes*' [emphasis added].[12] Finally, the appeal to the Catholics had to be seen in the context of a situation of rising neo-fascist strength in which the Catholic middle class, never wholly won over to parliamentary democracy, might once more fall for the appeals of reaction, as it had in 1922.

This was the element in Berlinguer's strategy — the hand outstretched to the ruling Christian Democracy — that has received most attention. But from a closer reading of the text, it seems to have been less central to his intentions in 1973 than it would become in later practice. First, only a short section of his very long article was dedicated to the PCI's relations with Catholics. Second, the DC was named as only one of the *three* elements in the Catholic world — the Church and catholic social organizations were the others — demanding the PCI's attention. Third, and most important, the term 'historic compromise', introduced only in the last sentence of the article, did *not* refer only to the DC, but to an alliance 'among the forces that gather together and represent the great majority of the Italian people.'[13] The appeal to the DC was only one element in a three-pronged strategy consisting of social alliances, anti-fascist defense, and social and political dialogue with Italian Catholicism.

It was events after 1973 that would lead the PCI's relations with the DC to emerge at the center of political debate and, eventually, at the core of the PCI's strategy. Four of these appear to have played a contributory role. First, the DC lost heavily in the divorce referendum of 1974, convincing even the PCI, which had long been convinced of Italy's Catholic soul, that much of the country had a secular mind. Second, the high level of mass mobilization of the 1969-73 period quickly subsided as the post-1973 economic crisis set in, turning PCI attention from social to political alliances and from mass mobilization to elite politics. Third, the profound moral crisis already evident in the Catholic world was capped by a series of scandals which would eventually touch some of the DCs highest leaders.[14] Finally, no party in power for thirty years could have escaped responsibility for Italy's economic crisis, and the DC, with its massive system of state patronage, was particularly susceptible to blame.

These events left the DC, especially after its electoral defeats of 1974 and 1975, more open to PCI pressure for collaboration than Berlinguer could have imagined in 1973. They thus led the PCI to emphasize the *political* leg of its strategy — a broad non-ideological elite coalition — and to downplay the aspects of social alliance-building and mass mobilization that had also been evident in the 1973 line. By the time the left crystallized its gains in the legislative elections of 1976 — making it impossible for the DC to govern any longer without Communist abstention — the die was already cast. Berlinguer and his party were now no longer ready for a strategy of mobilization, even though some of the PCI's biggest gains had been in the working class neighborhoods of Italy's northern cities.[15] Thus the party would *never seriously consider* the alternative of a government of the left in 1976, although a majority of the Socialists favored one at the time.

The historic compromise, a strategy of social alliances, mass mobilization and of dialogue with Catholicism at *all* levels of Italian society, had moved, through the impact of events, towards the practice of political alliances, to an absence of mass mobilization, and to an entente with the Christian Democracy at the summit. Our first question can now be answered; instead of a new political strategy, the historic compromise was an extension of an old one, Togliatti's *Via italiana al socialismo*. The dramatic increase in PCI strength after 1973 was not the fruit of the new strategy; it was rather the result of events in the system and in the international environment. And rather than shaping these events, the party's strategy was shaped by them, with consequences that are only now becoming clear.

II. LEGITIMATION, THE PCI
AND THE ITALIAN SYSTEM

How to combine combativeness with alliances, mobilization with consent, social alliances from below with a broadened political coalition at the top? To these old dilemmas in PCI strategy was added another as the country plunged into a spiral of recession, unemployment, terror on the extremes and crisis in the center; how could the PCI insert itself into the *governing* process — a necessity that all the major parties now appeared to accept — without assuming responsibility for the economic crisis, for a crumbling state, and for the hard policy choices needed to support it? And how could the party exercise its increased political weight without losing support from the workers, peasants and radical intellectuals who constituted the core of its political base?

Mirror-image problems affected the DC and the system of state-financed clientelism it had built up over the past thirty years. How could a party that governed through a broad coalition for patronage under a hard veneer of anti-Communism with a substratum of popular Catholicism afford to bring the PCI into a governing coalition without sacrificing its claim to govern or its control over state patronage? The legitimacy of the DC's system — in the intensifying climate of economic crisis, moral decline and physical insecurity of 1976 and 1977 — would be threatened by the one political solution that would give the DC votes with which to govern — bringing the Communists into the coalition. The DC could not govern without the Communists, and it would not govern with them.

Two events made a provisional solution to this dilemma possible. First, the political power of the center-right majority in the DC was temporarily broken by the party's electoral reversals, and a new left-center coalition took over within the party under the leadership of Zaccagnini and Moro. Second, the PCI appeared willing to compromise its more extreme demands for a share of power in return for symbolic conquests like the election of Communist Pietro Ingrao as President of the Chamber of Deputies and the allocation of a number of parliamentary committee chairmanships to Communist legislators. Most important, the PCI was willing to turn its propaganda fire away from the DC in exchange for recognized consultation on major policy issues and administrative appointments.

The political solution appeared in three stages: first, in a 'government of abstentions' in 1976 led by Christian Democrat Giulio Andreotti, a man with impeccable anti-Communist credentials, whose major role was to stop the erosion of Christian Democratic power while the other parties were binding their wounds and the Communists were consolidating their gains; second, the six-party accord, hammered out in June and July, 1977 in relative secrecy by the party secretaries, and adopted 'independently' by the Andreotti government as its program. The latter had been passed sequentially, beginning with the least controversial plank — fighting terrorism — and passing gradually through more controversial issues like nuclear energy to the linchpin of the program — a policy of austerity and productivity which still remained to be carried out in mid-1978. Third, the PCI was brought explicitly into the majority — but not into the government — in early 1978 in a compromise worked out under the auspices of master negotiator Aldo Moro, President of the DC. The PCI cooperated in Parliament, urged the workers to make greater compromises and, through a 'medium-term program', emphasized its desire to streamline and modernize — but hardly liquidate — the capitalist system.[16]

The DC had solved its legitimacy problem — at least temporarily — by quieting the Communist fox while avoiding the charge of allowing it into the Catholic henhouse. It was true that Communist leaders now had to be consulted on major appointments; that they demanded action on social legislation that might cause the government political problems, such as a reform of the country's antiquated rent law; and that they continued to consolidate their gains in Parliament and in the local and regional governments they had won in 1975. But DC leaders could hope that the reviving economy, fueled by the wage discipline that the Communists would force upon trade union colleagues, would redound to the government's credit, and that the Communists — long regarded as the most efficient managers in Italy — would be revealed as mere mortals, trying to govern ungovernable cities like Rome and Naples and struggling to fashion complex legislation to cut through the underbrush of the country's bureaucracy. Besides, PCI pressure could be resisted as long as the DC held on tight to the major ministries and para-state holding companies.

The result was that the legitimacy problem was now greater for the

Communists than for the DC! For the arrangements of 1977-78, while they added up to much more than a backroom political deal, reflected not the original goals of Berlinguer's *compromesso storico*, but the evolution of those goals in a far more moderate direction in response to the events of the years 1974 through 1977. The Communists may be close to a hand on power, but the working class is not. On the contrary, the six-party accord of July 1977 was developed in a political vacuum by the party secretaries and implemented by a Christian Democratic government which consulted its allies in secret and called its relation-ship to the Communists a *confronto* and not a coalition. As for the mobilization of the masses and the social alliances projected by Berlinguer in 1973, they have taken second place to the PCI's con-solidation of institutional positions won since 1975. There was little sign in 1978 of that combination of alliances and combat − in Berlin-guer's curious terminology of 1973, 'alliances of combat' − that could augur an aggressive social and political strategy at the summit and the base of the political system.

This is the heart of the PCI's problem of legitimacy. Students of Italian politics have focussed recently on the 'legitimation' of the Communist party vis-a-vis non-Communist opinion, but there is also a threat of undermining the party's legitimacy among its traditional voters, militants and intellectuals. By the fall of 1977, evidence began to accummulate that all was not well inside the PCI's ranks. Member-ship had gone down in the FGCI, the young Communist league; several local elections were lost, though probably for localistic reasons; federa-tion secretaries complained of a widespread unease in the party's ranks; and a poll of party members showed that while a large majority approved of Berlinguer's policies, over 30 percent thought the PCI stood to lose the most from the *accordo a 6*. The mood in the party was summed up by venerable party leader Giorgio Amendola, who remarked that though he saw no evidence of *dissenso* in the party, there was little sign of *consenso* either!

It was these internal strains − rather than the crisis in the country − that led Berlinguer to demand Communist entry into the majority in early 1978. If all he could show for the party's electoral gains after two years of negotiations with the DC was semi-clandestine consultation on policy, the restlessness at the base would turn rapidly into dissent. Already in late 1977 there were signs of revolt when CGIL head Luciano Lama was literally driven off a platform in Rome and the so-called *autonomi* could assemble a massive demonstration against the party in its citadel, Bologna. If Berlinguer had not acted in early 1978, his control over the base might have been effectively challenged.

But what did the PCI get out of its closer relationship with the DC in February 1978? But for a few minor changes, the Andreotti government that was installed at that time was exactly the same one that Berlinguer had criticized as do-nothing for the past three months! The *non*-change in government revealed a weakness in the PCI's basic strategy: in exchange for legitimation, it was willing to cede continuing policy control to the DC, which uses it to continue its old way of doing business. This dilemma, which had already appeared in negotiations over the new regional law,[17] gave the parties to the immediate right and left of the PCI support for their position that the communists were selling out their reform program in exchange for a finger on the levers of power. It was also accompanied by an intensification of the threats to the survival of the state represented by the extremist groups of left and right and particularly by the *brigate rosse*.

It was no accident that the kidnapping of Aldo Moro occurred in March 1978, nor that the man chosen for assassination was the architect of the PCI-DC entente. The tragedy of his death was felt by the Communists for two reasons; first, there was no visible Christian Democratic leader who could take his place in fashioning the DC side of the historic compromise; second, the climate of tension generated in the country forced the PCI to come down even harder on the side of defense of the state and repression of extremism than it had done in the past. Even the trade unions were swept up in a campaign against terrorism when the extremists demonstrated their power to hit the productive process by destroying a shipment of cars from the Alfa Romeo plant. But 'revolutionary vigilence' was a slogan that had mixed connotations for a working class movement that had lived through the rigors of stalinism, fascism, de-stalinization and de-fascistization.

The PCI even turned nasty against those of its own intellectuals who would not vocally condemn extremism of every kind, and doubly so against former-Communist intellectuals like Rossana Rossanda, who — appalled by the red brigades' depredations — admitted nonetheless that she heard in their slogans the echoes of words remembered from 'a family album'. Dissenters from the PCI's line of 'defense of the democratic state' could still have letters published in party journals, but the heavy air of conformity began to weigh on the conscience of the Left. When the small parties of the Left found themselves once voting on the same side in Parliament as the fascist party, they were castigated by the

PCI as part of a 'libertarian-fascist' opposition.

It is easy to counter the charge of PCI conformism by saying that only a small group of intellectuals and middle class 'democrats' are likely to be offended by it, as against the vast mass of the party's following. But when the party, at the same time, embraces its traditional enemy, the DC, and demands of the workers discipline, productivity and wage restraint, then what is left to differentiate it from the DC, in defense of the state, and from the non-communist left in social policy? With only a little exaggeration, it can be maintained that the PCI's policy on public order has played into the hands of the Christian Democrats while its social and economic policy has given an electoral advantage to the non-Communist left.

Such an interpretation, which the Communists would have denounced as demagogic in the past, begins to have some support since the partial local and provincial elections of May 1978. Coming on the heels of Moro's assassination, the DC could not fail to gain votes from the upsurge of public sympathy for the slain leader's family and ideology. But given the ruling party's denunciation by his family for refusing to deal with the kidnappers and the government's appalling inefficiency in carrying out the investigation, massive gains could not have been predicted on the basis of Moro's death alone. But the DC gained fully 5 percent over the previous local elections, 6.7 percent over the regional elections of 1975 and 3.6 percent over the legislative elections of 1976 in the communes with over 5,000 population in which local elections were held in May 1978. The DC made its greatest gains in the South and in the Islands – where the 'Moro factor' may have played a great role – but made only moderate gains in the Catholic Veneto – where it might have been expected to have been greater – and made big gains in progressive Liguria and Emilia-Romagna, heartland of the PCI's subculture.[18]

It was not just the 'party of order' that won more votes in these partial elections; the Socialist Party made a remarkable recovery too, with 13.3 percent of the vote, compared to its low point in the 1976 legislative elections, where it had sunk to 9.2 percent of the vote in the communes in which elections were held in 1978. The PSI recovered a part of the ground it had lost to the Communists in the South and the Islands, and even gained with respect to its 1976 vote in the Center-North. The PCI lost fully 9 percent compared to its performance in 1976 in the communes above 5,000 inhabitants in which elections were held in 1978, gaining ever so slightly over its 1972 peformance.

Proportionally, the biggest losers in the 1978 elections were the small parties (except for the Republicans), especially the Liberals, neo-Fascists and Social Democrats, who lost, in total, one-third of their support. But psychologically, the biggest loser was the PCI and its strategy of collaboration. In some ways the most dramatic defeat was a victory: the strengthening of the leftwing governing coalition in the city of Pavia, especially its Socialist component, which allowed the PSI mayor to claim the results as a victory for the strategy the PCI had rejected in 1976:*l'alternativa.*

The ink was barely dry on these electoral results when the PCI was thrown into another difficult fight: the defense of the tough new law-and-order law challenged by the dissident Left in a referendum held in mid-June. The party's dilemma was that, while in opposition, it had *opposed* such a law as being overly repressive; now, in the majority, it was forced to defend it as essential for the defense of the republican constitution. A good deal of political courage was required to defend such a switch in the face of the party's recent electoral defeat, but perhaps even greater courage would have been required to have joined its opponents, thereby contradicting its recent support of law and order.

An answer can now be hazarded to our second question: 'is the PCI legitimizing the system or the system legitimizing the party, or is there a risk of de-legitimation for both?' The DC's legitimacy had clearly survived its low point in 1974-75 by the end of 1977, and the Berlinguer demand for a stronger PCI role in government was intended to challenge it before it had become to strong to challenge. The non-change in the Andreotti government that followed, but even more so the Moro affair and the May 1978 partial elections, showed that the ruling party could co-opt the PCI into the government without being swallowed up in the process. The PCI's legitimacy among its working class clientle will probably survive the changes in its image and allies, but its adoption of a policy of order, austerity and collaboration has nibbled away at its electorate, challenged its 'liberal' image and given its competitors on the Left a new lease of life.

But what of the survival of the Italian political system itself as a more-or-less recognizable variant of Western parliamentary democracy? Is Italy moving, as Di Palma provocatively asks, from 'uncertain compromise' to 'historic compromise?' Or has it merely moved from one uncertain compromise to another? The answers to these questions must be most tentative of all, and will depend on the nature of the arrangements worked out at the summit and the base of the political system.

III. HISTORIC COMPROMISE OR
WANING OF OPPOSITION

What are these arrangements? A classical Italian *connubio*, or coming together at the center for a mere division of the spoils? A realization of the *compromesso storico* strategy boldly set out by Berlinguer in 1973? Or the replacement of a system of government versus opposition by a structured cartel arrangement for sharing power between a Marxist left and Catholic center-right that continue to maintain their separate identities? A classical *connubio* would erode the policy differences between left and right, while an implementation of the historic compromise would be accompanied by an aggressive PCI strategy at the summit and the base, and the third alternative − what I will call, with some hesitation, a 'waning of opposition' − would emphasize power sharing at the summit at the cost of both mobilization and social alliances at the base through a well-oiled system of *proporz* in the allocation of resources and maintaining each party's control over its respective subculture.[20]

Students of Italian history will not recognize a classical *connubio* in Italy's current governing arrangements. The nineteenth century *connubio* was the co-optation of a portion of the opposition by a strong national leader − a Cavour or Depretis − in the context of a weak party system and a narrow electorate. The current accord includes virtually the entire spectrum of political elites in the context of an organized party system and of a highly mobilized electorate. Besides, the policy differences between left and right are *not* eroding. The typical PCI leader still seems to be as much a policy radical as he was when Robert Putnam analyzed Communist parliamentarians in the late 1960s,[21] while Christian Democratic politicians − always programmatically diverse − seem to have as much policy resistance to the Communists as when they governed hegemonically.[22]

But the current arrangement does not appear to fulfill the goals of Berlinguer's *compromesso storico* either. For it leaves the working class carefully insulated from the governing process and its programmatic core − the six-party accord − was developed in a political vacuum and is being implemented by a Christian Democratic *monocolore* government that consults its allies in secret and calls its agreement with the Communists a *confronto* and not a coalition. As for the other aspects of the Berlinguer strategy — social alliances and mass mobilization — they have received mainly lip service as party leaders concentrate on consolidating the institutional gains made since 1975. There is certainly little evidence of that combination of alliances and combat that augured an aggressive strategy both at the summit and at the base of the political system in 1973.

Even Berlinguer's approach to the Catholics — as revealed in his October 1977 answer to the letter of the Bishop of Ivrea — shows a preference for incorporating existing Catholic social and educational institutions within the Italian state over secularizing the state and dealing at the base with the forces of popular Catholicism. It is a strange version of mass mobilization and social alliances that is realized through the absorption of the traditional structures of Catholic charity within the secular state! The PCI obviously prefers a deal with the Vatican to the patient and conflictual task of extending its hegemony to the Catholic masses.

What we see in Italy in 1978 is a progressive decline of opposition — not the decline of *the* opposition, for the PCI is stronger than ever organizationally — but a decline in the level of dialogue, both between government and opposition and between the summit and the base, that is the hallmark of classical parliamentary democracy. Decisions are made behind closed doors and only publicly ratified. Parliament has become a rubber stamp for the party secretaries and the government a technical instrument for implementing decisions arrived at elsewhere. One price of this new reconciliation at the summit of the political system has been the stultification of the lively process of political exchange at the periphery which has been one of the hallmarks of the Italian system since World War Two.[23] Another, probably more serious, is the sense of many Italians, rightly or wrongly, that where everybody governs, nobody governs. A third is the danger to representative government itself.

In many of its particulars, in fact, the arrangement worked out in Italy in 1978 resembled the waning of opposition in parliamentary regimes that made its appearance in the early 1950s in central Europe. Decisions made in secret by conclaves of party leaders; the reduction of parliamentary power; the reinforcement of the parties' organizational control; the dampening of policy initiative at the base; policymaking by proportional allocation of resources; even an emphasis on policy issues that unite, rather than divide, the parties to the agreement. This does not mean that the parties agree on all issues. There is room for the exploitation of differences that do not threaten programmatic agreements (such as the vote on abortion in May 1978). Even this characteristic of the Italian scene reminds one of the waning of opposition in past wartime or crisis situations elsewhere in Europe.

But there are differences, and these make the probability of a permanent cartel solution in Italy extremely tenuous. Consider the history of 'grand coalition' politics in Austria, from which Kirschheimer first derived the concept of waning of opposition. (1) There was a strong party system, with demands from the periphery limited and the base of each party's organization under tight control from the summit. (2) There were never more than two parties involved, thus lowering the possibilities for friction and facilitating the proportional allocation of policy resources. (3) There was an expanding economy, thus allowing some economic margin for the inevitable inflation in public spending that follows from policy *proporz*. (4) There was no major extra-parliamentary opposition, the extreme nationalist fringe having been silenced by the collapse of the Third Reich. (5) There was a propitious international environment, with the Russians and Americans agreeing to keep their hands off Vienna as long as it followed a policy of formal neutrality. (6) Neither party to the agreement had any need to prove its legitimacy to govern to the other or to the electorate as a whole and, therefore, neither had much to fear from revolts within its ranks on the part of militants who saw themselves as the guardians of orthodoxy.

Let us look at Italy in 1978 in the light of this earlier experience:

(1) The party organizations are strong, but there is considerable factionalism within the major parties, especially the DC, and the control of each party's leadership over the base cannot be assumed, especially in the light of the crisis of various sectors of each's support base (e.g. the unemployed and young people for the PCI, farmers and small business for the DC). In the latter party, a dynamic young conservative faction may be encouraged by the party's recent success in local elections to move back to a form of 'anti-red' propaganda that lumps together PCI and *brigate rosse*.

(2) A six-party accord (or five-party, since the Liberals' defection in February, 1978) differs from a two-party cartel in important ways, first because the temptation is great for the smaller parties to gain marginal advantage by opting out and, second, because there are risks of friction in the delicate allocation of resources with so many parties to be

satisfied. The PSI's 1978 national conference in Turin showed how skilled leadership could differentiate between current and conditional support for the coalition and permanent, enthusiastic support, seizing on the new embrace between Communists and Catholics to establish independent political space for itself. The 1978 election results will encourage this line.

(3) Even if the minor parties can be assuaged, policy allocation through *proporz* is a delicate operation, especially when structural choices about reviving a flagging economy come up. Even in normal times, policy allocation by proportional representation is inflationary, which is exactly what the Italian economy cannot stand. Yet without proportional allocation of resources, neither the minor parties nor the PCI may be able to support the government for long.

(4) There is an extra-parliamentary opposition that has made a mockery of public security by walking off in broad daylight with one of the country's foremost leaders and by forcing him to attack his colleagues in the press before being disposed of. The 'legal' extra-parliamentary opposition has been marginalized by these traumatic events; but the reaction in the country shows that there is an 'extra-governmental' opposition that will not be reduced so easily by PCI accusations of demagogy. Finally, there is an 'extra-political' force in the country — the Vatican — whose moral authority re-emerged powerfully during the Moro affair, with power that can be held in reserve and be mobilized against a DC that tries to give away its privileges.

(5) The international system of which Italy is a part still feels itself threatened by PCI presence in the circles of power, and possesses important financial and propaganda resources that could be imposed at virtually any time. Although the USSR is now more tranquil than in the past with the PCI's line — a mixed blessing — its current aggressive international posture cannot help the Italian communists, nor can the clamorous change in French communist strategy since 1977. Indeed, instead of a southern European wave of the future, Eurocommunism is looking more and more like a Spanish-Italian fringe phenomenon, with the PCI well in the rear of its more adventurous Spanish communist colleagues.

(6) To many, the main difference between what we see in Italy in 1978 and the 'cartel governments' of the 1950s and 1960s in central Europe is the Communists. The PCI, it is argued, is inherently different from the social democratic parties that participated in these earlier coalitional experiments. But history is not always determining; the very

Social-Democrats sitting complacently in power in Bonn and elsewhere now were once feared with the same certainty reserved for the Communists in Italy.

I think the 'leigitimacy' problem of the PCI is another: that it is constantly torn between demonstrating its legitimacy and representing the interests of its clientele, and lacks the cultural hegemony over its followers that will allow it to do both at once. To explain; every party has problems of reconciling the support of its mass base with the legitimacy of exercising power. There are two solutions to the problem: repression and legitimation. The PCI, it seems clear to all except its most ardent opponents, has chosen the latter path. But three factors limit the PCI's ability to span the contradictions between support and legitimacy through hegemony. First, its support base is remarkably diverse, especially since 1975; second, legitimacy is much harder to achieve in coalition with the DC than it appeared to PCI leaders to be a few years ago; third, the hegemony necessary to bridge the gap depends upon a comprehensible and coherent ideology of power and social change, and cannot be based on the pot pourri of slogans, catch-phrases and mutually contradictory polarities that the PCI has substituted for programs over the past few years.

Berlinguer would come to power on the basis of a system of 'alliances of combat'; the Italian crisis will be solved by a process of 'transformative reconstruction'; extreme leftists who cry neither with the state nor with the red brigades are 'objectively taking the side of terrorism'. Hegemony will never be built on such contradictions, at least not as long as there are political opponents capable of pointing them out. There remains the possibility — not to be discounted in the surge of conformism, 'vigilance' and repression of extreme left groups following the Moro affair — that the PCI's 'defense of the republican consitution' will turn into something very different.

Thus I do not think that Italy in 1978 reflects the coming of the historic compromise, either in the form of true government by cartel or in the hegemonic form outlined by some observers.[24] In an emergency situation, a floundering, but still dominant, moderate party succeeded in coopting the support of a dynamic and flexible opposition party to keep the economic wolves at bay and preserve its power. A share of this power, probably an important one, has been given up, perhaps forever. (If nothing else, the DC will never again be able to shrug off opposition by claiming that the Communists are an 'unacceptable' party of government).[25] But the costs to the Communists have also been great, both

internally – in the restlessness at the base – and externally – in its loss
of electoral support, however partial or temporary were the 1978
results.

There are strains in the relations between the actors as well, in the
fear of the DC that its control of the state would crumble if the PCI
were allowed too firm a hand on the controls, of the Communists that
they would lose face by too direct a governing responsibility, and by
the minor parties that they would be squeezed out by too close an
embrace between the two giants. Not to mention the restraint represented by the tremendous power of the United States and other
conservative countries to act if the communists are given too much
power.

There are also dangers in the continuation of the relationship
beyond the Presidential elections in 1979. Though the economy has
shown a mini-revival, unemployment, investment, reconversion all
remain to be dealt with. The reform of local governmental finance is
still on the agenda and the nationalized industries continue to be a
drain on the treasury. More important are the political dangers. It is
true that the DC in power unchecked would govern the state poorly,
and that the PCI represents a prod in the direction of reform But its
marginal position between government and opposition has turned the
PCI into a party of public order and ideological conformism, with all
the dangers to democracy that this represents. Finally, with the PCI on
the edge of the state, who governs the opposition? The experience of
1978 shows a definite correlation between the Communists' move to
the right and the intensification of political terror. And where terror
governs the opposition, government becomes a beseiged citadel which,
in fighting for its life, may take the essentials of democratic government
along with it.

NOTES

1. These quotations are all from Berlinguer's key *Rinascita* article, 'Rifles-
sioni sull'Italia dopo i fatti del Cile', 28 September, 5 October and 9 October
1973, republished in his *La 'Questione' Comunista; 1969-1975*, Vol. 2, Antonio
Tatò (ed.), (Rome: Editore Riuniti, 1975), pp. 621, 633-34.

2. See the arguments by Communists and non-Communists in 'Il marxismo e lo Stato: il dibattito aperto nella sinistra italiana sulle tesi di Norberto Bobbio', special issue of *Mondoperaio* 6 (June 1976).

3. See Stephen Hellman's contribution to *The Elections in Italy, 1976* (Washington D.C.: American Enterprise Institute, 1978) for an excellent discussion of the development of PCI strategy during these years.

4. Berlinguer, op.cit., pp. 592-608.

5. See Donald Blackmer's argument to this effect about Togliatti's use of Khrushchev's reforms to justify a largely-unrelated policy breakthrough in PCI domestic strategy in his *Unity in Diversity* (Cambridge: MIT, 1967).

6. Ibid., p. 619.

7. Palmiro Togliatti, *Il Partito* (Roma: Editore Riuniti, 1964), pp. 69-70.

8. Berlinguer, op.cit., pp. 628-29.

9. Ibid., p. 622, quoting Luigi Longo from an uncited source.

10. For a summary, see Peter Weitz's 'The CGIL and the PCI: From Subordination to Independent Political Force', in Donald L. M. Blackmer and Sidney Tarrow (eds.), *Communism in Italy and France* (Princeton: Princeton University Press, 1975, 1977), Chapter 14.

11. Berlinguer, op.cit., pp. 630-31.

12. Ibid., pp. 629-31.

13. Ibid., p. 639.

14. Gianfranco Pasquino, 'Crisi della DC e evoluzione del sistema politico', *Rivista Italiana di Scienza Politica* 5 (December 1975), pp. 443-72.

15. I am grateful to Stephen Hellman for sharing with me the preliminary results of his analysis of the 1976 elections.

16. See *Rinascita,* September and October 1977, for the discussion of this program.

17. For a brief summary, see my 'Regional Autonomy in Italy and France: Lessons for Spain?' I.P.S.A. Roundtable Conference on the Politics of Mediterranean Europe, Athens, Greece, 29 May – 1 June 1978. The PCI in this case compromised its established support for regional devolution so as to protect the programmatic accord, leaving the PSI in opposition.

18. Celso Ghini, 'Analisi del primo voto dopo il 16 marzo', *Rinascita* 19 maggio, 1978, p. 3.

19. Ibid. By some ingenious presentation of data, Ghini leaves the impression that the bulk of DC gains came from Liberal, Social Democratic and neo-Fascist losses, which would have been difficult, given that the DC gained 9 percent while the others' total losses equalled 5 percent!

20. In Otto Kirchheimer, 'The Waning of Opposition in Parliamentary Regimes', *Social Research* 23 (Summer 1957), pp. 127-56; republished in part in *European Politics: A Reader*, Mattei Dogan and Richard Rose (eds.), (Boston: Little Brown, 1971), pp. 280-95.

21. Robert Putnam, 'The Italian Communist Politician', in Blackmer and Tarrow, op.cit., chapter 5.

22. Gianfranco Pasquino, 'Recenti trasformazioni nel sistema di potere della Democrazia cristiana', in Graziano and Tarrow (eds.), *La crisi italiana* (Turin: Einaudi, 1979).

23. See my *Between Center and Periphery: Grassroots Politicians in Italy and France* (New Haven: Yale University Press, 1977), chapters 6 and 8.

24. For a balanced inquiry into the alternatives open to the party in a hypothetical future, see Peter Lange's 'PCI e possibili esiti della crisi italiana', in Graziano and Tarrow (eds.), *La Crisi Italiana*. For Luigi Graziano's stimulating attempt to place the historic compromise in the theory of comparative party systems, see his 'Compromesso storico e democrazia consociativa: verso una "nuova democrazia" ', ibid.

25. PCI leaders correctly stress the importance of the dropping of this bar for the future.

14

PATTERNS OF CHANGING SUPPORT FOR CHRISTIAN DEMOCRACY IN ITALY: 1946-1976

Paolo A. Farneti
University of Turin, Italy

The second early elections in the history of postwar Italy, those of 20 June 1976, were followed with suspense by political observers both within and outside the country. These elections were one year after the elections for renewal of the regional assemblies (15 June 1975), in which Christian Democracy suffered a loss of about 4 percent of its support in comparison with both the regional elections of 1970 and the Parliamentary elections of 1972. On 15 June 1975, the Communist Party gained almost 6 percent of votes when compared with the regional elections of 1970, and about 7 percent when compared with the votes gathered in May 1972.

The results of the election of June 1976 were the following: the Communist Party (PCI) reached 34.4 percent of votes for the Chamber of Deputies and 33.8 percent for the Senate; Christian Democracy (DC) reached 38.7 percent of votes for the Chamber of Deputies and 38.9 percent for the Senate.[1] The PCI had reached a level of support that was sufficient grounds for a plausible claim at sharing power. The DC had recovered from a bad loss and remained the major party of the Italian political alignment.

The minor parties of the center — the Liberals (PLI), Republicans (PRI) and Social Democrats (PSDI) — had suffered a great loss of votes that had responded to the emergency appeal of the DC. Therefore no center coalition was numerically or politically feasible. The Socialists (PSI) had remained at the 9 percent level, whereas according to pre-electoral forecasts the PSI should have reached the respectable size of 14 percent. No center-left government was politically feasible with a frustrated Socialist party.

The *Catholic tradition*, represented by the DC, has kept its major position in the political alignment, and the *Socialist tradition*, now clearly monopolized by the PCI, has been slowly but constantly advancing. Differently from both of these, the *Lay, Liberal tradition* represented by the center parties and also by the PSI, has suffered from continual setbacks since 1948. The last setback was the electoral result of 1976. The DC had held out, thanks to the voters that had abandoned the lay parties, and limited the defections of the dissenting Catholics in favor of the opposition. The PCI had increased its votes thanks to the continuous defections from the area of the lay Liberal left and primarily from the PSI. The two traditional political cultures of Italian history had come to a confrontation. Both had attracted the new enfranchised voters, although the majority had turned to the Left.[2] The Liberal tradition, on the other hand, had failed even in appealing to the younger generations.

What is this 'Catholic tradition'? What made the DC hold out, adapting to a new, more challenging situation in which the PCI, abandoning a great deal of Leninist verbiage, had become a dangerous pole of attraction for many non-Communist voters? The Catholic tradition has undergone remarkable changes during the last thirty years. It seems to me that these changes converge in making the DC a *conservative mass-party*, that maintains confessional reference grounds especially during major crises of legitimacy, but which is essentially a 'Sammelpartei' oriented towards secularization.

This paper deals with the changes in support for Christian Democracy by the Catholic tradition. First, we draw an outline of the indicators used to analyze the process of secularization and adaptation of the DC electorate as a part of the Catholic tradition. Then we will analyze the features of the DC electorate, as can be inferred from public opinion data gathered by several agencies during the last thirty years. In doing this we want to point out any eventual changes in the direction of secularization of the Catholic tradition and transformation of the DC into a conservative mass party. Finally, within the same conceptual framework we will analyze the changes which occurred in the crucial 1972-76 period. Greater changeability of the electorate seems to be the result of a process that was at work during all the previous thirty years. But it was accelerated by three main factors: the change in PCI and DC party strategy; the growing political autonomy of women voters; and the input into the political arena of 18 to 21-year-olds.

This is true for the Catholic tradition and its political representative, the DC; it is also true for the Socialist tradition and the PCI. The PCI started as a Leninist mass party, with some modifications due to the intelligent and prudent leadership of Togliatti. It then moved from the model of the revolutionary 'ghetto-partei' to the model of the 'multi-class' party led by intellectuals, oriented towards gaining the electoral majority and some 'national' autonomy from the USSR. The choice of electoral consensus which was made by the PCI in 1946-48, instead of the choice of a take-over of power consequent to a crisis situation, marked the first basic differences between the PCI and other more 'Stalinist' parties in continental Europe. The slow but constant moving farther away from the slogan of 'Proletarian Internationalism' (and − to some extent − from the USSR's leadership) marked the second important 'difference' of the PCI, representing a secularization of the Socialist, 'Massimalista' tradition of the early Twenties.

Have these two traditions, with all these changes, reached a point where they can cooperate according to a 'consociational' model? Or are they rather moving towards a model of alternation in power according to the characteristics of parliamentary democracy? The two Catholic and Socialist traditions cannot be compared with the 'blocs' that make up the consociational model of Dutch politics.[3] The latter is based on a possibility of non-interference within the blocs, and of course of non-osmosis of votes. This is far from being the Italian case, in which there is both distrust of eventual alliances of one's own party with other parties and osmosis of votes from one party to the other, often as a consequence of durable party alliances. This was the case of the relationship between the DC and the center parties. To some extent it ws also the case of the relationship between the PSI and the DC, during and after the center-Left governments, and between the PSI and the PCI after the split of the PSIUP from the PSI in 1963. Of course intra-tradition osmosis of votes is by far higher than inter-tradition osmosis, but there has been some of the latter between the DC and the PCI, which might increase after an eventual 'historical compromise'.

This leads us to what I would call the *Italian paradox* of today. On one side, as we will see later in more detail, the two historical and political traditions, the Catholic and the Socio-communist, have undergone a serious process of secularization. On the other side this means a lessened capacity of the political parties representing these traditions (or their functional equivalents, such as the Catholic organizations in the case of Christian Democracy) to be gatekeepers of political values and guardians of votes. The paradox is that, the moment the two traditions are more secularized, and therefore more capable of political coalitions and alliances, they are also more vulnerable to each other and therefore less disposed to such alliances and coalitions.

AN OUTLINE FOR ANALYZING THE SECULARIZATION PROCESS OF A POLITICAL TRADITION

The secularization process we are concerned with here has to do with *the ways* in which a given sector of the population *legitimizes* the role of a political party. Secularization appears to be a complex process through which certain values, which once were dominant, become less important (although they rarely disappear completely). At the same time other values which once were unimportant become leading and decisive. In this case the basic principle of loyalty towards a political party becomes the leading principle of adaptation to the new realities. The simple voter as much as the militant prefers 'to change the party from within' rather than change the party himself.

Too often we have thought of political traditions in terms of black and white. Too often we have devoted attention to the decline of traditional norms, as foundations of party legitimacy, without giving attention to the flexibility of political traditions, in coping with new and unpredictable challenges. Here we are trying to apply these considerations to a small, possibly workable scheme of variables of continuity and change of certain political values as parts of a political tradition.

Let us point out a set of possible techniques aimed at gathering support in the population. We are referring mainly to a governmental party, i.e. a structure capable of mobilizing such resources as institutional devices and economic provisions that are not usually available to a party in opposition, such as the Italian DC.

(1) In the first place there are arrangements, such as mechanisms in the electoral system, that are meant to channel the popular vote towards one or more parties, deterring the formation of splinter groups or new parties, or by encouraging electoral coalitions. This is a technique of support in the sense that it structures the alternatives available to the electorate: 'forced consent' perhaps, but consent. The creating

of institutional structures — in the loose sense of the word — belongs to similar 'constitutional engineering'. These are, for instance, the formation of new administrative agencies (for example regional, decentralized authorities as poles of 'tension management', or, to move to another field, creation of top judiciary authorities as guardians of an insecure constitution, and so forth).

(2) 'Cultural' arrangements are means of support when they include the three types of legitimacy indicated by Max Weber: charisma, tradition and legal order. These include 'charismatic' appeals, 'symbolic' personalities and ethico-ideological principles (which can have a charismatic function similar to that of personalities). An ideological and ethical core has been, for instance, the communism-anticommunism cleavage, the appeal to *religion* in the case of Catholic parties, and the appeal to *history* in the case of Socialist and Communist parties. Both ideological sets are ambivalent. In fact, a party can appeal to religion in order to encourage ideological intransigence and readiness to fight. However, it can equally appeal to religion in order to encourage moderation and conciliatory attitudes towards opposing parties. Similarly, a Leftist party can appeal to history in order to encourage disposition to class struggle and revolutionary revolt, just as it can appeal to history in order to encourage gradualism and acceptance of opposition. Finally, the appeal to legality and to the constitutional order (in the Weberian sense) belongs to the same category of legitimation techniques, a set of valid rules issued through manifest and formal procedures.

(3) Finally, there are 'contractual' arrangements, through governmental action. These include differential allocation of economic resources (salaries, etc.) to given categories of citizens, incentives and rewards to other categories (for instance businessmen and shopkeepers). Therefore they include rewards in both the distributive and the productive system.

Therefore, techniques of legitimation or of support-gathering can be of three kinds: *institutional,* in the sense of operating in the structure of political alternatives and targets of identification or opposition (regional authorities, etc.); *cultural,* in the sense of appealing to charisma, tradition or the legal constitutional order; and *contractual,* in the sense of gathering support through differentially allocated economic rewards. The DC in effect tried these techniques with different success. It tried to change in favor of the winning coalition the electoral system in 1953 but failed. It tried the charismatic appeal with

De Gasperi and, later, tradition and order until recently. But most important — through the control of a huge set of resources ('sotto-governo') — the DC was able to establish durable contractual relationships with a great number of social strata and organized interests.[4]

When we turn to analyze a parallel model of legitimation on the side of the population, the problem of an empiracal analysis of support becomes more complex.

First, we can identify *secularization in the support of institutions,* or regime-support.[5] In the case of post-war Italy regime support was identifiable in people's attitudes towards democracy versus Fascism, and the republic versus the monarchy, the implementation of institutions such as the Constitutional Court, the Higher Council of the Judiciary, the role of the President of the Republic, and so forth. As far as these institutions were concerned secularization meant the progressive separation of people's judgement from powerful 'opinion agencies' such as the Catholic Church, the parties, the media and any other organized influence-structures.

Secondly, we can identify a secularization process as *emancipation of politico-electoral choice.* In our case, since there are *two* political traditions, Catholic and Socialist, we can first distinguish a secularization of the support for a party that makes constant reference to a dominant religion, such as the DC and the secularization of the support for a party that makes constant reference to hegemonic ideology, such as the PCI. For the latter, clear indicators of non-secularization can be identified in the following domains: (1) acceptance of the influence of the international working class movement as represented by the leading Socialist country, the USSR, over domestic issues; (2) the close tie between ideological identity, for instance 'communism', and allegiance to a given version of this identity, such as that of historical institutions of the Socialist countries (USSR, etc.); and (3) the close tie between allegiance to the party in general and obedience to party-political instructions over certain specific issues.

These are simple examples of how we would like to go about testing the secularization of a Leftist tradition as exemplified by the relationship between a Communist party and a Socialist tradition. But our main interest is in the secularization of the political choice of a party with a Catholic tradition. In this sense we can distinguish three main areas of secularization:

(a) the refusal — rather than acceptance — of the influence of the clergy over given issues, in the *laicism-clericalism* dichotomy (not necessarily anti-clericalism);

(b) the refusal − rather than acceptance − of an absolute bond between religious allegiance and party-loyalty, along the dichotomy *non-confessionalism-confessionalism*; and

(c) personal acceptance − rather than refusal − of the existence of personal religious allegiance and disobedience to the religious 'authorities' over certain specific issues according to a *secularism-traditionalism* dichotomy.

Thirdly, we have a meaning of *secularization as the refusal of the principle of deference towards authority, which can eventually become a critical attitude towards a political party.* This is a step forward in the process of secularization. It is not only an autonomous making up of one's mind about politics, but it is also a choice with a specific *content* oriented toward the political party. We can identify three indicators of this concept of secularization:

(a) approval or disapproval of party-policies because of trust or mistrust in the party, versus approval or disapproval because of critical evaluation of party-performance, either by the party in government or by the party in opposition;

(b) approval or disapproval of party-policies versus friends and foes, i.e. *party alliances* as referred to the identity of the party; and

(c) presence or absence of a sense of *effectiveness* of one's opinion over the political elite of the political party, according to an *elitism-democracy* dichotomy.

It is possible to divide the *techniques of support* used by Christian Democracy over the last three decades and the *ways in which a relevant sector of the population has granted support* to the governmental party into *periods.* According to available data the periods of both techniques and ways tend to be quite the same. From the point of view of the DC's techniques of gathering support we can distinguish three main periods.

(1) The period of so-called 'collateralismo', meaning that the Church organizations worked side by side with the loose DC organizations. In this period, from 1946 to 1958, it was more the Church that channeled the population's support towards the DC with its powerful and diffused associational network rather than the other way around. This primacy of church organization in the Cathlic tradition of course lasted longer than the collateralismo period: until about 1966-68.[6] The DC's appeal rested on the Catholic tradition and the anti-Communist offense, the 'charisma' of De Gasperi's personality and, especially in 1953, the

'protection' of the governing coalition through a modification of the electoral system.

(2) The period from 1958 to 1968, in which the motive of the DC granting economic development without traumatic changes ('progress without adventure') followed a technique of support, stated around 1953. After the defeat of the electoral law the DC started to penetrate into the governmental structures controlling the economy. It managed differential allocations of rewards to given categories of citizens. It was clearly a 'contractual' model of support-technique, in the specific sense of 'contractualism' used in this paper, based on a differential distribution of benefits.

(3) The third period, from 1968 to 1976, was characterized by the electoral ups and downs that we well know, with the economic crisis that made the appeal to economic expansion 'without adventure' less plausible, and the tensions that marked the crisis of public order and individual security. Until 1974-75 the DC had appealed to the traditional motives of (a) reinforcement of public order, eventually made through amendments brought to the criminal code and the legal order but both considered to be too permissive; and (b) the continuous Leftist-Communist threat — to the achievements of the country under DC leadership — and preservation of religious values, for example against divorce. Christian Decmocracy revived old motives after the defeat of the anti-divorce front, with the loss of votes in 1975, and the peculiar recovery of 1976. It revived the three pillars of its legitimation throughout the last thirty years: 'protected' democracy as opposed to the excesses of full democratization; revival of family and religious values; and state-intervention as a mediation between Capitalism and state-Socialism, i.e. centre-progressivism to cope with the economic crisis.

This is, of course, a very sketchy outline of the techniques of support used by Christian Democracy in Italy, as the party in government, to obtain the consent necessary to govern. Perhaps this outline will be sufficient to understand the major steps undertaken by the Catholic electorate on the way to becoming a secularized, conservative, mass party, similar to the other (perhaps more consistent from this point of view) conservative blocs of Continental Europe both in a situation of 'alternance' in power or of 'consociational' democracy.

'SECULARIZATION' OF THE
DC'S POLITICAL TRADITION: 1946-72

The first concept or 'step' of *secularization* that has been indicated above is the *emancipation of one's political choice*. The first indicator of confessionalism is widespread legitimation of the clergy's intervention in private and public matters. As we have seen, during the years of the 'collateralismo' the clergy intervened quite often in private and public matters.[7] As Table 1 shows, it was not only the DC electorate that justified intervention of the clergy in several matters. There were sizeable minorities of 'clerical' people (sometimes majorities) within the PCI and the PSI, and even in the so-called 'lay' parties that belonged to the area of the center.

TABLE 1

Indicators of Secularization as Emancipation of One's Political Choice in the DC Electorate and Other Electorate: 50s, 60s and 70s

People who answered 'Yes' to the question whether the Clergy has the right or not to have a say in several matters, by party preference: 1958

Matters	Party preferences								
	PCI	PSI	PSDI	PRI	DC	PLI	PMP	MSI	N
TV programs	13	23	43	32	62	39	36	31	2,272
Movies	21	31	51	29	68	49	50	37	
School programs	18	33	50	57	62	51	39	47	
Labor union issues	1	7	19	11	30	8	16	8	
Lay marriages	9	20	42	34	63	36	42	35	
Private life of catholics	20	34	48	32	61	44	47	40	
Domestic politics	–	3	11	–	29	14	11	5	

Source: Pier Paolo Luzzatto-Fegiz, *Il Volto Sconosciuto dell'Italia*, vol. 2, a serie Milano: Giuffre, 1966, pp. 1, 294-98. No subtotals are indicated in the original text.

The attitudes of the party electorates towards the divorce issue in April 1974 can be considered a limited but decisive functional equivalent of a complex set of attitudes towards clerical intervention in public (and private) matters in the late Fifties. By that time the position of the Church and of political parties on the issue was clear, and there was certainly no lack of information in the future electorate. From Table 2

Legitimation of Regimes

we see a relevant secularization of 10 percent of the DC electorate. In view of the fact that the issue was presented by the DC leadership of a plebiscite on *all* the values continually sustained by the DC (preservation of the family, education of children, etc.) and as a means of stopping the advance of the Left – mainly the Communist Left – the 30 percent of the pro divorce DC electors is a sizeable minority.

TABLE 2

Propensity to Vote *in Favor of Divorce* by Party Preference in 1949 and April 1974

PCI		PSI		PSDI Sinistra		PRI		PLI		DC		MSI MON.	
1949	1974	1949	1974	1949	1974	1949	1974	1949	1974	1949	1974	1949	1974
62%	91%	58%	83%	55%	73%	55%	83%	36%	61%	20%	29%	37%	52%

N (1949) = 2,356; N (1974) = 2,000.
Source: Giampaolo Fabris, *Il Comportamento Politico degli Italiani,* Milano: Franco Angeli, 1977, p. 62, Table 3.8. For the 1949 data, see P. Luzzatto Fegiz, op.cit., p. 399. Since party preferences are compared by asking which newspapers the respondents usually read, I have arbitrarily attributed PSDI and PRI preferences in 1963 as preferences for 'papers of the Left' in 1949 and the 1963 PLI as 'Independent papers' in 1949. The results seem to be plausible.

A second indicator of *secularization as emancipation of political* choice is the *separation of political from religious allegiance.* This can also be expressed as compatibility between religious allegiance, such as 'being good Catholics' and political allegiance, such as belonging to a party that is condemned or manifestly disliked by the Church. Again, the element of party strategy and (purposive) location of parties in the ideological spectrum as revealed by their being inside or outside the government, and their attitudes towards the government in general, is a crucial variable of secularization. The compatibility between being a Catholic and a PSI voter was very low within the DC electorate in 1953. It almost tripled ten years later, not just because of the time elapsed, but because the PSI was already part of the governmental majority. More interesting, perhaps, is the data concerning more committing compatibilities, such as that of being Catholic and Communist (Table 3).

TABLE 3

Sympathizers for the DC who answered 'Yes' to the following questions:

'Do you think that one can be both a good Catholic and a good Socialist?'		'Do you think that one can be both a good Catholic and a good Communist?'	
1953	1963	1953	1963
15%	43%	5%	16%

N (1953) = 874; *N* (1963) = 2,492.
Sources: For the data of 1953 see P. Luzzatto Fegiz, op.cit., vol. 1, pp. 874-75 and for 1963, P. Luzzatto Fegiz, op. cit., vol. 2, pp. i, 301-2.

The legitimacy of the presence of the two roles in the same person tripled over the ten years. It is likely that this was the consequence of more general 'openness' to the Left in 1963 and, at least in the beginning, the favorable attitude of the PCI towards the center-Left governments. These could be interpreted by the DC electorate as greater proximity to the DC.

The picture of the DC electorate that emerges from these scattered data that often cannot be cumulated is that of a slow but increasing process of autonomy of political choice from traditional religious allegiance. This is far from being a completed process, or even a completed first step. It is a general direction; having to do with deeply rooted principles (what Pareto called 'residues'), once they change, their change is irreversible.

It will be remembered that the second step of secularization is the tendency critically to evaluate party activity or performance, government performance and the performance of the opposition. It stresses 'experimentation' rather than 'blind trust', and value-rationality rather than traditional and emotional attitudes. 'Policy orientation' is a loose concept as far as the DC is concerned; being the major party in the government, the voter has difficulty in making a clear-cut distinction between the DC as a party and the DC as government. Again, when we draw a distinction between the party's rank and file and the party elite, the latter has a clear meaning when the party concerned is not in government. It has a different weight as 'governmental elite' when the party is in government.

There are several indicators of this second step of secularization: levels of interest and information, of party trust, and of acceptance of alliance, whether or not/this is connected with party identity and so forth. In general, whereas the first set of data indicated a trend towards the *de-confessionalization* of the Catholic tradition, in the sense of systematic observance of the Church for political guidance, the second step, the autonomy of political choice as an experimental rather than a traditional fact, is far from being completed (if it has been initiated at all). In this sense it seems fair to conclude that at least until 1972 *political Catholicism remained a fairly consistent bloc, with all the characteristics of the 'tradition' without being necessarily bound to specific mechanisms of confessionalism and clericalism.* This is hardly a novelty in the history of political cultures. In France, for instance, political Catholicism has secularized, in as much as it has largely abandoned the Church's guidance in daily political matters, even fore-saking the principle of 'the party of all Catholics'. Yet it remained deeply rooted in French political culture, mainly converging with the Gaullist choice and even the personality of Charles De Gaulle.[8] It is no wonder that this second step is so hard to take in a more clerical country like Italy.

A fairly important syndrome can be inferred from the *Ciser* data of the fall of 1963, which still give us the idea of the 'impermeability' of the DC electorate. As Table 4 shows, this electorate was unable to think of any choice alternative to the DC, at any time. Whatever happened, the constant, the only party, was Christian Democracy. As Gianfranco Poggi has perceptively pointed out, the DC is unanimous in attributing preferences to the DC in any alternative in which this is possible.[9] Certainly there was a solid majority of DC choice within the rural electorate! But the city-countryside cleavage is a variable of rather limited power when facing the appeal of the party as such (Table 4 again).

Thirty years have gone by since 1948, with great changes in the structure of Italian society and, at least since 1968, in the attitudes of mass-media. Despite these changes, the DC electorate has shown impres-sive continuity that only a deeply rooted tradition can explain. There is, in effect, some sense of not being removed from the political process, as the Sani-Barnes researches have shown.[10] From the point of view of the 'subjects' it shows a 'paternalistic' consciousness or 'care' by the DC leadership, and once again a sense of trust. This was certainly reinforced by the 'contractual' technique of gathering support, used, as we have seen, by the DC since the early Fifties. Yet support must be rooted in the minds of the people through deeper mechanisms than

TABLE 4

What DC and PCI Followers would Choose in a 'Polarized' Alternative, by Occupation (1963)

	Non-rural non-manual	Non-rural manual	Rural	Upper and middle upper SES house-wives	Lower and middle lower housewives	Total
	Between Partito Comunista and Democrazia Cristiana they would choose *Democrazia Cristiana*					
DC Followers	100	100	100	100	100	100
PCI Followers	45	15	7	32	25	22
	Between DC and PSI they would choose *Partito Socialista Italiano* (PSI)					
DC Followers	1	–	–	–	–	–
PCI Followers	82	85	95	77	76	83
	Between PSI and PCI, they would choose *Partito Comunista Italiano* (PCI)					
DC Followers	–	–	–	2	–	–
PCI Followers	29	66	82	45	59	60

Source: Gianfranco Poggi, *Le Preferenze Politiche degli Italiani,* Bologna: Il Mulino, 1968.

simple exchange of votes and benefits. There can be no formal 'interest' in politics, but at least until 1972 the DC electorate had some sense that the party and its leadership, the governmental bloc or whatever could be viewed in power at that moment, took some care of them. About 60 percent of the electorate have had a sense of government impact on their lives during the last five years. Therefore, so far the pattern of DC support appears to be the following: the DC political tradition had secularized in one direction, namely as emancipation of political choices from such external legitimizing agencies as the Catholic Church. In other words the tradition was felt to be something more internal to the individuals, that is principles that were not identical to the Church's viewpoints. Precisely because this remained a tradition, it had not secularized in the direction of a greater 'check' over the policies of the party in power. The two last rows of the Sani-Barnes studies show that the 'lack of interest' and of information did not affect either the people's willingness to choose or their sense of government impact over their private lives.

If this is true, then change that might have taken place (how durable, however, we do not know) between 1972 and 1976 can only be due to factors *external* to a tradition, such as changes in the *structure of the politically relevant population* and in the voluntary aspect of action of political leaders, namely party-strategy, the importance of which has repeatedly be shown through these data. If this is plausible (we dare not say 'true' with the existing amount of data), it would validate the hypothesis that a *political tradition, as a tradition in general, changes not only from internal 'push', a force from within such as ethical consistency, for instance the 'corruption' of its leadership, but also and above all from a push from outside, unpredictable, external forces that impinge upon a customary set of norms and behavior.*

The second indicator of secularization is the people's concern with the party's position on specific issues and problems felt to be important in a certain moment of national life. The data we provide are very limited because of the difficulty in comparing the widely different issues to which the respondents are exposed in different times and after many years. In general, what emerges from these data is a diffused tendency to ask for immediate provisions for general improvement rather than for specific reforms. There is no such thing as massive demand for a reform or even for reforms in general. Rather, as appears from most public opinion polls, there was a generic request for improvement of the general situation. The DC electorate rates neither better nor worse than the other electorates, including that of the PCI.

Perhaps one might add that after more than two decades there is an increasing articulation of opinions. However, this seems to be a characteristic of the whole electorate, and not just of that of the DC. Moreover, many of these differences could depend upon the more sophisticated 'stimulus' that the researcher has been able to provide in his sample. But if what these researchers reveal were true, then it would be comprehensible that the Italian political struggle primarily developed around general issues of symbols and identity, continuity and alliances, rather than on specific policy issues, reforms and changes within the system. More than an ideological struggle, in the rigorous sense of the term, according to these tables political life seems to be a cultural struggle. Within this struggle the choice of one battle field rather than another has a general meaning of life style which it is hard to articulate in pragmatic points. This is hardly new in recent Italian history. In fact, this has been a permanent theme of politological research in Italy.[11] However, what strikes us here is the *basic continuity* of this cultural pattern, whose breakthroughs, however, can come either from external, uncontrollable factors or from internal exhaustion, as indicated by many cases of *corruption.* Unfortunately there is no data available on the Italian electorate's perception of the corruption of its respectable

leaders. However, we can hypothesize that because of its simplicity as
an issue and moral tone, corruption can be a breakthrough force within
this tremendous continuity pattern of political choice, trust and allegiance.

The attitudes towards the party's possible alliances has been considered a further indicator of a secularization process in terms of
concern with policy issues. We have already seen the difficulty with
which the DC electorate accepted an alternative to the DC. Here (see
Table 5) we can say that it was a matter of cultural and ideological
identity. Even today there is a threshold that a DC political leader can
hardly cross without suffering a loss of legitimacy, and that is the
threshold of party identity intended by its electorate as party integrity.
Located in the center of the political alignment in the minds of these
respondents, Democrazia Cristiana could hardly move to the Right or
to the Left of the alignment without suffering a loss of votes. Of course
it could use some of its leaders to enduce its people to accept an
alliance.

TABLE 5

Indicators of 'Secularization' as Availability to
DC — Alliances with Other Parties

a		b		c	
Favor of DC respondents for a government DC-PSI (April 1956)		Choice of DC respondents for different government coalitions (July 1964)		Choice of DC respondents for different parties to be in government with DC (April 1976)	
	%		%		%
Yes:	6	DC Left:	5	PCI	: 6
No:	58	DC, PSDI,		PSI	: 20
Don't know		PLI, PRI	61	MSI-Dn	: 5
No answer:	36	Other	24	PSDI	: 26
N = 1,473		Don't know	10	PLI	: 16
Source: P. Luzzatto-Fegiz, op.cit., Vol. 2, p. 649		N = 1,550		PRI	: 27
		Source: P. Luzzatto-Fegiz, op.cit., Vol. 2, p. 693		Other	: .3
				None	: 13
				Don't know	
				No answer	: 19

Source: G. Fabris,
op.cit., p. 106

Since 'trust' was given a party more for what it stood for than for what it actually did, attention was polarized on the preservation of a given cultural identity. It is impressive that even in April 1976 (referring to Table 5) centrism remained the basic choice of an electorate that could not ignore that a DC, PSDI, PLI and PRI alliance had no numerical majority, either in the Chamber of Deputies or in the Senate, and therefore was equivalent to a DC minority government, i.e. the so-called 'monocolore'. However, there is a slight change in the direction of a possible alliance with the Left: 26 percent indicate it as a possible alliance as opposed to 5 percent twelve years later (Table 5). This shows a small change indeed, but it is change.

YOUTH, WOMEN AND
PARTY STRATEGY:
1973-1977

There are several interpretations of 'what happened after 1972'. The basic factors of change that seem to emerge from this literature are 'external' to the political system. First there is the generation of young people, from 18 to 21 years old, who went to the polls for the first time in 1975, thanks to the lowering of the voting age from 21 to 18 by the Chamber of Deputies. The second factor has been indicated as that of a greater autonomy and political consciousness of women, including the 'housewives' that, as we have seen in all the public opinion data we have considered so far, generally favored a 'traditional' choice.

These two factors are proper to a 'new' population; Antonio Gramsci would define them as populations passing from 'passivity' into 'activity', and in his conceptual framework they are basic elements of an 'organic crisis'.[13] I would like to add a third factor, namely the *party-strategy*, of the PCI first and the DC second. But before getting to this factor, which in my opinion is further evidence of the formidable capacity of political parties, as leadership structures, to assimilate and redefine social change, let us consider the first two.

Youth seems to have been a basic variable of political change after 1972. As has been convincingly demonstrated by analyses of data collected in 1975, the 'young cohort' showed considerable *diversity* in his political mentality as far as *political choice* was concerned. This is a group of people who were born betwen 1948 and 1958 and became eligible to vote in the years 1969 and 1976 and that therefore actually voted in 1972 and 1976. In particular, the age group that voted for the first and second time in 1972 was approximately more than three million people. The one that first voted in 1976 was more than five million people. All together they represented about 21 percent of the electorate, i.e. eight-and-a-half million people.

This was indeed a sizeable segment of the electorate. Therefore we are dealing with a population that altogèther had a chance to influence, in a considerable way, the features of the political outcome of elections. This electorate was particularly active because of the two early parliamentary elections, a referendum on divorce (the second in Italian political history, after that of 1946 on the monarchy versus the republic) the regional elections. In what sense can we say that it is *different* from the traditional Italian electorate of the postwar years? First of all, in its partisan preference; this electorate was about 2 percent more Communist and 6 percent more Socialist than the whole 1976 electorate. Had it been for this electorate (the one that answered about its political preference), the DC would hardly have recaptured in the parliamentary elections of 1976 the votes lost in the regional elections of 1975. Secondly, this group of young voters was about twice as interested in politics as is older fellows. It was also twice as active in politics (including such activities as occupation of plants, traffic blocks, writing slogans on the walls and wild-cat strikes). It was also about twice as alienated from the system and more libertarian. In only one item were these youngsters similar to their older fellows: the non-response abut their political preference. If it is likely that this non-response (as has happened in the pre-electoral polls) was made of DC-sympathizers, then the DC as such would have received simply 'secular' support from these young people. As such, the data on secularization would *not* be modified. This means that the generational factor was so powerful that it aggregated a general secular opinion of the youngsters across party preferences. In other words, the generational factor seems to have been more powerful than region, sex, community-size and social status in making for a manifest secular mentality in the majority of the members of the younger generation. This did not mean (and does not mean) a lack of religiosity. It meant a decline of ritualistic attitudes and 'religious' deference towards authority.

Finally, by a percentage difference of almost 21 percent, there are more offsprings with DC-oriented fathers choosing Leftist allegiance

than offsprings from fathers of PCI or PSI allegiance choosing DC or
other center-parties, in this sense, the Leftist 'tradition' seems to hold
more than the Catholic one, if the 'consistent' children are more than
eighty percent within the group having a PCI father and almost sixty
percent within the group having DC fathers (Table 6).

TABLE 6

**Political Choice of Offsprings Versus
Political Choice of the Fathers:
1968-75**

1968				1975	
		Father's party preference		Father's party preference	
		Center-Right	Left	Center-Right	Left
Offspring	Center Right	74%	17%	66%	9%
Party Preference	Left	26%	83%	34%	91%
		N = 138	N = 101	N = 505	N = 483

1968
Source: Elaborated from, Paul Abramson, 'Intergenerational Social Mobility and
Partisan Preference in Britain and Italy, A cross-National Comparison', *Comparative Political Studies* VI (2) (1973): 227.

1975
Source: Giacomo Sani, *Generations and Politics in Italy*, Turin: Einaudi Foundation, Seminar on 'Italy: Crisis or Transition', 1977, Table 36, A.

The 1975 regional elections, however, were an exceptional case from
this point of view. About three million youngsters, suddenly enfranchised, voted in such a way as to give a 10 percent difference in
favor of the Left. In 'normal' turnover, this would have been probably
5 percent. This is an electoral change compatible with the relative
stability of the major political forces. In this case the 1976 electoral
outcome would be more a consolidation rather than a transition, more
a terminal rather than a transit station.

Let us now see the second factor of change between 1972 and
1976: the process of emancipation of women. More durable in the
direction of emancipation, however, this process is also likely to be very

slow. If the generational factor is able to mark 'jumps forward' and then consolidate as long as the 'young' become less young, the eventual secularization of women is likely to be a less dramatic but steadier process. Let us go back to our indices of secularization, and see how women have changed in a more secularized direction.

The political continuity of Italian women, their 'traditionalism' reinforced by a life spent entirely within the family, being 'casalinghe', (housewives), reading very little and being interested in politics even less — these were their characteristics. In 1970, after the passing of the divorce bill by Parliament, the attitude of women changed in favor of divorce in the following years, until 1974.[14] I think that the divorce issue has had a profound function in emancipating the women's political attitudes from the traditional role they seemed to have acquired. The data collected by Sam Barnes in 1968 and that of Sani-Barnes in 1972, both show an irrelevant change in women's politico-ideological attitudes as compared to those of ten, twenty or even thirty years earlier. Versus this solid continuity in traditionalism of Italian women from 1946 through 1977, there is evidence of a remarkable change in the electorate concerning divorce, political allegiance and even the problem of abortion, which is so delicate and important in a Catholic country like Italy. The most impressive change was over divorce, probably because it directly concerned the freedom and emancipation of women (Table 7,A). However, this does not extend to the woman's freedom to give birth or not to a child (Table 7B). Today the woman is in a period of transition, the direction of which is towards emancipation.

In sum we have the tendency of an electorate that through several generational experiences of women versus men, of Catholic versus non-Catholic, of Communist versus non-Communist, tends to erode the preconditions of political allegiance in being loyal to extra political entities, such as the Church and the International Working Class Movement. Certainly there is a long way to go before attaining this sort of electorate, but the DC electorate seems to be oriented more and more towards the model of *secularized, conservative mass-party*, due to the crisis of these extra-political (but politically relevant) allegiances. Certainly the emancipation of the political choice goes through the phases of its most stressed subalternation: the stressing of being Catholic, of being a Worker, of being Young, of being a Woman; the walls, Durkheim would say, of a segmented society. As is the case young and women, sometimes *old segments are eroded by new*

TABLE 7

Indicators of Secularization of Women

A. Divorce-Issue: Percentage of Women in Favor of Divorce

1947	1955	1965	1971	1974 (April)
19%	27%	19%	49%	55%
N = (including men):				
2,110	1,235	968	2,333	2,000

Sources: (1947) P. Luzzatto-Fegiz, op.cit. vol. 1, p. 397; (1955) P. Luzzatto-Fegiz, op.cit., vol. 2, p. 349; (1965) P. Luzzatto-Fegiz, op.cit., vol. 2, p. 349; (1971), Maria Weber, *Il voto dell donne,* Turin: 'Biblioteca della Liberta', 1977, p. 70, Table 1.2; (April 1974), Giampaolo Fabris, op.cit., p. 50, Table 3.2.

B. Women in Favor of Abortion

1974	1976
26%	31%
N = 464	N = 1,500

Sources: 1974, Giampaolo Fabris, 'Il Problema dell'Aborto', *Ricerche Demoscopiche* I (3) (1974): 14; 1976.

segments, and not by a sudden 'liberalization' of 'Utopian' character. This seems to be the case in Italy today, and political parties are trying to adapt their strategies accordingly.

Since the initiative of the 'historical compromise' (November 1973), the DC leadership has made some attempts to adapt its party strategy to the rapidly changing situation. The relative capacity of the PCI in gaining the votes of both the working class Catholics and the middle class by doing away with the strategy of frontal collision, and opening to the DC as leadership and as electorate, has been an unpredictable and formidable example for the DC. The PCI was able to do this without losing its traditional basis, although it certainly faced (and still is facing) considerable discontent among the party militants. However, the 'fire-test' for the PCI had taken place earlier, in 1968, when some of the PCI's young leaders left the party and joined the extra-parliamentary Left. In 1973 the PCI had partially overcome the crisis of identity of the Leftist tradition, of intellectual and political orthodoxy, and had freer ground for such daring innovations as that of a general alliance with a traditional enemy.

The example of the PCI could hardly be imitated by a party whose tradition was less cohesive and whose organization was more loose. In effect since 1968 the strategy of the DC has been that of absorbing outside novelties rather than innovating or even taking initiative itself. This is a strategy of defense rather than a strategy of attack. Of course a good defensive strategy could also be necessary for a while, in order to 'modernize'. This only seems to be the case for a very limited part of the DC leadership. While the Catholic tradition continues, and is stronger than many observers were — and are — disposed to recognize, DC leadership is exhausted. The traditionalists have expressed their willingness several times to change personnel in the government but not to change party, but the DC leadership is divided. In fact, the DC has exhausted the alliances compatible with its tradition. Its strategy can only be that of getting the PCI to accept center-Left rather than Leftist, policies.

The center location in the political alignment has become a compulsory location that risks becoming a *political cage*, whereas when there was frozen opposition in the Fifties and Sixties this position was grounds for relative freedom of innovation. The DC is divided between two party models: the old, popular party, *Sammel* or *Volks-partei*, encompassing all the social cleavages: party of the working class as much as party of the middle classes; party of the periphery as much as the center; party of the countryside as much as of the city; unique point of reference for active Catholics and an eventual port of call for disoriented laymen. The other model is that of the *conservative mass party*: urban rather than rural; middle and entrepreneurial classes rather than working and middle-lower classes; center rather than periphery; state intervention within the premises of free enterprise; and last but not least, international integration rather than national specificity.

The Catholic tradition is *not*, per se, incompatible with this second model, but it needs active participation by the cadres of the party that, on the contrary, are more attracted by the model of the old 'popular' party. Such cadres as 'Communion and Liberation', which have given great help to the party and have perhaps been the most responsible for the victory in the elections of the school-councils (November, December 1977) are far from being 'modern', 'neo-capitalist' and 'liberal democratic'. Rather, they are 'integralist', generically anti-capitalist, perhaps democratic but certainly not 'liberal'. With such leadership the objective task of becoming a modern conservative mass-party, which much of the DC leadership feels to be necessary, inevitably has great difficulty.

Moreover, the old 'partito popolare' model, a strategy of great popularity within the DC as a party, but objectively a losing strategy, is provisionally reinforced by the now compulsory center-location of the DC. It cannot go towards the existing Right because the 'constitutional Right', i.e. the Liberals (PLI), no longer exist (5 deputies and 2 Senators). The other Right, the radical MSI, has become the party of violent marginals, partly of *Lumpeproletarier* and Southern resentment. The only strategy in that sense is to gain the MSI electorate; in fact, the split of the MSI between a moderate, pro-DC Right and a radical Right will probably have a postive outcome for the DC. However, this is hardly in the direction of the modern conservative party. No way on the Left; the Left is being monopolized by the PCI, unless a strategy is set up by the DC in order to call back the Catholic votes that went to the PCI in 1975 and 1976. If these were middle class votes, the task could be successful: people who have broken once with a tradition – the Catholic – can break again with the new (and still provisional) tradition – the Socialist. After all, the culture of the country rewards the prodigal sons. But if, as some have convincingly shown, these votes come mostly from the working class,[15] then the task is far more difficult, as there are reinforcement effects to keep the votes Communist, such as the unemployment crisis of opportunities, etc.

These are, of course, the difficulties of the DC. Yet even this defense strategy has contributed to the secularization of the Catholic tradition. First, during the center-Left governments the DC accepted a general liberalization and democratization of society, pushed forward by the PSI: universal access to high school, workers' statute, reform of penal procedure (rights of the defendants), equality of men and women in the family law, etc. Secondly, the DC leadership has always penalized the most 'integralist' and Right-wing tendencies within the party (such as that once represented by Senator Fanfani). Thirdly, party activism and militancy, at least since the middle Seventies, tends to be independent from the clergy, i.e. to be completely lay activism. From this point of view even 'Comunione and Liberazione' has nothing to do with the confessionalism of the old Catholic Action. These are indicators of a party strategy that is oriented at slow secularization. It is hard to tell how much this will contribute to the implementation of the model of a conservative mass party of 'pluralistic' nature. A great deal will depend upon the secularization of the PCI, which we have only pointed out as a subject worthy of analysis.

NOTES

1. According to the Italian electoral system, individuals at 18 are eleigible to vote for the Chamber of Deputies. The voting threshold was lowered immediately before the regional elections of 1975.

2. See, Giacomo Sani, 'The Italian Elections of 1976, Continuity and Change', Paper presented at the APSA meeting of the Conference Group on Italian Politics, Chicago, 2-8 September 1976.

3. See Arend J. Lijpart, *The Politics of Accommodation, Pluralism and Democracy in the Netherlands,* Berkeley: University of California Press, 1975 (1968).

4. See Giuliano Amato, *Economia, Politica e Istituzioni in Italia,* Bologna: Il Mulino, 1976.

5. For a recent discussion of the concept of 'support', see, Richard Rose, 'Dynamic Tendencies in the Authority of Regimes', *World Politics* XXI (4) (1969): 602-28, and David Easton, 'A Re-Assessment of the Concept of Political Support', *British Journal of Political Science* VI (5) (1974): 435-57. For an interesting 'operationalization' of the concept, see Philip E. Converse, *The Dynamics of Party Support, Cohort-Analyzing Party Identification,* Beverly Hills and London: Sage Publications, 1976.

6. This and the following periodizations must be taken 'cum granu salis': they are oversimplifications of patterns that overlap each other.

7. For the 'public mood' of a period in which the bishop of Prato, Monsignor Fiordelli, could publicly condemn a couple for living together without being married, see Filippo Barbano, *Partiti e Pubblica Opinione nella Campagna Elettorale,* Torino: Giappichelli, 1960.

8. See, Jean Charlot, *Les Francais et De Gaulle,* (IFOP), Paris: Plon, 1971, especially chapter IV.

9. See, Gianfranco Poggi, *Le Preferenze Politiche degli Italiani,* Bologna: Il Mulino, 1968, pp. 66-67.

10. See, Giacomo Sani, 'L'Immagine dei Partiti nell'Elettorato', in Mario Caciagli e Alberto Spreafico (eds.), *Un Sistema Politico alla Prova* Bologna: Il Mulino, 1975, pp. 85-126 and Samuel H. Barnes, *Representation in Italy, Institutionalized Tradition and Electoral Choice,* Chicago and London: The University of Chicago Press, 1977, especially chapter 7.

11. See, for instance, Joseph La Palombara, 'Italy: Fragmentation, Isolation and Alienation', in Lucian W. Pye and Sidney Verba (eds.), *Political Culture and Political Development,* Princeton: Princeton University Press, 1965. For the

public opinion polls of this period, see Institute of Public Opinion Research (IPOR), 'Codebook of the Research on Italian Political Attitudes', mimeographed copy, p. 32, Table 22, and G. Fabris, op.cit., p. 76.

12. This part draws heavily on the work of Giacomo Sani, 'Generations and Politics in Italy', Seminar on Italy: Crisis or Transition, Turin, Einaudi Foundation, 24-27 March 1977.

13. Antonio Gramsci, *Prison Notebooks*, New York: International Publishers, 1975 (1971) p. 210 and ff.

14. See, Maria Weber, *Il Voto delle Donne*, Torino: 'Biblioteca della Liberta', 1977, pp. 33-39, and Alberto Marradi, 'Analisi del Referendum sul Divorzio', *Rivista Italiana di Scienza Politica* IV (3) (1974): 589-644.

15. See, Arturo Parisi e Gianfranco Pasquino, *Continuita' e Mutamento Elettorale in Italia,* Bologna: Il Mulino, 1977, and Guido Martinotti, 'Nuove Ricerche Sul Voto degli Italiani', *Mondoperaio* XXX (12) (1977): 79-84. The 'change in the perception of the representatives of interests' by social groups, the third variable of electoral change indicated by the author in the article, can be assimilated into the concept of secularization presented here.

15

THE STATE AND LATE CAPITALIST DEVELOPMENT:
The Case of Brazil

Sylvia Ann Hewlett
Barnard College, USA

> More than ever before men now live in the shadow of the
> state . . . . . It is for the state's attention, or for its control,
> that men compete; and it is against the state that beat the
> waves of social conflict . . . . It is possible not to be interested
> in what the state does; but it is not possible to be unaffected
> by it. The point has acquired a new and ultimate dimension
> in the present epoch; if large parts of the planet should one
> day be laid waste in a nuclear war, it is because men, acting in
> the name of the state and invested with its power, will have
> so decided, or miscalculated.
>
> *Ralph Miliband*

The state is an increasingly dominant fact of twentieth century life, with a new and frightening ability to shape the political and economic fate of mankind. The adoption of state managerialism to combat the Depression, the expansion of executive power in World War II, and the growth of state regulative and welfare functions since the war, have all contributed to increasingly powerful central governments in advanced industrialized countries. In the underdeveveloped world, the role of the modern state is even more dramatic. This is because contemporary growth processes require that governments play a dominant part in structuring economic and social reality.

But, despite these conspicuous developments, contemporary political and economic theory is surprisingly unhelpful in coming to terms with the modern state. Alfred Stepan has described the situation in his discipline:

> While almost everywhere the role of the state has grown, one of the few places it has withered away is in the theoretical schemes developed in political science.[1]

And the situation is equally depressing in economics. Bodies of theory do exist to deal with socialist states and with regulatory functions in advanced democracies, but neither of these conceptual frameworks are particularly relevant to the military dictatorships of the Third World — which are neither socialistic nor democratic.

Perhaps the most influential threads running through postwar 'Western' political and economic analysis are: a static model of the political process called liberal-pluralism; and a linear or 'Rostowian' evolutionary dynamic. Both of these theoretical constructs have tended to downplay the state as an autonomous force.

According to the liberal-pluralist perspective, society should be allowed to regulate itself, with as little interference as possible from the state:

> The general rule is nothing ought to be done or attempted by the government. The motto or watchword of government, on these occasions ought to be — *Be Quiet* . . . . With few exceptions, and these not very considerable ones, the attainment of the maximum of enjoyment will be most effectually secured by leaving each individual to pursue his own maximum enjoyment.[2]

This harmony of interests is arrived at by men and women freely pursuing their own selfish ends. In the economic universe we have the doctrine of the 'invisible hand'.[3] This describes a free enterprise system unconsciously coordinating producers and consumers through a system of prices and markets so as to achieve the best good for all: any interference with free competition by the government, is almost certain to be detrimental to the general good.

The political universe is dominated by the same atomistic, equilibrating mechanisms. Individuals pursue their own selfish ends, but because people have various interests, there is a tendency to associate with numerous and different pressure groups whose interests criss-cross. Multiple, overlapping group membership is a crucial element in pluralistic theory for it denies the existence of a dominant group or class; it assumes that through bargaining and compromise all interests are weighed in the political arena.

The liberal-pluralist perspective rules out the possibility that the state needs to intervene on behalf of the weak or underprivileged. Since it assumes that all interest groups are in on the political balancing act, it essentially denies that some groups are powerless or illegitimate. This would seem to contradict reality, for in most societies, throughout most of history, interest groups have not been at liberty to combine freely, but have been strictly chartered by the state. Doctrines of the invisible hand and the harmony of interests are cold comfort if one happens to be a worker in a country where an authoritarian regime has outlawed trade unions in the name of economic progress.

The net result of liberal-pluralist theory has been to minimize the role of the state as an independent actor. It has also reduced the need for political and economic theorists to come to grips with the intensely moral question of what the state ought to be doing. In the nineteenth century Hegel wrote: 'The State is the Divine Idea as it exists on Earth'.[4] Modern social scientists are distinctly uncomfortable with such notions, and the intellectual bias of both economists and political scientists has been to solve societal problems with mechanistic, scientific, and supposedly objective tools. The self-regulating market mechanisms of Adam Smith and the atomistic, egoistic assumptions of utilitarian philosophers have been easier to deal with, if less illuminated, than those that are more explicitly bound up with value-laden judgements.

A second powerful thread running through contemporary political and economic theory has been a linear, evolutionary dynamic. In simple terms this means a smooth, continous and cumulative progression from various states of economic and political backwardness to representational democracy and high mass consumption for all. During the 1960s the rhetoric and part of the reality could be made to support this upbeat theme. In Latin America the Alliance for Progress, LAFTA, high growth rates, and a veneer of democracy spawned a brand of academic euphoria and Rostowian theories of continuous development in several disciplines:

> David Lerner, Karl Deutsch, Gino Germani and Gabriel Almond all taught us how societies develop from tradition to modernity, from isolation to communication, from reduced to expanded political participation, from political underdevelopment to political maturity, from national isolationism to international integration.[5]

This doctrine of continuous progress left little room for repressive dictatorship or increasing poverty, two of the dominant facts of political and economic life in the 1970s.

I want to point to yet another intellectual bias common to the

contemporary social sciences. It is the expectation that the underdeveloped world would or should comply with the evolutionary pattern
of Western Europe and North America, that it is 'the history of
advanced or established industrial countries which traces out the road
of development for the more backward countries'.[6] For generations,
economists and political theorists have taken for granted the essential
similarity of the development processes of the past and those that are
taking place at the present time. Two elements in this intellectual
conditioning are particularly important in coming to grips with the role
of the state in the development process at the periphery of the
capitalist world.

First it should be accepted that many Third World countries are not
becoming well-behaved representational democracies. Authoritarian
states are here to stay, and it is necessary to set up a theoretical
framework that describes the raison d'être of stable, reactionary, and
autocratic regimes. It no longer suffices to borrow the goals and
programs of western democracies.

Secondly, the crucial fact of late development should be taken into
account when analyzing the political imperatives of underdeveloped
nations. The extent and pace of change in economic structures have
been consistently overlooked by Theorists preoccupied with evolutionary perspectives. Capitalism in the latter half of the twentieth
century is an entirely different animal from what it was in the seventeenth and eighteenth centuries, when the currently developed nations
entered their take-off phase. Laissez-faire democratic perspectives
become singularly irrelevant when a strong interventionist state is a
necessary condition for economic growth or even survival in many
'underdeveloped' contexts. The liberal state is no longer 'the best
possible political shell for capitalism',[7] and many nations are currently
choosing a route from the pre-industrial to the modern world that
encompasses reactionary autocratic regimes superimposing modernization from above with scant regard for democratic niceties.[8]

A central task of this paper is to create a conceptual framework that
will illuminate the nature of the interaction between the Brazilian state
and late capitalist growth.[9] A preliminary step is the rejection of the
dominant theoretical models of 'Western' social science and the intellectual biases that pervade them.

A THEORETICAL FRAMEWORK
FOR BRAZIL

The first and most fundamental element in my analysis is that the role of the state is intimately related to the successive structural crises of late capitalist development.[10] During the early development of Brazil, the political economy was bound up with the fact of being a primary commodity producer, and economic growth was contingent upon the international market. The world depression of the 1930s constituted the first structural crisis of late development, drastically undermining the viability of export-based economies in the Third World. Brazil, along with several other countries, began to emphasize domestic industrialization. The first phase lasted from the 1930s to 1964, and is often called the era of 'easy' import-substituting industrialization.

It certainly was a stage in which the simple or expedient solutions to industrialization were adopted with a minimum of forethought or planning.[11] The state created protective barriers, and both national and foreign companies participated in a concerted attempt to replace imports by domestic production. But 'easy' import-substituting industrialization was far from problem free. By the early 1960s the chronic tendency to inflationary and balance-of-payments pressures had provoked stagnation and a second structural crisis. It seemed that a drastically revised economic strategy was called for if Brazil was to get back on the growth path. Hence, the ruthless solutions of the post-1964 era, a period which was marked by successful stabilization, repression, and a much more export-orientated industrialization policy.

Secondly, the solution to these successive crises of late development has involved various types of inclusionary and exclusionary authoritarianism, and an accelaration of state participation in economic affairs. The structural crisis of the 1930s provoked a distinctive brand of inclusionary authoritarianism which had marked populist overtones and self-consciously coopted the emerging industrial working force. The crisis of the early 1960s, on the other hand, was resolved by resorting to an exclusionary and repressive form of authoritarianism. Although the current regime has many characteristics in common with an earlier period — developmentalism, nationalism, anticommunism, centralization, to name just a few — it has, by and large, excluded the working force as well as the masses from the fruits of economic growth. These changes in the form and function of the state have gone hand in hand with increased economic activism. The Brazilian state has become a powerful regulator of economic activity, an important agent of protection and subsidy, a significant producer of basic industrial goods and infrastractural items, and *the* determinant of the direction of national economic development.[12]

Thirdly, it is necessary to stress that one cannot go from an economic crisis to the political solution of that crisis without talking about motivating forces. There is nothing automatic or inevitable in the link between economic cause and political effect. But, given a driving force — in this case the tremendous emphasis given by successive Brazilian regimes to national economic success — a strong, authoritarian state has become a necessary component of the answer to structural crisis in this underdeveloped economy. The dominant ideology of Brazilian political leaders since the 1930s, whether democratic or autocratic, has comprised a mixture of developmentalism and nationalism.[13] In the earlier phase this ideology was most clearly articulated by the *Tenentes* (a group of young army officers) and by Vargas himself; in the 1950s by Kubitschek and by the ISEB (*Instituto Superior de Estudos Brasileiros*); and in the post-1964 period, the military establishment, particularly the ESG (*Escola Superior de Guerra*), has been the most skillful exponent of these central political goals.

This leads us to a final element in my conceptual framework — the balance of power between the various economic actors in the growth process. The timing and format of Brazil's structural crises, together with the authoritarian political response, has largely dictated the roles played by national, state, and foreign capital — the *ménàge a trois* of Brazilian development.

Brazil is a late developer and, as a result, national capital has been unable to capture the dynamic sectors of the economy. Multinational corporations, the industrial giants of the advanced world, have a multifaceted technological edge and have preempted the most profitable areas of consumer goods production, while the state has become increasingly dominant in basic industry and in infrastructural investment. This latter fact is also a function of late development and the economic facts of life in the twentieth century: economies of scale and long gestation periods make the state rather than the private investor the natural agent for this type of industrial growth. Political factors have undoubtedly exacerbated this structural tendency in favor of the multinationals and the state. For example, post-1964 authoritarian governments have generally been receptive to foreign capital and demonstrably tolerant of state control of the economy, all in the name of speeding up the rate of economic growth. In several instances this receptivity and tolerance has exceeded that which would have been possible under a democratic regime responsive to a vocal and liberal national bourgeoisie. Striking examples of this trend include the repeal of the profit remittance law (1964), and the 1964-67 squeeze on domestic sources of credit.

In short, industrialization cycles in Brazil have been marked by a progressive strengthening of the multinational corporation and the state. During certain stages the multinationals have advanced faster than the state; at other, vice versa; and most stages have featured the assimilation or cooptation of national capital, which has become a rather shadowy member of the *ménàge a trois*. This constellation of economic actors becomes a result of late capitalist development when the political project is national economic success defined in terms of annual growth rates.

With these 'bare bones' of a theoretical framework, one can begin to understand some of the more blatant contradictions of the contemporary Brazilian state: it is fiercely developmentalist, and yet has exacerbated poverty for the mass of the population; it is firmly nationalistic, but has linked Brazil even more closely to foreign capital; it favors a free enterprise market economy, yet it has created in practice something akin to state capitalism. But, before allowing myself to be carried away by the explanatory power of my conceptual framework, I need to substantiate my case by looking more closely at the facts.

THE BRAZILIAN STATE
IN HISTORICAL PERSPECTIVE

For the purpose of this analysis the historical evolution of the Brazilian economy is best divided into three periods: (1) the 'colonial' economy, based on the export of primary commodities and dominated by a planter-exporter elite, which lasted from the sixteenth century until the Great Depression;[14] (2) the phase of 'easy' import-substituting industrialization, which spawned a distinctive brand of inclusionary or populist politics and spanned the years 1930-64; and (3) the post-1964 period of stabilization and export-led growth which is heavily identified with repressive, military regimes. All three periods saw considerable and accelerating state participation in economic affairs, but the nature if not the goals of government intervention changed substantially over time.

In the colonial period the Brazilian domestic economy was integrated into an international capitalist market system where it functioned as a supplier of raw materials and as a consumer of manufactured goods. The power elite of this period comprised the rural landlords and the export commercial and financial intermediaries, who did not hesitate to call upon the state to assume a major supportive and regulatory role. Large-scale subsidized immigration and government supported railroad are examples of state initiative in this period. But perhaps the best illustration of the way in which the state intervened on behalf of the planter-exporter elite was in the sphere of price supports for coffee.[15]

In the sphere of industrialization, however, economic liberalism held sway. The pre-1930 era saw various attempts by domestic industrialists to gain tariff protection and more liberal credit policies from the Brazilian state. But they were largely unsuccessful.[16] Not only did state intervention on behalf of industry collide with laissez-faire liberal concepts of Brazil's 'natural' role as a producer of primary commodities, but it also threatened the self-interest of the landed oligarchy, who obviously benefited from free trade. The relatively weak class of domestic industrialists proved incapable of galvanizing the state on their behalf.

The year 1929 is an important watershed in the economic history of Brazil and of most Latin American nations. The world depression hit the region with particular ferocity 'bowling over the props of the area's export-based economies and causing widespread internal dislocation.'[17] In Brazil, the value of exports fell from US $445.9 million in 1929 to US $180.6 million in 1932.[18]

This collapse of the primary product, outward-oriented growth model was the first major structural crisis of Brazil. The 1930s saw the beginnings of a new phase of economic growth with an emphasis on domestic industrialization; this was accompanied by a regrouping of political actors and a more direct and expanded role for the state. But let us examine this new stage in more detail.

First, the economic dimension. Brazil did have some small-scale industry prior to the 1930s, but it was technologically backward and could not begin to compete with the manufactures of the advanced industrialized nations. Tentatively in the 1930s, and more thoroughly in the late 1940s and 1950s, domestic manufactures were encouraged through protection and subsidy. Some of this encouragement took the form of self-conscious state policy, but some support was indirect – a function of programs primarily designed to bolster the coffee sector or ease a balance-of-payments crisis. The net result was that both national and foreign firms were provided with the incentive and opportunity to manufacture goods for the Brazilian market and replace imports with domestic products. This first cycle of import-substituting industrialization was immensely successful in growth terms, and by the early 1960s Brazil was the most important industrial nation in Latin America.

Some of the initial state encouragement of industrialization was indirect or unselfconscious. For example, the first few years of the Vargas regime were marked by a rather desperate attempt to compensate the coffee growers for the disastrous fall in prices, and industrialization was a somewhat inadvertent, though welcome, byproduct of these policies. The purchase of coffee surpluses by the state created a major source of deficit financing and prevented Brazil from experiencing the grave collapse in domestic demand which the loss in export earnings implied. The resulting maintenance of internal demand, coupled with exchange controls and a progressive currency devaluation, proved to be a powerful stimulant to the growth of domestic light industry. Consumers, unable to satisfy their needs through imports, turned to Brazilian manufactures, and domestic investment, which once had gone into the export sector, was attracted by the higher profits to be earned in industrial production.[19]

This type of 'spontaneous' industrialization was aided and abetted by self-conscious and considerable state intervention. Vargas thoroughly repudiated the doctrine of economic liberalism and, during his first term in office, the state expanded its authority to direct the economy in two major ways: first, the manipulation of fiscal measures, exchange controls, import quotas, and credit controls, to protect and subsidize domestic manufacturing; secondly, direct state intervention in areas such as railroads, shipping, public utilities, and such basic industrial areas as oil and steel.

The intervention of the state in the Brazilian economy was further exaggerated by World War II. Brazil's formal entry into the war in 1942 provided the occasion for a full-scale economic mobilization effort; in particular, the obvious need for raw materials and manufactured goods vital to the war effort gave new urgency to the Vargas program of state-financed enterprises.

By 1943 Vargas had committed himself unequivocally to systematic industrial development. In that year he proudly announced that, on the strength of its iron and steel plants, Brazil was forging:

> ... the basic elements for the transformation of a vast and scattered agrarian community into a nation capable of providing its fundamental necessities.

A year later, in a speech to the military, he stressed:

> Our first lesson from the present war was that... the only countries that can really be considered military powers are those that are sufficiently industrialized and able to produce within their own frontiers the war materials they need.[21]

This linking of national security matters with the economic development of the nation was to become a dominant theme in the ideology of the Brazilian state. In the recent period it is heavily associated with the ESG and the military establishment.

But before launching into a more thorough analysis of the postwar period, a word on the political framework of the first Vargas era.

THE POLITICAL FRAMEWORK
OF THE FIRST VARGAS ERA

The new industrialization strategy of the 1930s did not take place within a political vacuum. The first structural crisis of Brazilian economic development was accompanied by a profound shift in the Brazilian balance of power. The installation of Getulio Vargas as the President of Brazil in November 1930 brought to a close a 41-year period during which the rural landholding oligarchies of São Paulo and Minas Gerais were in control. Vargas was the creator and spokesman for 'the new urban middle class and for industrial sectors against the traditional centrifugal interests of the pre-1930 rural political and economic elite'.[22] The hallmark of the new regime was modernization — defined as industrial growth under the aegis of a centralized, paternalistic state with strong anti-communist, pro-Western overtones. The formal structure of the state evolved through virtually every political form. According to Skidmore, the years 1930-37 witnessed:

> ... agitated improvisation, including a regionalist revolt in São Paulo, a new constitution, a popular front movement, a fascist movement, and an attempted Communist coup.[23]

In 1937 an exhausted Brazil ended political experimentation and began eight years of authoritarian rule under the *Estado Novo*.

However, under the apparent politcal turmoil of the 1930s it is possible to detect the formation of a strong populist coalition which was to dominate the national scene until 1964. Vargas put together an alliance of the landed oligarchy, the urban middle class, and the industrial work force in pursuit of economic growth under the new rules of the capitalist game. In the wake of the 1929 crisis this meant a much more inward-looking development strategy with an emphasis on domestic industrialization. As O'Donnell has put it, 'industrialization and nationalism were the ideological glue of the new coalition'.[24]

It is crucial to note the 'inclusionary' characteristics of this era. Populism is generally seen as:

> [T]he guise within which change orientated segments of the middle class sought to construct multiclass coalitions powerful enough to gain control of the state and underwrite programs of structural transformation.[25]

In the Brazilian case, this seems to be an accurate account of what actually happened. The multiclass coalition involved the absorption and cooptation of a pre-existing elite group (the landed oligarchy via price supports for coffee) and the manipulation and cooptation of an emerging class (the industial work force via various types of material rewards).[26]

Aside from being nationalist and developmentalist, what was the ideological content of populism? In Brazil the goals and purposes of an inclusionary populist state were first articulated by the *Tenentes*, a group of young military officers who gained access to Vargas in the years 1930-32 and were able to set the tone of his thinking on many social and economic question.[27] Their vision of Brazil included the following elements: the assertion of national economic independence; the breaking of semi-feudal structures so as to liberate human and material resources for economic development; and the promotion of social justice. These goals were to be achieved by a strong state supported by a multiclass coalition. Populism was therefore 'statist' but not socialist. Indeed, it rejected in rhetoric both socialism and capitalism and advocated a third route to development unique to Brazil. However, despite the veneer of anti-capitalism and anti-imperialism, at a practical level the ideologues of the Vargas era took the position that the conditions of underdevelopment made any break with capitalist structures inadvisable. Rather, the task was to expand state power so as to reform and regulate those structures and achieve an evolutionary process of controlled economic development. At base, the Brazilian version of populism was nationalistic, capitalistic, statist and, most importantly, elitist.

Conventional images to the contrary, the first Vargas era was not exactly a bonanza for the people. There was a controlled, limited cooptation of the most crucial lower-class group – industrial workers – and a reorganization of labor on the basis of functional representation.[28] In each *municipio* employers and employees set up unions (*sindicatos*) for the various trades and industries. These coalesced into ·state federations in each field of activity, and came together at the national level as confederations representing workers or employers in such broad spheres as industry, commerce, etc. The system gradually evolved in the 1930s and was codified in 1942 (*O Consolidaçao das Leis do Trabalho*). At this stage, state control of the unions took several forms. First, only those unions recognized by the Ministry of Labor were legal. Secondly, the government placed its own agents in position of influence, thus excluding militants from the union leadership. Finally, compulsory membership dues (the *imposto sindical*, a tax of one day's wages per year to be deducted from the worker's paycheck) gave the state almost complete control over the labor movement, as the funds were only to be distributed by the Ministry of Labor to government-approved unions for official activities.

Under Vargas, Brazilian labor unions became government sanctioned interest groups whose main function was the administration of the extensive social services created by the *Estado Novo*. Workers became 'objects to be manipulated and controlled... the passive recipients of paternalistic social policies'.[29]

This prolonged attempt by Vargas to coopt the emerging industrial work force had two purposes: it bought worker loyalty for his brand of government, and it preempted the Left of the political spectrum. The material 'goodies' handed over to this segment of the work force were considerable; they included medical services with some hospitalization privileges, subsidies after the first fifteen days of illness, grants upon birth or death, old-age pensions, and some limited assistance with purchasing low-income housing. The Vargas legislation also included a 'tenure' law, which provided that no employee with more than ten years of service in the same firm could be dismissed, and a minimum wage law for some categories of urban workers. In the 1930s and 1940s this was an impressive list of social security benefits for a country at

Brazil's level of development, and it did serve to buy off the industrial work force, the labor aristocracy of the Brazilian lower classes. Vargas accurately saw this segment of the population as being increasingly crucial in a country that was entering an era of large-scale industrialization. As long as industrial workers supported state policy there was no need to worry about mass mobilization and a challenge from the Left. The 70-80 percent of the population that existed at subsistence levels on the *fazendas* and in the *favelas* of Brazil were illiterate and politically inert. Because of the cooption of the only articulate segment of the lower classes, 'the urban mass, the base of the left in Brazilian politics' remain 'a mass rather than a class'.[30] In Hobsbawm's words, Vargas broke the identification between the laboring classes and the dangerous classes.[31]

THE 1946-64 ERA

The year 1946 is normally seen as an extremely important date in the evolution of Brazil. However, despite a 'Rebirth of Democratic Politics' and a change in the formal political structure of the state, the 1946-64 period was very much a continuation of the 1930s.

In terms of economic policies, industrialization was accelerated, but developmentalism and nationalism remained the key notes of state policy, and there was a continued emphasis on import-substituting industrialization. Changes were in degree rather than in kind.

For instance, Vargas's second term in office (1951-54) and, even more dramatically, the Kubitschek years (1956-61) saw much more explicit and forceful state control and encouragement of domestic industrialization. There was a deliberate attempt to eliminate the structural bottlenecks (inadequate transportation, insufficient electricity), sectoral legs (in chemicals and the metal working industries), and regional disequilibria (between the hinterland and the coast) in the Brazilian economy by means of state control and public investment. Steps in this direction included the creation of a National Bank for Economic Development (BNDE) which was intended to 'eliminate or reduce the infrastructure deficiencies which impede the regular development of the Brazilian economy';[33] the setting up of Electrobras and Petrobras (the state monopolies in electricity and oil); and the building of the new capital Brasilia.

However, it would be wrong to characterize the 1950s as an era dominated by public investment. Both Vargas and Kubitschek made direct appeals to private investors, both domestic and foreign. The state offered Brazilian businessmen liberal credit policies and high levels of domestic demand and gave foreign firms special incentives to make direct investments in Brazil. For example, the Kubitschek government made liberal use of SUMOC Directive no. 113, issued in 1955 during the Cafe Filho government. This regulation encouraged foreign firms to bring into Brazil badly needed industrial equipment by waiving the need to provide foreign exchange 'cover' for imported machinery.

In short, it is possible to identify in both the Vargas and the Kubitschek regimes a pragmatic approach to an already mixed economy. The overriding aim was to achieve the most rapid rate of growth possible by encouraging expansion in both the private and the public sectors, and by taking advantage of both spontaneous and deliberate industrial incentives. The effect was to deepen the import-substituting process. During these years Brazil became self-sufficient in an increasingly sophisticated range of consumer goods and made considerable progress in basic industrial ,products. Growth rates were impressively high, particularly in the latter half of the 1950s. Kubitschek promised fifty years' progress in five, and there is little doubt that from 1956 to 1961 Brazil did record remarkable real economic growth (7 percent per year, or three times the Latin American average).

The dominant ideology of these years was nationalist and developmentalist. Nationalist sentiment hinged on a vision of a powerful and independent nation: it was Brazil's 'destiny' to undertake a drive to development based on rapid industrialization. Kubitschek made a special point of involving nationalist-minded intellectuals who were attracted by this upbeat image of the future. He financed the Institute of Advanced Brazilian Studies (ISEB), which became a mecca for research and teaching on Brazil's problems as conceived from this enthusiastic perspective. The Institute published a stream of books and lectures offering a rationale for industrialization and explaining the cause and effect of underdevelopment in every sector of the economy. The hundreds of young professionals who attended the one-year course at the Institute were profoundly influenced by the 'developmentalist' mystique.

Let us now turn to the political structures of the 1946-64 period. Despite the obvious change in formal appearances – the new constitution of 1946, the creation of political parties, and the advent of elections — the political reality was not significantly altered. The much-enlarged executive created during the *Estado Novo* remained intact, as did many of the policies of the previous regime. And, since the electorate was confined to literates, well over half of the Brazilian population was excluded from the new democratic processes. There was no reason why the mass of the population should enter the policy calculus any more in 1946 than they had done in the 1930s. A particularly important thread of continuity was the emphasis on populist or inclusionary economic policies.

Kubitschek, like Vargas before him, attempted to find something for everyone — everyone of course meaning those segments of the population that possessed political force. The state-promoted industrial-ization program drew enthusiastic support from industrialists, both domestic and foreign. The landed oligarchy were appeased by con-tinued price support for coffee and the assurance that Brazil's archaic pattern of land tenure would remain intact. The urban middle class was effectively wooed through more jobs — in the vastly expanded state bureaucracy, in the public enterprises, and in private industry. Finally, the industrial working class — the only mobilized segment of the lower class group — was coopted by means of generous wage settlements. In short, the Kubitschek brand of developmentalist nationalism was care-fully designed to gain maximum sympathy from the articulate classes.

A combination of vigorous state-directed industrial growth and these inclusionary policies spawned chronic inflation and balance-of-payments problems; these were to become increasingly difficult to deal with and were largely to blame for the second structural crisis of Brazilian development and the military *coup* of 1964. But let us examine the origins and consequences of these crucial problems which go a long way toward explaining the raison d'être of a repressive exclusionary authoritarian state in modern Brazil.

A recurrent theme in Brazilian economic policymaking from World War II to 1964 is the repeated but largely unsuccessful attempt to control inflation. For example, there were incomplete attempts at stabilization in 1953-54, 1955-56, 1961, and 1963-64. Until the 1960s the failures did not prevent a resumption of growth, but the infla-tionary distortion increased, and by 1964 it was doubtful if any elected regime could carry out the draconic stabilization program that was needed to resume growth.

Where did these inflationary pressures come from and why was it so difficult to control them? It is my contention that inflation in Brazil is far from being a superficial problem; rather, it has been, and still is, the least tractable manifestation of late industrialization. Skidmore stresses the critical issue of inflation in 1954:

> The problems that had proved to be beyond Vargas' ability to solve and thereby contributed to the political crisis that cost him his life were inflation at home and payments deficits abroad.[34]

And the frenetic rate of inflation under Goulart was an extremely important and well-known catalyst of the Right-wing *coup*.

A SIMPLE MODEL

In order to understand the full implications of these cumulative inflationary pressures, I would like to develop a simple model that conforms to the Brazilian situation.

Let us start with certain assumptions: a country has a low per capita income; it possesses a few large centers of commercial and industrial activity; it depends for export earnings on one or two primary commodities; it needs to import capital goods, raw materials, intermediate goods and consumer durables; and at some initial point in time it has a stable price level and balance-of-payments equilibrium. A final assumption is that this country is politically committed to insuring a high rate of economic growth into the future.

Let us now suppose that export earnings begin to fall relative to the growth of imports. Let us further assume that foreign exchange reserves are not adequate to keep imports at an unchanged level for more than a short time. The value of imports thus has to be curtailed in order to match export receipts. The state can do this in a number of ways (import control, tariffs, currency depreciation, etc.), but if it wishes to maintain growth rates it will seek to structure imports so that items essential for industrial growth flow into the country at an undiminished rate. That is to say, imports of consumer goods bear the brunt of import curtailment.

In this situation price increases and inflation are inevitable. Initially, domestic purchasing power remains unchanged but the amount of available consumer goods will have decreased; import substituting industries will experience substantial increases in profit rates due to their ability to charge higher prices for the newly-scarce goods. This might encourage domestic manufacturers to increase capacity and/or invest in additional import-substituting industries. Since the situation facing the country is one of long-run decline in the earning power of its export staple, the state is likely to favor such investment activities and will provide various forms of subsidy and protection — further exacerbating inflation. This is due to several factors: tariff barriers often provide a 'captive' home market which generates abnormal profit margins; threshold size and economies-of-scale constraints mean that firms are initially operating at less than full capacity and this pushes prices up; and finally, certain domestic factors of production (particularly skilled labor) will become increasingly scarce and therefore increasingly expensive. The net result is a rise in the average cost of manufacturing and enhanced inflationary pressure.

A final point: it should always be remembered that increased industrial activity will undoubtedly aggrevate the foreign imbalance in he short run as there will be increased need for capital goods imports, and this will intensify inflationary pressures.

The above scenario should be familiar: it accurately describes some of the key dynamics in the Brazilian import substitution strategy and demonstrates why inflationary pressures are so clearly associated with balance-of-payments crises. Inflation is an inevitable concomitant of late development when the state faces a continuously declining ability to import; is committed to high rates of economic growth; and meets the situation by promoting import-substituting industries. In the Brazilian case these 'inherent' inflationary tendencies were further exacerbated by the extremely active role played by the state in furthering growth. The building of Brasilia and the great expansion of the government bureaucracy were not clearly tied to the import-substitution process, but they had a dramatic effect on domestic rates of inflation since they were largely paid for through deficit financing.

However, if inflation is predictable in a late-developing country, it is also functional to the growth process. Through higher prices and lower real wages the inflationary process is capable of penalizing consumers and transferring resources to national industrial development. Domestic entrepreneurs charge higher prices for goods, realize bigger profit margins, and have both the wherewithal and the incentive to channel new investment into manufacturing. Such a transfer would not be possible if consumers were strong enough to force an increase in their money earnings to compensate for inflation, for this of course would raise labor costs and decrease profit margins, thus reducing the incentive for new investment. In short, a lag in wage adjustment is a necessary condition for making the inflationary process compatible with economic growth. It was this lag that the inclusionary regimes of Vargas, Kubitschek, and Goulart failed to sustain. They failed because their political survival depended upon the goodwill of the urban working class. Time and time again wages were allowed to catch up with, and even surpass, the rate of inflation, and when stabilization programs were hatched to deal with the ensuing 'stagflation', they failed because it was tantamount to political suicide to suppress the real wage rate for any length of time. Indeed, not only did inclusionary politics mean the inability to deal with inherent inflation, they also tended to add another, more specific, dimension. Brasilia and an enlarged bureaucracy did not grow out of thin air; they were products of the need to galvanize popular support in an inclusionary political arena. By 1964, stagflation of both the inherent and the specific kind had become untenable. If Brazil was to resume growth within the capitalist framework, authentic stabilization was essential and an exclusionary authoritarian regime became a necessary condition for such a program. Campos and Bulhoes (the Planning and Finance Ministers of the first military government) succeeded where their predecessors failed because they were given great latitude by a military government to ignore public opposition.

THE POST-1964 ERA

I would like to begin this section with an examinaion of the ideology of the modern period. Since 1964 Brazil has been particularly well endowed with a sense of direction. An ideology based on the inter-relationship between national security and national development has emanated from the higher echelons of the military establishment, and has served to further refine and focus the national project of the Brazilian state.

In earlier periods it is possible to see ways in which national security and economic development were related issues in the minds of the Brazilian power elite. The writings of the Tenentes and of Vargas himself point to the inseparable nature of these issues. In the late 1950s and early 1960s this interrelationship took on a new significance. The success of guerrilla warfare techniques against conventional armies —

the most dramatic example being, of course, Cuba in 1959 — led the military in both the developed and underdeveloped world to turn more attention toward preventing domestic revolution. An essential ingredient in this program was accelerated development and the eradication of economic grievances.

The most concrete expression of the new ideology was the *Escola Superior de Guerra* (ESG) which was set up after the war with the express intention of formulating a more coherent and sophisticated doctrine of national security and development.

The origins of the ESG are both interesting and relevant. The Brazilian contribution to the war effort, the *Force Expendicionaria Brasileira*, had been firmly integrated into the US army corps in Italy. Because of this connection, the Brazilians looked to the American military for advice in setting up their new War College. A US advisory mission was invited to Brazil and remained there between 1948 and 1960 with the result that the ESG came to be modelled after the US national War College both in its organization and its focus. Indeed, some of the distinctive characteristics of the post-1964 military governments in Brazil — pro-Americanism, anti-communism, a favorable attitude toward foreign capital, and a distaste for 'excessive' nationalism — can be directly traced to the early collaboration between the military establishments of these two countries.

However, it would be wrong to assume that American ideas were adopted en bloc; the Brazilian military very much attempted to shape conventional wisdom to fit the special problems of underdevelopment. As General Golbery, chief theoretician of the ESG, put it:

> The planning of national security is an imperative of the hour in which we live. . . for us in the underdeveloped countries. . . planning assumes aspects of another order which puts everything else in relief.[35]

The chief threats were seen to be:

> . . . localized conflict, and above all indirect communist aggression, which capitalizes on local discontents, the frustration of hunger and misery, and just nationalist anxieties.[36]

It should be remembered that Latin American fears of communis were very much bound up with the rise of Castro and the unsuccessful guerrilla movements in Venezuela and elsewhere. The contemporary reality seemed to indicate that conventional military techniques and even counterinsurgency measures were no longer sufficent to contain revolution. For the ESG national security became a function of:

> ... rationally maximizing the output of the economy and minimizing all sources of cleavage and disunity within the country.[37]

'National-building' and global development plans became central ideological themes as the military recognized modernization as a key ingredient in the fight against communism.

Another Brazilian innovation was the determined effort to incorporate civilians into the life of the ESG. Precisely because the military were concerned with all aspects of national development, it was thought appropriate to include government officials and private individuals from such areas as education, industry, communications, and banking in its academic program:

> The decision to include civilians as a central part of the ESG proved to be crucial for the development of the school. It brought military officers into systematic close contact with civilian leaders. This gave them civilian allies who shared many of their ideas on development and security and also gave the military confidence to discuss problems on terms of equality with civilian specialist.[38]

It is time to turn our attention to the *coup* of 1964 and delineate the part played by this military ideology in the resolution of the second structural crisis of Brazil.

Along with the worsening economic situation of the early 1960s — a state of affairs which encompassed inflation, balance-of-payments difficulties and stagnation — there was a growing sentiment among the military that corrupt politicians were encouraging economic chaos and political subversion. In particular, the military became increasingly doubtful as to whether any democratically elected president could carry out the stabilization program that was essential if Brazil was to resume growth within a capitalist framework. As the military saw it, it was either stabilization under an authoritarian government, which at least in the first instance should be controlled by themselves, or social revolution from the Left. They made sure that the crisis was resolved in their favor.[39]

It is important to remember that by this date the military establishment did have the practical ability to present an alternative government. It possessed a finely-honed, if limited, ideology that saw a fundamental connection between internal security and national development, and therefore a narrowing gap betwen military and political spheres of influence. Through the activities of the ESG there existed a body of military officers and civilian technocrats who held common perceptions of the problems of Brazil and had evolved a coherent program of action. The fact that the ESG was an important actor in the *coup* of 1964 is borne out by the fact that of the 102 generals on active duty at that time, those who had attended the ESG, were markedly over-represented among the active plotters against Goulart. Indeed, the new president himself, Castello Branco, had been director of the Department of Studies at the ESG betwen 1956 and 1958, and General Golbery, the 'father of the ESG', became director of the important (*Servico Nacional de Informaçoes*) SNI under the new government.

In short, the events of March 1964 were neither unexpected nor arbitrary. The link between economic cause and political effect in this particular context is provided by a military caste with a highly developed, if narrowly conceived, view of the world. The content of this ideology was in tune with the beliefs of earlier incarnations of the Brazilian state and dovetailed with the attitudes and needs of the contemporary bourgeoisie, but it owed something to the specifics of the modern military establishment. Militant anti-communism, pro-Western rhetoric, and criticism of 'excessive' nationalism are characteristics of post-1964 regimes that can only be understood in terms of the origins, loyalties, and evolution of the Brazilian military.

Now, a word on the ways in which the military has reflected the attitude and needs of the Brazilian bourgeoisie in the post-1964 period. First, it is necessary to stress that the military *coup* was supported by all segments of the bourgeoisie. Faced with stagflation and an increasingly militant labor movement, the bourgeoisie cheerfully swopped 'the right to rule for the right to make money'.[40] The structural crisis of 1964 provoked an almost unprecedented degree of elite cohesion. In Nun's words:

> [T]he movement of April 1964 amalgamated all the property owning classes of the society: the agrarian sectors out of fear of reform, the industrial sectors out of fear of loss of their mechanisms of security, the middle class out of their panic at seeing the social distance separating them from the masses shortened, and all of these sectors out of the even greater fear... [of communism].[41]

Faced with the choice between military rule or socialist revolution, the Brazilian bourgeoisie opted, quite decidedly, for the former.

Secondly, once the crisis was over and the military ensconced in power, there were distinct patterns of interaction betwen the military and different segments of the bourgeoisie.

The national bourgeoisie became increasingly neglected and increasingly disaffected. As noted earlier in this paper, national capital has become a progressively 'shadowy' member of the *ménàge a trois* of Brazilian development. The state has therefore been able to neglect the interests of this sector with impunity. But neglect of the national bourgeoisie has not been willful or arbitrary; rather it has been part of the drive for fast growth rates. The efficient or 'natural' agents for rapid industrialization in late-developing nations are undoubtedly the state and the multinational corporation, *not* national capital. Domestic entrepreneurs have objected (witness the recent 'destatization' debate) but, given the ultimate alternative (communism), even this neglected segment of the Brazilian bourgeoisie has accepted the rules of the game as laid down by a military state.

The powerful segments of the elite are the internationalized bourgeoisie and the state bourgeoisie.[42] The internationalized bourgeoisie comprises those Brazilians who manage and control the operations of multinational corporations in Brazil. As key beneficiaries of the post-1964 period, this segment of the elite naturally constitutes an enthusiastic support base for the contemporary Brazilian state.

As far as the state bourgeoisie is concerned, i.e. the government bureaucratic and planning elite and the managerial echelon of the state enterprises, they are keen supporters of the military state for two reasons. First, the post-1964 regimes have dramatically increased the role of the state in economic affairs, thus promoting the expansion and prosperity of these segments. Secondly, through the activities of the ESG, many of the representatives of the 'public sector' have been directly involved in the construction of national goals and policies.

The net result is that the economically powerful internationalized and state bourgeoisies have given their support to military control of the state, while the less important national bourgeoisie has grudgingly accepted its presence as the least of several evils.

With this 'consensus of the powerful' as their support base, the military moved into action in 1964 with 'authentic' stabilization as the most crucial issue on their agenda. They were successful. Campos and Bulhões were able to dampen inflation because they were given great latitude by the new exclusionary and repressive military government to ignore public opinion. Time was the essence of the problem. Previous inclusionary regimes had been able to promote unpopular policies for limited periods; but stabilization needs a two- or three-year time span to break the public's well-established inflationary expectations, and elected politicians shrink from this extensive and ruthless economic therapy.

The most unpopular component of the stabilization package was the deliberate policy of letting wage increases lag behind increases in the cost of living. This reduction in real wages, which amounted to 25 percent by 1967, was justified as the lag effect of lowering inflationary expectations, and was billed as being 'temporary'. But, however imaginative the explanation, it is difficult to see how such a policy could have been carried out by a government that had to face elections — even under the imperfectly democratic framework of pre-1964 Brazil.

The industrial working class was the chief victim of the stabilization policies, but it would be wrong to assume that it was the only segment of the Brazilian population asked to pay for lower rates of inflation.

The Campos-Bulhões stabilization policy also penalized the interests of national capitalists. In an effort to lower prices within the industrial sector, the government reduced the level of effective protection and put an end to the policy of providing publicly subsidized credit from the central banking system in times of liquidity crisis. As a result, Brazilian business went through a painful shake-out phase during which multinational corporations were able to acquire Brazilian firms that could not find domestic sources of credit. This was surely a type of inflation control that few elected governments could aspire to for long!

Policies designed to eradicate the federal deficit also resulted in political unpopularity. Previous inclusionary regimes had seen a vast expansion of public spending in state enterprises and in government bureaucracy: failure both to increase prices for goods and services and to raise taxes had resulted in large deficits financed by monetary issues. This was highly inflationary, and the Castello Branco government moved quickly to settle both accounts. By increasing the price of services — a step that directly increased the cost of living in the short run — the huge deficits in the state-owned railroads, shipping industry, and oil industry were wiped out. Covering costs meant that long deferred investment could be made in these public enterprises, thus increasing productivity and lowering costs for the future, but it is doubtful if any elected regime could have withstood the storm of protest over costlier bus fares and other public services.

Even more important than 'corrective inflation' in eliminating the deficit were the taxation policies of the new regime. In the crisis year of 1964 almost one-third of total government spending was in the red; by 1968-69 there was a budgetary surplus, mainly through the device of expanding receipts even faster than expenditures and passing the burden on to the tax-paying public. The military state was, and is, extremely proud of the fact that it has imposed and stringently enforced collection of taxes on income. As Schmitter observed:

> The specter of fearful middle- and upper-class citizens paying direct taxes for the first time has been used by the regime to enhance its socially neutral technocratically efficient image both domestically and internationally.[42]

There is no doubt that income tax revenue has risen — by as much as 70 percent in 1968 alone, but indirect taxation has risen roughly twice as fast again. The 'squeezing' of the rich must be placed in context: the urban working class, the main target of indirect taxation, has been squeezed even harder.

Nevertheless, the point remains that in the area of taxation the military regime has demonstrated its ability to make all classes of Brazilians pay for development. The burden has fallen disproportionately on the working class — and regressive indirect taxes are particularly difficult to bear when real income is stagnant — but even the middle and upper classes, the principal beneficiaries of the development programs, have been forced to contribute significant sums. Such a dramatic increase in the effectiveness of taxation is often extremely difficult under inclusionary, democratic regimes in the underdeveloped world. Such a program seems to need the repressive and disciplinary powers of a military state that can afford to alienate politically mobilized segments of the population.

The foreign sector is yet another policy area where programs adopted after 1964 would have been difficult under an elected government. On the eve of the *coup*, Brazil faced a crushing short-term international debt, a product of the cumulative balance-of-payment pressures described earlier in this paper. It could be renegotiated only if the new government could convince the country's creditors, specifically the IMF, that domestic stabilization plans were both serious and likely to be successful. The Castello Branco government fell over itself to do a convincing job on this front. The first task it set itself was to repudiate the exaggerated economic nationalism of the Goulart regime. The profit remittance law passed by Congress in 1962 was repealed, and there was a rapprochement with foreign private investors. This was important since the government hoped for a rapid increase in private foreign investment to strengthen the balance of payments and to take up the slack resulting from the deflationary squeeze on Brazilian business. Such a rapprochement could also be offered as proof to the international agencies and the United State government that Brazil was firmly committed to capitalist development. These policies were successful. From 1964 to 1968 United States economic assistance averaged $312 million a year; after this date Brazil's economic recovery rendered aid less urgent and the United States cut back its support. The World Bank and IADB, on the other hand, have maintained high levels of lending throughout the recent period.

In summary, it should be obvious from the above paragraphs that an exlusionary and repressive state was an absolutely necessary condition for successful stabilization, and that, in its turn, successful stabilization was an essential prerequisite for a new cycle of capitalist growth within the Brazilian domestic economy.

In 1968 Brazil entered that period of boom that is often referred to as the 'miracle'. Annual real growth of GDP, which averaged only 3.7 percent between 1962 and 1967, averaged 10.1 percent in the years 1968-74. Industry was the leading sector, expanding at yearly rates of 12.2 percent. Within manufacturing the highest growth rates were achieved by such sectors as transport equipment, machinery, electrical equipment, and chemicals (sectors dominated either by the multinational corporations or by the state). Traditional sectors such as textiles, clothing, and food products experienced much slower rates of growth; these sectors remain the preserve of private national capital. In short, the recent period has witnessed extremely impressive, if uneven, rates of growth in Brazil.

CONCLUSIONS

A recurring theme of this paper is that there is no simple mechanical relationship between economic cause and political effect. Cardoso warns us of simple-minded economic determinism:

> [A]ll too frequently analysts do not take into account either theoretically or empirically, the dynamic, mutually shaping interrelationship between politics and economics.[43]

The seemingly logical and remorseless progression from structural crisis to authoritarian rule, both in 1930 and in 1964, is only intellectually convincing if one recognizes and accepts the maximization of the rate of growth of GNP as the overwhelming goal of the Brazilian power elite. The modern military have couched their ultimate goal in terms of a secure and strong nation, but for the immediate future this boils down to rapid growth with scant regard to democratic or egalitarian considerations. In essence, the contemporary exclusionary and authoritarian framework becomes a result of late development *only* when the political project is national economic success defined in terms of growth rates per year.

This leads us to a related issue. The Brazilian state since 1964 may have had an extremely strong sense of direction, but does this constitute legitimacy either in the eyes of the elite or in the eyes of the mass of the population?

Many theorists have distinguished between: (a) the effectiveness of the political system, which in contemporary contexts often relates to performance in achieving modernizing goals; and (b) their legitimacy, which refers to a belief by the populace that a regime has the right to exercise political authority.[45] This right is normally grounded in such factors as traditional roots, historical continuity, commonly-held value systems, and participation in the political process. Effectiveness and legitimacy obviously interact. For example, a high level of effectiveness in meeting the modernization goals of the state may purchase at least some legitimacy for an initally illegitimate political regime.

By applying these concepts to the evolution of the Brazilian state it is possible to distinguish ways in which the pursuit of effectiveness in the modern period has driven this particular nation farther away from the realization of legitimacy. The original drive towards industrial take-off (the era of easy import substitution) was based on the enthusiastic cooperation of the articulate members of the population. The populism of the 1930s and the limited democracy of the 1946-64 period did ensure that the urban industrial classes as well as the landed aristocracy were included in the political process and benefited from the fruits of economic progress. Without overdrawing the extent or depth of this process — it should always be remembered the mass of the people were excluded in both the economic and political sense of the word — this first phase of industrial development was both effective and legitimate. This cannot be said of the post-1964 era. By this stage in the game, high rates of economic growth were firmly entrenched as essential components of the national project and of effective government. However, due to the economic problems that had accumulated during the previous stage of development — particularly inflationary distortions — rapid growth could not be attained without a repressive military regime and a ruthless stabilization program. As we have seen, this meant a withering of the political process and extended belt-tightening for certain segments of the urban population. This scenario has little historical precedent and flies in the face of elite opinion which has always valued concensus and cooperation between and amongst the articulate classes.

We are left with an important question: How long can effectiveness substitute for legitimacy in this national context? I would suggest not very long. After all, effectiveness is fairly narrowly defined as rapid economic growth — an inherently unreliable commodity. The best economic management cannot cure capitalistic growth of its cyclical and fluctuating properties; it therefore provides a poor long-run substitute for legitimacy. The lifespan of this particular autocratic military regime would appear to be limited.

NOTES

1. Alfred Stephan, 'State and Society in Latin America', Lehrman Institute Seminar paper, (February 1975): 2.

2. Jeremy Bentham, 'A Manual of Political Economy', in Bullock and Deaken (eds.), *The Liberal Tradition,* New York: New York University Press, 1957, pp. xxiii-xxiv, 28-29. Emphasis in the original.

3. The doctrine was of course originally elaborated by Adam Smith in *The Wealth of Nations,* vol. 1, London: J. M. Dent and Sons, Everyman's Library Edition, 1954, p. 398.

4. Quoted in Harold J. Laski, *The State in Theory and Practice,* New York: The Viking Press, 1935, p. 3.

5. Simon Schwartzman, 'Back to Weber: Corporatism and Patrimonialism in the Seventies', in James M. Malloy (ed.), *Authoritarianism and Corporatism in Latin America,* Pittsburgh: University of Pittsburgh Press, 1977, p. 89.

6. Alexander Gerschenkron, *Economic Backwardness in Historical Perspective,* New York: Praeger, 1965, p. 6.

7. Lenin, quoted in Peter B. Evans, 'Industrialization and Imperialism: Growth and Stagnation in the Periphery', *Berkeley Journal of Sociology* 20 (1975): 132.

8. This is one of the routes to development outlined in Barrington Moore; see his *Social Origins of Dictatorship and Democracy*, Boston: Beacon Press, 1966, pp. 433-53.

9. In this paper I restrict the use of the phrase 'late development' to those countries of the Third World that began industrialization in the 1930s and 1940s. In some more vigorous sense they should perhaps be called late, late developers (Southern Europe and the USSR being the original late developers). This distinction is irrelevant to my argument.

10. O'Donnell was perhaps the first political scientist to lay stress on this analytical point. See Guillermo A. O'Donnell, *Modernization and Bureaucratic-Authoritarianism: Studies in South America Politics*, University of California at Berkeley: Institute of International Studies, 1973. I would like to stress that some of the recent work by theorists such as O'Donnell, Cardoso, Stephan, Hirschman, Collier, and Kaufman does go beyond the conventional models outlined in my introduction. I draw upon these theorists in constructing the elements of my framework.

11. This point is stressed by Albert O. Hirschman, see 'The Turn to Authoritarianism in Latin-America and the Search for its Economic Determinants', mimeo, Princeton, New Jersey: Institute for Advanced Study, February 1977.

12. State activism was built up through the process of accretion of roles. Schmitter stresses that the entire Brazilian sistema was based on sedimentation rather than metamorphosis. See Philippe C. Schmitter, *Interest Conflict and Political Change*, Stanford: Stanford University Press, 1971, p. 378.

13. The term 'metality' is often thought to describe the philosophical content of authoritarianism better than 'ideology'. See Juan J. Linz, 'An Authoritarian Regime: Spain', in Erik Allardt and Stein Rokkan (eds.), *Mass Politics: Studies in Political Sociology*, New York: The Free Press, 1970. Linz states that '... ideologies... are systems of thought more or less intellectually elaborated and organized, often in written form by intellectuals... and mentalities... are ways of thinking and feeling, more emotional than rational, that provide non-codified ways of reacting to situations' (p. 257). According to these definitions, Brazilian authoritarian regimes would appear to have an ideology. Over the last four decades there has been a relatively formal and rigorous development of the goals of the state. However, I do want to overstate the tightness of my definition. My use of the term 'ideology' does not correspond to a rigid political or religious doctrine, rather it approximates Mannheim's use of the term as 'an integrated set of ideas for systematically ordering and evaluating social reality'. See Karl Mannheim *Ideology and Utopia*, New York: Harcourt, Brace, and World, 1966.

14. I use the term the 'colonial' economy to describe the primary-exporter orientation so typical of colonized parts of the Third World. In the case of Brazil this phase outlasted explicit colonial role, which officially came to an end in 1815.

15. See Celso Furtado, *The Economic Growth of Brazil: A Survey from Colonial to Modern Times*, Berkeley: University of California Press, 1963.

16. Despite instruments such as the *Caixa de Conversao*, which did favor the import of machinery and raw materials between 1910 and 1914, the overwhelming direction of domestic policy was against industrialization. For example, Brazilian industry blossomed during World War I due to the fact that supplies

were cut off from Europe. The end of the war and the resumption of free trade provoked a recession in domestic manufactures, and the state steadfastly resisted pleas from Brazilian industrialists for a measure of protection. For an interesting study of the sentiment favoring industrialization in Brazil, see Nicia Vilela Luz, *A Luta Pela Industrializacao do Brasil,* Sao Paulo: Corpo e Alma do Brazil, Difusao Europeia do Libro, 1961.

17. Malloy, *Authoritarianism,* op. cit., p. 8.

18. Werner Baer, *Industrialization and Economic Development in Brazil,* Homewood, Illinois: Richard D. Irwin, 1965, p. 20.

19. As Marini has put it, the crisis in the coffee economy presented domestic industrialists with 'an economic surplus which it did not need to expropriate, since it was spontaneously put to its disposal'. See Ruy Maruo Marini, 'La dialectica del desarrollo dapitalisto en Brasil', *Cuadernos Americanos* XXV (3) (1966): 137.

20. Getulio Vargas, A Nova Politica do Brasil (Rio de Janeiro, 1938), x: 168; quoted in Thomas E. Skidmore, *Politics in Brazil, 1930-1964,* New York: Oxford University Press, 1967, p. 45.

21. Skidmore, *Politics in Brazil,* op.cit., p. 45.

22. Robert M. Levine, *The Vargas Regime,* New York: Columbia University Press, 1970, p. 175.

23. Skidmore, *Politics in Brazil,* op.cit., pp. 7-8.

24. O'Donnell, *Modernization,* op.cit., p. 57.

25. Malloy, *Authoritarianism,* op.cit., p. 8.

26. This is elaborated in Philippe C. Schmitter, *Interest Conflict and Politcal Change in Brazil,* Stanford: Stanford University Press, 1971, p. 375.

277. See Edgard Carona, *Revolucoes do Brasil Contemporaneo, 1922-1938* Sao Paulo, 1965, and John D. Wirth, 'Tenentismo in the Brazilian Revolution of 1930', *Hispanic American Historical Review* XLIV (2) (May 1964): 161-79.

28. For an up-to-date and extremely comprehensive view of the organization of Brazilian labor, see Kenneth Paul Erickson, *The Brazilian Corporate State and Working Class Politics,* Berkeley: University of California Press, 1977.

29. Malloy, *Authoritarianism,* op.cit., p. 12.

20. Frank Ackerman, 'Industry and Imperialism in Brazil', *Review of Radical Political Economics,* 3 (Spring 1971): 26.

31. E. J. Hobsbawm, *Laboring Men: Studies in the History of Labor,* New York: Doubleday, 1967, pp. 272-315.

32. Skidmore, *Politics in Brazil,* op. cit., p. 70. Foreign Exchange Reserves of $709 million were wiped out during this period. Satisfying domestic demand by importing manufactures no longer worked in Brazil. Aggregate income had increased 50 percent over 1929 while the importing capacity of the country had remained the same.

33. Skidmore, *Politics in Brazil,* op.cit., p. 94.

34. Thomas E. Skidmore, 'The Politics of Economic Stabilization in Latin America', discussion paper in Economic History, University of Wisconsin, February 1975.

35. Golbery do Couto e Silva, *Geopolitica do Brasil,* Rio de Janeiro: Jose Olympio, 1967, p. 198.

36. Ibid., p. 199.

37. Alfred Stepan, *The Military in Politics: Changing Paterns in Brazil,* Princeton: Princeton University Press, 1971, p. 178. This is not without a parallel in contemporary American writings; for example, Lucien W. Pye sees the army as 'a vigorous champion of progress and development'. See his *Aspects of Political Development* (Boston: Little, Brown, 1966), p. 173.

38. Stepan, *The Military,* op.cit., p. 176.

39. The specter of revolution was a very real fear goven the events of the Goulart period, particularly the increasing militancy of the labor movement.

40. As Cardoso has put it, 'in its attempt to contain the pressure from below the bourgeoisie supported measures that essentially destroyed its own direct political expression'. See Fernando Henrique Cardoso, 'Associated-Dependent Development: Theoretical and Practical Implications', in Alfred Stepan (ed.), *Authoritarian Brazil,* New Haven: Yale University Press, 1973, p. 147.

41. Jose Nun, *Latin America: the Hegemonic Crisis and the Military Coup,* Politics of Modernization Series No. 7, Institute of International Studies, University of California at Berkeley, 1969, p. 31. This point is also stressed in Maria da Conceicac Tavares et al., 'The Gwoth and Decline of Import Substitution in Brazil', *Economic Bulletin for Latin America* IX (1) (March 1964): 37.

42. I am adopting Cardoso's terminology; see his 'Associated-Dependent Development', op.cit., pp. 142-79.

43. Philippe C. Schmitter, 'The "Portugalization" of Brazil?', in Stepan, *Authoritarian Brazil,* op.cit., p. 193.

44. Cardoso, 'Associated-Dependent Development', op.cit., p. 142.

45. See Seymour Martin Lipset, *Political Man,* New York: Doubleday, 1959, ch. 11.

NOTES ON CONTRIBUTORS

J. Bowyer Bell is a Senior Associate of the Institute of War and Peace Studies at the School of International Affairs of Columbia University. He is a prolific author, having published a number of volumes on terrorism. His latest volume is *Thunder Out of Zion,* a biography of Begin, 1977.

Bogdan Denitch is Professor of Sociology and Executive Officer, PhD Program in Sociology at the Graduate School of City University of New York. He is primarily interested in working class parties of Western Europe and developments in Eastern Europe. He is co-editor of *The Opinion-Making Elites in Yugoslavia,* Praeger, 1973, and author of *The Legitimation of a Revolution: The Yugoslav Case,* Yale, 1975, *Society and Social Change in Eastern Europe,* American Association for Advancement of Slavic Studies, Columbus, Ohio, 1978, and of numerous articles.

Paolo Farneti is Professor of Political Science, University of Turin, Italy. He is a regular contributor to *Il Mondo* and his chapter on 'Trade Unions and Working Class Parties in Italy 1946-76' was included in *Government and Opposition in Italy* (1978) and his work on 'The Take-Over of Fascism' in Linz and Stepan (eds.), *The Breakdown of Democracies* (1978).

Franco Ferrarotti is Professor of Political Science at the University of Turin. He obtained his PhD in political sociology from the University of Columbia, USA, in 1968.

G. Lowell Field is at the University of Connecticut. He is the author, with J. Higley and K. Graholt, of *Elite Structure and Ideology: A General Theory with Applications to Norway,* 1976.

Sylvia Ann Hewlett is Assistant Professor of Economics at Barnard College at Columbia University. She is a specialist in problems of development and modernization and has written extensively on Brazil.

John Higley is Fellow in Sociology at the Research School of Social Sciences in the Australian National University. He has recently completed a study of Australian elites.

Irving Louis Horowitz is Hannah Arendt Professor of Sociology and Political Science at Rutgers University. He is also Director of Studies in Comparative International Development. Other writings of his on the theme of political legitimacy appear in *Three Worlds of Development* and *Ideology and Utopia in the United States.*

Branko Horvat is Professor of Economics at the University of Zagreb. He is the author of numerous volumes, including *The Yugoslav Economic System,* 1977, and is co-editor of *Self-Governing Socialism,* 1975.

Charles Kadushin is Professor in the Center for Social Research of the Graduate School of the City University of New York. He has written on elite and networks, and has published several volumes, the latest one being *The American Intellectual Elite,* 1974.

David Lane is Lecturer in Sociology and Politics, University of Cambridge, and Fellow of Emmanuel College, Cambridge, UK. He is the author of *The Roots of Russian Communism, Politics and Society in the USSR, The Socialist Industrial State,* and, with F. O'Dell, *The Soviet Industrial Worker.*

Robert Lane is Eugene Meyer Professor of Political Science, Yale University. He is past president of the American Political Science Association (1970-71) and is the author of *Political Man,* 1972, *Political Thinking and Consciousness,* 1969, and *Political Ideology,* 1962.

Peter C. Ludz is Professor of Political Science at the University of Munich. He is author of *The Changing Party Elite in East Germany,* 1972. His recent publications include *Ideologiebegriff und marxistische Theorie,* 1977, and *Die DDR zwischen Ost und West: Politische Analysen 1961 bis 1976,* 1977.

Joseph Rothschild is Professor of Political Science at Columbia University. He is a specialist in Eastern European political history, and his latest publication is *East Central Europe Between the Two World Wars,* 1974.

Andreas Svrakov is a PhD candidate in Political Science at Columbia University.

Sidney G. Tarrow is Professor of Political Science at Cornell University. He is a specialist in West European communist parties, particularly those of France and Italy. His more recent publications include *Between Center and Periphery: Grassroots Politicians in Italy and France,* 1977, and, with Luigi Graziano and Peter J. Katzenstein, *Territorial Politics in Industrial States,* 1978.